Studies In The New Testament

Robert G. Hoerber

Distinguished Service
Professor Emeritus of Classics
Westminster College
Fulton, Missouri

Professor Emeritus of Exegesis
Concordia Seminary
St. Louis, Missouri

STUDIES IN THE NEW TESTAMENT

Biblion Publishing has received permission to republish Dr. Hoerber's studies as they appeared in *Concordia Theological Quarterly*, *Concordia Journal* (formerly *Concordia Theological Monthly*), *Christian News*, and *Affirm*.

ISBN 0-9620063-5-1

God's Word To The Nations Bible Society
Biblion Publishing
P.O. Box 26343
22050 Mastick Road
Cleveland, OH 44126
1-800-937-9050

To My Sister

Melba H. Siefert

Contents

Editorials in *Concordia Journal*

Foreword

Under Christ the Head of the church and under His Holy Spirit who gives talents to the various people who constitute that Christian church, it is an honor to present this volume of studies from the pen of Robert G. Hoerber.

This collection of lifelong writings is offered to the church by God's Word To The Nations Bible Society, parent organization of Biblion Publishing and NET, its Bible-publishing division.

God's Word To The Nations Bible Society regards Dr. Hoerber and his family as dear friends in Christ and servants in the cause of bringing God's Word to the nations. Because of Robert Hoerber's significant role in the translation process of *God's Word to the Nations: New Testament* in the New Evangelical Translation (NET) text, the Bible Society has deemed it a great privilege to publish his shorter works.

It is my personal privilege to introduce this collection of studies in behalf of Bob, my dear friend and fellow worker. He has patiently taught me as we have labored together and has often has been like a father to me through difficult times.

In a sense, Robert Hoerber is "a man for all seasons." He spans the spectrum from conducting himself as a serious, energetic scholar...to being a capable administrator...to finding time for his family on a daily basis...to knowing how to enjoy himself thoroughly at the Cardinals' ballpark in St. Louis. I have known only two people who can outwork me in length of hours—Bob Hoerber is one of them.

The present volume includes the autobiography that I requested Robert to draft, along with his theological studies. Except for "Notes on the Greek Article," all of these writings have appeared in print before.

Those not acquainted with the works of Dr. Hoerber will soon recognize the expertise developed during his more than forty-five years of research and teaching on the college and seminary level.

His scholarly depth is revealed in these studies, while his concern for students of the Bible is reflected in the NET New Testament (NET Publishing, 1990). Dr. Hoerber's brilliant classroom technique is ably transferred to the printed page in his book *Reading the New Testament for Understanding* (Concordia Publishing House, 1986), one of the ten best books I have read.

With stewardship of time and finance representing absolute necessities at God's Word To The Nations Bible Society, we decided to reproduce the Hoerber articles photographically, rather than typeset them a second time. This saved time and money; it also negated the possibility of introducing errors, especially in Greek spellings. The photographing option, of course, accounts for the different type styles and layouts. An occasional correction is made by pen because of limitations dictated by our printing method.

This volume, then, represents some of the talents given to Dr. Robert G. Hoerber by the Spirit for service in behalf of Christ's people. May it be received and used on this basis!

BIBLION PUBLISHING

Dr. Phillip B. Giessler
Biblion Editor in Chief

Autobiographical Introduction

To preach or to teach, that was the question! The decision to teach resulted from the tremendous influence that some of my instructors had on me—Dr. Leonard J. Dierker at St. John's Parochial School in St. Louis; Dr. Walter H. Wente at St. John's College in Winfield, Kansas; Dr. William Arndt at Concordia Seminary in St. Louis; and Dr. Thomas Duncan in the graduate school of Washington University.

Dr. Wente deserves special mention, since he introduced me to the study of Greek and also encouraged me to apply successfully for a scholarship at the University of Chicago. There I studied with such scholars as Professor Werner Jaeger of world-wide reputation as a classicist.

Also meriting special recognition is Professor Thomas Duncan, my mentor at Washington University, where I received a fellowship in Greek and Latin. Professor Duncan, who took his doctorate at Johns Hopkins University under Professor Basil Gildersleeve, was a scholar and a gentleman, giving generously of his time to his students—the same professor under whom Dr. William Arndt and Dr. Martin Scharlemann earned their doctorates.

I would be remiss if I did not include the influence of my parents Eugene T. and Adele A. Hoerber. Their Christian example will always be remembered. Also, their financial assistance made it possible for me to devote full time and attention to my studies at St. John's College, Concordia Seminary, and Washington University. As a result, for three years I took classes at the seminary in the mornings and spent the afternoons in courses at Washington University, receiving my M.A. before I was scheduled for vicarage. Then after two years of intensive graduate studies I was fortunate to have earned my Ph.D. before I entered my final year at Concordia Seminary.

Last, but not least, was the encouragement of my wife, formerly Ruth Hanser, who gracefully acquiesced in all of my professional decisions relative to our "pulling up stakes" and moving to various small towns—Mankato, Minnesota; Fulton, Missouri; Northfield, Minnesota; back to Fulton; to Concordia Seminary, and back again to Fulton.

Bethany Lutheran College

After receiving my doctorate in Greek and Latin from Washington University in May 1944, I returned to Concordia Seminary for the summer semester to begin my last year of theological education. In June I was contacted by President S. C. Ylvisaker and was extended a call to the faculty of Bethany Lutheran College in Mankato.

After prayerful consideration and with a definite preference for teaching, I accepted the call to Bethany on the basis of the following choice: a divine call to immediately utilize my graduate training *versus* a possible opportunity to teach twelve to fifteen years down the road. I could not picture myself before my Maker some day confessing that I did not make use of any specialized talent because of the advice of some administrators.

At that time the Synodical Conference consisted of the Missouri Synod, Wisconsin Synod, Evangelical Lutheran Synod (the smaller Norwegian group, which maintained Bethany College), and the Slovak Synod. A number of scholars from the Missouri Synod had been utilized by Bethany over the years. During my first year at Bethany, five of us were from the Missouri Synod: Dr. John Klotz, Dr. Paul Zimmerman, Pauline Spitz, Dr. Alfred Fremder, and myself.

The three years at Bethany (1944-47) were both enjoyable and profitable through my close contacts with the students and with fellow faculty members.

A most positive event took place during these years. At that time relations within the Synodical Conference and in the Missouri Synod became strained through the rise of the so-called "Forty-four" who published *A Statement* in September 1945 and a volume, entitled *Speaking the Truth in Love*, which contained unsigned articles. One unsigned chapter was on Romans 16:17. Other pamphlets and papers on this verse soon appeared by the dozens. After studying all of these attempts at the exegesis and application of the passage, I noticed that both the "conservatives" and the "liberals" did not comprehend some basic points of Greek grammar—particularly whether the prepositional phrase, "contrary to the doctrine," is adjectival or adverbial, and whether the articles before "divisions" and "offenses" are specific or generic. The faculty heard my oral presentation on this text and requested that I put it in written form, which the Evangelical Lutheran Synod then printed and sent out to every clergyman in the Synodical Conference under the title, *A Grammatical Study of Romans 16:17*.

The first edition was published in 1947; a second printing was issued in 1963. (It is still available from the Lutheran Synod Book Company at Mankato, Minnesota.) This thirty-two page monograph made my reputation as a Greek scholar. After its appearance the "liberals" ceased using this passage in their discussions with the "conservatives." A later publication, credited to Dr. Behnken, assisted by Professor Martin Franzmann, referred to my monograph as follows: "The translation 'the well-known' [for the definite articles] rests on a misapprehension of the nature of the specific use of the definite article, as Robert George Hoerber has shown in his careful and objective study of the grammatical questions of our passage" (*Exegesis on Romans 16:17ff.*, May 11, 1950, p. 4).

Westminster College

In 1947 I accepted the position of Professor of Classics at Westminster College in Fulton, Missouri—a prestigious Presbyterian school, founded in 1851, with an enrollment of 600-700 students—where I taught Greek, Latin, Ancient History, and Mythology for approximately thirty years. In 1965-67 I took temporary leave to become the chairman of the Classics Department at St. Olaf College in Northfield, Minnesota—a school I would rate as one of the best Lutheran colleges in the country.

At Westminster I experienced "heaven on earth." The registrar allowed me to choose the hours and classes I wished to teach—usually from 9 to 12 noon Monday through Friday. We had no summer school and very few committee meetings in the afternoons. So with the time available for study I began preparing papers for meetings of the various classical societies; I published articles and book reviews in over ten professional journals in this country and abroad. My rationale was—and still is—that research not only makes one a superior teacher because of increasing knowledge of the subject, but that one also becomes more sympathetic to the struggles of students, who are facing challenges in a foreign language studied for the first time—parallel to the instructor's unsolved problems in his current research. During these years my publications totaled about 400 items, and I was promoted to Distinguished Service Professor of Classics. In the summer of 1956 I taught in the graduate school at the University of Missouri as Visiting Professor of Classical Languages and Archaeology.

My research and publications in Classics centered primarily on Plato—particularly in two areas. One began with my doctoral dissertation, *The Theme of Plato's Republic* (published at Eden Publishing House, 1944), in which I proposed that interpreters of the *Republic*, beginning with Aristotle, incorrectly assume that Plato's *Republic* is *political* in theme. My conclusion was that Plato presents his political views in the *Laws*, the *Politicus*, and some *Epistles*. His threefold division of the ideal city-state into (1) the "philosopher rulers," (2) the "professional warriors," and (3) the "multitude" is essentially an enlarged model of his division of the human "soul" into three parts, namely, (1) the "rational element," (2) the "high-spirited element" or the "will," and (3) the "appetitive element" or the "passions." This view concerning the *Republic* at that time was similar to telling a group of conservative preachers that the Bible is not the word of God. Over the past forty-five years, however, more and more scholars are adopting this newer approach to Plato's *Republic*.

In fact, while my volume was being set in type, Professor Werner Jaeger published his second volume of *Paideia*, in which he said that the theme of the *Republic* was *educational* rather than political theory. Since I had studied with Professor Jaeger at the University of Chicago, I sent him a copy of my volume. He replied in a hand-written four-page letter from Harvard University (where he was teaching after he had left Chicago), stating that he read my dissertation and found much in it with which he agreed. He cautioned me: "You are young; later you will discover that a person points out mistakes to the world, and the world soon sinks back into error and finds itself happier in that situation."

The other area in my study of Plato concerns the interpretation of his shorter dialogues. Usually scholars treat Plato in one of two ways—either as a philosopher or as a literary genius. My view is that we should combine the two approaches—that his literary techniques work "hand in glove with," and substantiate, the philosophical content of the dialogues. My findings were published in six major articles—five in the European journal, *Phronesis*, and one in a periodical published by the University of Chicago. For anyone who wishes to evaluate this approach, here is a list of these studies:

"Plato's *Euthyphro*" (*Phronesis*, vol. III, 1958)
"Plato's *Lysis*" (*Phronesis*, vol. IV, 1959)
"Plato's *Meno*" (*Phronesis*, vol. V, 1960)
"Plato's *Lesser Hippias*" (*Phronesis*, vol. VII, 1962)
"Plato's *Greater Hippias*" (*Phronesis*, vol. IX, 1964)
"Plato's *Laches*" (*Classical Philology*, vol. LXXIII, no. 2, April 1968).

During my tenure at Westminster I continued my interest in the New Testament, writing several articles for the *Concordia Theological Monthly*. In 1954 I published *Saint Paul's Shorter Letters*—a translation of all of Paul's Epistles, except *Romans*, *1 & 2 Corinthians*—a monograph of sixty-four pages, currently out of print.

For two years (1971-72) I served as pastor of our local St. Paul's Lutheran Church *gratis* in addition to my duties at Westminster. These two years gave me valuable experience for my future service at Concordia Seminary—thanks to the willingness of Westminster in permitting me to carry the increased responsibilities at the local parish. But two years of such a load was a sufficient challenge to my physical endurance and to my family.

Westminster College is the place where Winston Churchill gave his "Iron Curtain" speech. To commemorate this memorable event, the president of the college, Dr. Robert L. D. Davidson (an excellent president under whom I had the privilege to work) masterminded the transferal of a Wren church in the heart of London, bombed during World War II, to the campus of Westminster at a cost of $3,000,000. The original structure dates back to the 12th century and is the place where John Milton was married and where William Shakespeare worshiped. Its official title is the "Church of St. Mary the Virgin, Aldermanbury." The architect who rebuilt it in 1677, after its destruction in the Great Fire of London in 1666, was Sir Christopher Wren, a celebrity known for his particular design of several churches in England. Today over 20,000 visitors come each year to visit the magnificent edifice and to see the numerous and valuable Churchill memorabilia in the undercroft.

An active Association of Churchill Fellows, of which I am proud to be a member, meets on campus annually and sponsors lectures and symposia. Past and present members include such celebrities as Walter Cronkite, Hugh Downs, Malcolm S. Forbes, Armand Hammer, the Honorable Dean Rusk, and the Lady Soames.

In commemoration of Churchill's speech, officially titled "Sinews of Peace," there is on Westminster campus a portion of the Berlin Wall, eighteen by ten feet, dedicated on November 9, 1990—the first-year anniversary of the breach of the wall. The accompanying architectural pieces—a man and a woman—were done by the granddaughter of Winston Churchill, Edwina Sandys, a sculptoress in her own right. The entire cost of the project ($250,000) was underwritten by friends of the college. It's a joy to have retired in a town with such cultural attractions and where my family and I enjoyed thirty years of most pleasant experiences.

During my years at Westminster I had the privilege of training preministerial students in Greek and Latin in preparation for their study at various first-rate seminaries such as Louisville Presbyterian Seminary, McCormick Seminary, Eden Seminary, and Southern Methodist Seminary. My reputation as a conservative theologian prompted a number of students to consult me concerning religious issues confronting them. This opportunity to present Biblical principles was one of my major satisfactions. Recently, while shopping at a mall in Columbia, Missouri, a person approached me, inquiring whether I was Dr. Hoerber. He turned out to be one of our Westminster graduates in the class of 1970, a non-preministerial student. He thanked me for having shared Jesus Christ with him at Westminster, and he informed me that after graduation he "became converted" and presently is an active lay member of a congregation in Columbia together with his wife and two sons.

The Lord truly "moves in mysterious ways His wonders to perform." Toward the end of 1957 I was offered the position of chairman of the Classics Department at Wartburg College in Iowa. I was strongly leaning toward acceptance, since I would be serving a Lutheran institution, when I consulted Dr. Martin Scharlemann for advice. He told me that he did not wish to thwart any decision of mine, but if I stayed at Westminster, he would like me to teach in the Graduate School at Concordia Seminary—of which he was Director—in addition to my classes at Westminster. The opportunity to teach at my Alma Mater and thus to pay back at least something for the training I had received in schools of the Missouri Synod persuaded me to remain at Westminster and to teach two seminars each year at Concordia on Thursday afternoons—one on *The Acts of the Apostles* and the other on *Advanced Isagogics*. These classes were most challenging and satisfying, since the graduate candidates for the Th.D. degree in my courses included such scholars as Martin Haendschke, Robert Smith, Kenneth Rogahn, Lorman Petersen, Raymond Schultze, and Walter Otten.

This experience lasted two years (1958-60) and no doubt would have continued longer, but for the unfortunate fact that Dr. Scharlemann was removed as Director of the Graduate School, and his successor apparently decided that I no longer was needed. However, these two years that I taught in the Graduate School helped prepare me for my later work at Concordia. When the newsmaking faculty/student "walkout" occurred in January 1974, my name came to the minds of both Dr. Scharlemann and Dr. Robert Preus (with whom I first became acquainted during my tenure at Bethany in 1944-47)—the two persons who, together with Gladys Suelflow, should be given special credit for keeping Concordia Seminary from closing during those times of tension. Yes, the Lord "moves in a mysterious way."

Concordia Seminary

My service at Concordia and at Westminster College overlapped not only in 1958-60, but also immediately after the "walk out" when forty-five of the fifty faculty members and administrators left the campus as a result of a prolonged dispute between the president, John Tietjen, and the Board of Control. To understand the background and developments in the Missouri Synod at this time, one must read the volume, *Preus of Missouri and the Great Lutheran Civil War*, by James E. Adams (Harper & Row, 1977); also, Kurt E. Marquart's *Anatomy of an Explosion* (Concordia Theological Seminary Press, 1977).

The "exiles," as those who walked out referred to themselves, expected that the Board of Control soon would recall them rather than close the school. Yet, here again "man proposes, but God disposes." Concordia did remain open—with about only 34 students, reduced from 700-800—thanks to the return to the classroom of four retired professors, a few faculty members who remained (Martin Scharlemann, Robert Preus, Richard Klann, and Lorenz Wunderlich), some profs who came once a week from the sister seminary in Springfield, Illinois, Dr. Horace Hummel who traveled from Gary, Indiana each week, and myself coming from Fulton every Thursday afternoon. As I later told my friends among the "exiles": I did not wish to see my Alma Mater closed; I had never heard in the history of education of a faculty walking out instead of allowing its president to fight his own battle with the Board. If they had not miscalculated, most of them probably could still be on campus.

When Dr. Robert Preus contacted me to teach a seminar each Thursday afternoon in the Spring Quarter of 1974, I received permission from the president of Westminster and accepted the offer. I taught one of the courses which I had presented in 1958-60. Then after a few weeks Dr. Scharlemann became ill and no longer was able to finish his course on *Romans*. Again Dr. Robert Preus phoned me and requested that I take over Dr. Scharlemann's seminar each Wednesday afternoon, which I did—now driving 200 miles twice each week. It was quite a burden, in addition to my full schedule of fifteen hours in the classroom at Westminster, but the Lord provided the energy to help out in the emergency. I taught also during the two summer sessions of 1974.

The individual who became the key person in preparing for the rebuilding of Concordia Seminary—especially after Dr. Scharlemann's sudden illness—was Dr. Robert Preus, assisted in the "nuts and bolts" by Gladys Suelflow. (It was also Preus who later became the efficient president of our sister seminary, responsible for building a fine faculty by adding several key persons with doctorates from outstanding American and European universities.) Dr. Robert Preus carried out his and Dr. Scharlemann's plans in arranging for eleven new men to be installed as professors for the beginning of the 1974-75 academic year—of whom I was one.

Since I was already scheduled to continue teaching at Westminster for that year, my call in June to Concordia Seminary presented a problem. Dr. Robert Preus urged me to accept the call and assured me that "something could be worked out." The solution for the 1974-75 school-year was that I taught a full load (minus one course) at Westminster on Mondays, Wednesdays, Fridays, plus a complete schedule (less one class) at the seminary on Tuesdays and Thursdays.

Again Westminster was cooperative enough to allow me to assume this load. Since I was coming from a non-synodical school, my "call" was limited to two years (*sic*!). Without any request on my part, the administration of Westminster, realizing that I could be "out in the cold" if the seminary should fold, graciously granted me a two-year leave of absence. After two years Concordia extended my appointment for an additional four years. Since no school was going to give me a six-year leave of absence, and since the seminary had greatly increased its enrollment in the first two years of rebuilding, I took advantage of early retirement at Westminster, where I am still on the faculty as Distinguished Service Professor Emeritus of Classics, taking part in numerous functions at the college.

Of the eleven *new* faculty appointees in September 1974, almost all were parish pastors converted overnight to seminary professors. Only two of us, Horace Hummel and myself, had previous experience in college and seminary teaching. No doubt that this is the main reason I was asked to assume numerous *administrative* duties. For example, in addition to teaching a full class load, for several years I served as chairman of a twelve-man *exegetical* department, acting director of all academic programs, chairman of the editorial committee of the *Concordia Journal*, marshal of the school, and secretary of the faculty—in addition to writing editorials, articles, and book reviews for the *Concordia Journal*.

Publications

During my fifteen years at Concordia Seminary it was my privilege to carry out several projects in publications. I was enlisted by Thomas Nelson Publishers to participate in the *New King James Version*, published in 1982—for which I have high admiration, since it sticks closely to the Greek text, and its presentation of beautiful English phraseology makes it very easy to memorize. Over the years I have traveled for Thomas Nelson to address pastoral conferences of various denominations on the advantages of the NKJV.

In October 1983 the Reverend Phillip Giessler of Cleveland, Ohio requested my assistance in the revision of *The Holy Bible; An American Translation* (AAT), affectionately known as the "Beck Bible." We had first met at a week-long conference of scholars in New Haven, Missouri in 1978, where I became acquainted with Dr. Siegbert Becker of the Wisconsin Synod—for whom I soon developed the highest admiration as a scholar. My reply to Giessler was positive with the suggestion that Sig Becker and I work separately on the project, conferring frequently with each other *via* telephone conference calls and letters. Much of our work was completed before Dr. Becker was called to his heavenly home.

After the demise of Dr. Becker I was privileged to be asked to read the galley proofs of his commentary, *Revelation: The Distant Triumph Song* (Northwestern Publishing House, 1985).

Professor David Kuske, also of the Wisconsin Synod, then took the place of Sig Becker on our New Testament Editorial Committee, which currently consists of Giessler, Kuske, and myself. What a joy it has been and continues to be to work with a scholar of Kuske's caliber, both in the Greek as well as the English language. For the past six years we together have evaluated suggestions from numerous pastors, professors, and laity. The result, I believe, is an excellent product, now in its fourth printing (each slightly revised, totaling 100,000 copies) under the title: *God's Word to the Nations: New Testament*, NET (for *New Evangelical Translation*). Work is presently progressing on the Old Testament. This version should prove to be one of the clearest and most reliable translations in the English language.

A John W. Behnken Presidential Fellowship from the Aid Association for Lutherans made it feasible for me during a part-time sabbatical leave to prepare the major portion of my book, *Reading the New Testament for Understanding*, published by Concordia Publishing House in 1986. It is an attempt to illustrate a *method of study*, more challenging than reading merely for information or attempting to accumulate facts. *Reading for understanding* demands extreme alertness for clues in the text concerning such items as the personality of the individual book's author, the type of addressees, the relationship of the writer to his original readers, and the occasion and purpose of each document in the New Testament.

The nearest most people come to *reading for understanding* is when they read love letters. I first became alerted to this type of reading through a volume by Professor Mortimer J. Adler, titled *How to Read a Book*. This kind of reading needs to be applied to the New Testament, and over the years I developed it more thoroughly in my courses at the seminary. *Reading the New Testament for Understanding* is written in a style easily understandable by young people of high-school age and attempts to teach our laity a most rewarding method of studying Scripture. To illustrate, I quote three paragraphs from the book (pages 13,14):

> The first 17 verses of Matthew might seem at first to be merely a dry genealogy. But through *reading for understanding* (by watching carefully for clues) we should see hints concerning the addressees, an aspect of Matthew's message, and a characteristic of the author.
>
> The genealogy of Jesus is traced to Abraham (not to Adam as in Luke) with David occupying a prominent position in the first verse. What may these facts tell us about the nationality of the addressees? That they probably were Jewish Christians, of course. Furthermore, in verses 3-6 Matthew lists the names of several women—even women who were not born Israelites—and what is more, several of them had blemished characters. Since we know that the Jews regarded women as second-rate persons, non-Israelites as outside the fold, and wicked women as debased people, could the presence of these names in Jesus' genealogy indicate that Matthew wishes to stress that God's mercy extends to all nations and all classes of people? This conclusion would seem logical. Finally, we may note that in verse 17 the author systematically divides the names into three groups of 14 each. What does that orderly arrangement tell us about the author? Does it not coincide with what we might expect of a tax collector (parallel to our Internal Revenue Service agent)—a person who was accustomed to keeping orderly records?
>
> And so by *reading for understanding* we turn a dry list of names into several helpful clues about the author, the addressees, and the message of the First Gospel.

After Concordia Publishing House accepted the manuscript of *Reading the New Testament for Understanding*, I was appointed to be General Editor of the *Concordia Self-Study Bible*, a volume of over 2,200 pages, which sold more than 100,000 copies within the first year after publication (1986). It is based on Zondervan's *NIV Study Bible* with numerous alterations. Two basic changes are the insertion of notes concerning the sacraments as means of grace (Baptism and the Lord's Supper) and the deletion of references to millennialism (especially in *Revelation*).

Three items were added. (1) An introductory essay, "Principal Teachings of Scripture," discusses six topics: The Grace of God; Through Faith Alone; Scripture Alone; Law and Gospel; Word and Sacrament: Means of Grace; and Christology. (2) To show how a common theme permeates all sixty-six books of Scripture, each book is introduced with a paragraph on "God's Grace in *Genesis*," "God's Grace in *Exodus*," etc. (3) Brief paragraphs (where available) from Luther's *Prefaces* were included. It was my honor to do the entire New Testament and to receive assistance for the Old Testament from Dr. Walter R. Roehrs (Pentateuch and Major Prophets), Dr. Horace D. Hummel (Historical and Poetic Books), and Professor Dean O. Wenthe (Minor Prophets).

The following year (1987) with the aid of Walter R. Roehrs I revised two volumes by Dr. William Arndt, *Does the Bible Contradict Itself?* (1926) and *Bible Difficulties* (1932). The revision, entitled *Bible Difficulties and Seeming Contradictions*, combines both of Dr. Arndt's books with numerous updatings and additions to the original works, also using the *New King James Version* of the texts.

Several years previous Baker Book House requested that I completely revise Richard C. Trench's *Synonyms of the New Testament*, which has been a best-seller since 1854. Back in the 19th century pastors generally could comprehend in the original languages (Greek, Latin, German, French) the copious citations from Classical authors (Plato, Aristotle, Cicero, Plutarch, Josephus, Seneca, *ad infinitum*), quotations from the Church Fathers, as well as quotes in foreign languages from later authors. This project took much of my time, but was most enlightening and enjoyable. The finished product of 425 pages was published in 1989 by Baker Book House.

In addition to the translation of all the quotations in foreign languages, (1) foreign language titles to works by Classical and Ecclesiastical authors are spelled out rather than abbreviated, (2) Greek and Hebrew words appearing in Scripture are coded according to *The New Strong's Exhaustive Concordance of the Bible* (Nashville: Thomas Nelson, 1984), and (3) other Greek words are citied with their meaning and pagination in Liddell-Scott-Jones' *A Greek-English Lexicon* (Oxford: Claredom Press).

The entire volume has been completely rewritten to modernize and simplify the English style, spelling, punctuation, and sentence structure. This brings it in line with the standards of current scholarly literature. The revised volume should prove to be as helpful to the present and future students of Scripture as the original work has enlightened its readers for the past 135 years.

This short autobiography would not be complete without mentioning the love that I have for my family, my dear wife Ruth, my son Bob, a teacher of finance and management at Westminster, my daughter-in-law Janice, granddaughter Jennifer, and another grandchild on the way.

In addition, many have been my associations with friends and colleagues such as Presidents Ralph A. Bohlmann, Karl Barth, and Wilhelm Petersen as well as Robert and Lois Davidson, Horace Hummel, Erich Kiehl, Robert Preus, August and Gladys Suelflow, and Leon and Barbara Wilkerson. I also mention our (Ruth's and mine) deep friendship with Alfred and Ernestine Fremder and Walter and Louise Roehrs.

In my retirement I am preparing papers regularly for the combined pastoral circuits of Columbia and Jefferson City. Also, much joy is being found in preparing a Biblical commentary on *Matthew*. This Greek-based work will serve as a companion volume to *The Holy Bible: New Evangelical Translation* (NET). It will be printed by NET Publishing (Cleveland, Ohio).

Deo volente, I plan to continue my research and writing, with daily prayer for divine guidance and with the hope that all my work may glorify God and benefit many Christians.

Soli Deo Gratia!

Studies In The New Testament

"This Is My Body"

"This is My body" is the English translation of the Greek, τοῦτό ἐστιν τὸ σῶμά μου, which occurs in Matthew 26:26, Mark 14:22, and Luke 22:19. St. Paul records a variation of the statement in 1 Corinthians 11:24: τοῦτό μού ἐστιν τὸ σῶμα τὸ ὑπὲρ ὑμῶν. The importance of this text in Lutheran, Reformed, and Roman Catholic theology is obvious. Its interpretation, therefore, must be based on sound grammatical principles. One point of grammar in the sentence which has caused much concern to theologians in their interpretation is the gender of τοῦτο. Carlstadt, for example, proposed that Christ must have pointed to Himself when He declared: "This is My body." [1] He perhaps could not understand how τοῦτο, being neuter, could refer to bread (ἄρτος), which is masculine.

Although Carlstadt's suggestion is ridiculous, the grammatical point involved has apparently vexed also Lutheran theologians. *The Conservative Reformation and Its Theology,* by Charles P. Krauth,[2] contains the following statements: "Those who have entered the lists against the doctrine of our Church [i. e., Lutheran] usually insist that 'this' qualifies 'bread' understood, that is, the pronoun *touto,* which is neuter, qualifies the noun, which is masculine. Determined to be fettered by no laws of language, they abrogate the rule — that a pronoun shall agree with the noun it qualifies in gender (p. 609). . . . The Church [i. e., Lutheran] does not consider the neuter pronoun as qualifying the masculine noun (p. 610). . . . Now, 'touto' does not agree in gender with 'artos,' and 'artos' may, therefore, not be supplied (p. 668). . . . Not one instance can be found from Genesis to Malachi, in the Septuagint, or from Matthew to Revelation, in the New Testament, in which such a conjunction must be made as that of *touto neuter* with *artos masculine,* in order to reach the full sense of a passage (p. 669). . . . The accepted view of the *Lutheran* theologians is

---

[1] Cf. Luther, Vol. XX: pp. 221—222 (St. Louis Edition, 1890); J. T. Mueller, *Christian Dogmatics,* p. 514.

[2] Philadelphia: The United Lutheran Publication House, 1871. Cf. *The Lutheran Commentary,* edited by Henry Eyster Jacobs (New York: The Christian Literature Co., 1895), Vol. II, pp. 319—320. *The Interpretation of St. Matthew's Gospel,* R. C. H. Lenski (Columbus, Ohio: The Wartburg Press, 1943), pp. 1025—1026. *Popular Commentary of the Bible — The New Testament,* P. E. Kretzmann (St. Louis: Concordia Publishing House, 1921), Vol. I, p. 146. *An American Commentary on the New Testament: Commentary on the Gospel of Matthew,* John A. Broadus (Philadelphia: The American Baptist Publication Society, 1886), p. 529. *The Greek Testament,* Henry Alford (London, 1863), Vol. 1, p. 266. *A Commentary on the Holy Scriptures: The Gospel According to Matthew,* Lange-Schaff (New York: Charles Scribner, 1866), p. 470. Cf. Krauth, *op. cit.,* pp. 672—673.

that *touto* cannot refer grammatically to *artos*. This is especially illustrated among those we have examined by Gerhard, Quenstedt, Calovius, Carpzov, Oliarius, Scherzer, Bengel, and the best of our earlier and later commentators (p. 671)."

The dogmatic character of Krauth's statements is amusing, for the point of grammar is rather simple and has numerous illustrations throughout classical literature. In brief, the demonstrative pronouns are frequently attracted in gender to the predicate nominative both in Latin and Greek. Since so many of our theologians are exposed to the dogmatic and confused treatment of Krauth, it should be of value to treat this point in more detail by giving copious examples from classical literature.

While reading Vergil's *Aeneid* in leisure moments, we noticed in the first six books several examples of the attraction of the demonstrative pronoun to the predicate nominative.

> Urbs antiqua fuit (Tyrii tenuere coloni),
> Carthago, Italiam contra Tiberinaque longe
> ostia, dives opum, studiisque asperrima belli,
> quam Iuno fertur terris magis omnibus unam
> posthabita coluisse Samo: hic illius arma,
> hic currus fuit; *hoc* regnum dea gentibus esse,
> si qua Fata sinant, iam tum tenditque fovetque.
> I, 12—18

Hoc refers to *urbs,* but is attracted into the gender of the predicate noun *regnum.*

> Trunca manu pinus regit et vestigia firmat;
> lanigerae comitantur oves; *ea* sola voluptas
> solamenque mali. III, 659—661

Oves is the antecedent of *ea; ea* derives its gender and number from the predicate noun *voluptas* (*est*).

> Hinc Drepani me portus et inlaetabilis ora
> accipit. Hic, pelagi tot tempestatibus actus,
> heu genitorem, omnis curae casusque levamen,
> amitto Anchisen; hic me, pater optime, fessum
> deseris, heu tantis nequiquam erepte periclis!
> Nec vates Helenus, cum multa horrenda moneret,
> hos mihi praedixit luctus, non dira Celaeno.
> *Hic* labor extremus, longarum *haec* meta viarum;
> hinc me digressum vestris deus appulit oris.
> III, 707—715

Hic and *haec* are attracted into the gender and number of *labor* and *meta,* respectively, although they refer to the death of Anchises.

> His ego nigrantem commixta grandine nimbum,
> dum trepidant alae saltusque indagine cingunt,
> desuper infundam, et tonitru caelum omne ciebo.
> Diffugient comites, et nocte tegentur opaca;
> speluncam Dido dux et Troianus eandem
> devenient. Adero, et, tua si mihi certa voluntas,
> conubio iungam stabili propriamque dicabo;
> *hic* Hymenaeus erit. IV, 120—127

Hic agrees in gender with the predicate nominative *Hymenaeus;* its antecedent is the description in lines 120—126.

> Sed nunc Italiam magnam Gryneus Apollo,
> Italiam Lyciae iussere capessere sortes;
> *hic* amor, *haec* patria est.
>
> IV, 345—347

Although *hic* and *haec* both refer to Italy, they are attracted into the gender of their respective predicate nominatives.

> Heu! Furiis incensa feror! Nunc augur Apollo,
> nunc Lyciae sortes, nunc et Iove missus ab ipso
> interpres divum fert horrida iussa per auras.
> Scilicet *is* superis labor est, *ea* cura quietos
> sollicitat.
>
> IV, 376—380

Is and *ea* agree in gender with *labor* and *cura,* respectively, although both refer to the thought of *Nunc augur . . . auras.*

> Talibus orabat dictis, arasque tenebat,
> cum sic orsa loqui vates: Sate sanguine divum,
> Tros Anchisiade, facilis decensus Averno
> (noctis atque dies patet atri ianua Ditis);
> sed revocare gradum superasque evadere ad auras,
> *hoc* opus, *hic* labor est.
>
> VI, 124—129

Both *hoc* and *hic* sum up the preceding line; they agree in gender with *opus* and *labor,* respectively.

> Hi tibi Nomentum, et Gabios, urbemque Fidenam,
> hi Collatinas imponent montibus arcis,
> Pometios, Castrumque Inui, Bolamque, Coramque:
> *haec* tum nomina erunt, nunc sunt sine nomine terrae.
>
> VI, 773—776

Haec is attracted into the gender of *nomina,* the predicate nominative, although its antecedents are the towns mentioned in the previous three lines.

An example of attraction occurs also with a relative pronoun in Vergil's *Aeneid,* VI, 608—614:

> Hic, quibus invisi fratres, dum vita manebat,
> pulsatusve parens, et fraus innexa clienti,
> aut qui divitiis soli incubuere repertis
> nec partem posuere suis, *quae* maxima turba est,
> quique ob adulterium caesi, quique arma secuti
> impia nec veriti dominorum fallere dextras,
> inclusi poenam exspectant.

Quae agrees in gender with its predicate nominative, although its antecedent is masculine in gender.

In order that no one may suppose that attraction in gender to the predicate nominative is limited to Latin poetry, we shall list a few illustrations from Latin prose before taking up examples in Greek. Caesar begins the fourth book of his *Commentarii De Bello Gallico* thus:

> Ea quae secuta est hieme, *qui* fuit annus Cn. Pompeio M. Crasso consulibus . . .

The relative pronoun *qui* is attracted in gender to its predicate nominative (*annus*), although its antecedent (*hieme*) is feminine.

The *Germania* of Tacitus contains numerous examples of the same principle.

> . . . et in proximo pignora, unde feminarum ululatus audiri, unde vagitus infantium. *Hi* cuique sanctissimi testes, *hi* maximi laudatores . . . Chap. 7

> Tum in ipso concilio vel principum aliquis vel pater vel propinqui scuto frameaque iuvenem ornant: *haec* apud illos toga, *hic* primus iuventae honos; ante hoc domus pars videntur, mox rei publicae. Chap. 13

> *Haec* dignitas, *hae* vires, magno semper et electorum iuvenum globo circumdari, in pace decus, in bello praesidium. Chap. 13

> Nec solum in sua gente cuique, sed apud finitimas quoque civitates *id* nomen, *ea* gloria est, si numero ac virtute comitatus emineat . . . Chap. 13

> Intersunt parentes aut propinqui ac munera probant, munera non ad delicias muliebres quaesita nec quibus nova nupta comatur, sed boves et frenatum equum et scutum cum framea gladioque. In haec munera uxor accipitur atque in vicem ipsa armorum aliquid viro affert: *hoc* maximum vinculum, *haec* arcana sacra, *hos* coniugales deos arbitrantur. Chap. 18

> Plurimis Chattorum hic placet habitus, iamque canent insignes et hostibus simul suisque monstrati. Omnium penes hos initia pugnarum; *haec* prima semper acies . . .
> Chap. 31

> Tencteri super solitum bellorum decus equestris disciplinae arte praecellunt; nec maior apud Chattos peditum laus quam Tencteris equitum. Sic instituere maiores: posteri imitantur. *Hi* lusus infantium, *haec* iuvenem aemulatio: perseverant senes. Chap. 32

> Iuxta Hermunduros Naristi ac deinde Marcomani et Quadi agunt. Praecipua Marcomanorum gloria viresque, atque ipsa etiam sedes pulsis olim Boiis virtute parta. Nec Naristi Quadive degenerant. *Eaque* Germaniae velut frons est, quatenus Danuvio peragitur.

The following two illustrations of attraction in gender to the predicate nominative are from Livy:

> Ianiculum quoque adiectum, non inopia loci, sed ne quando *ea* arx hostium esset.
>
> I, 33

> Inter consules ita copiae divisae: Sempronio datae legiones duae — *ea* quaterna milia erant peditum et treceni equites . . .
>
> XXI, 17 [3]

In Greek literature likewise "the demonstrative pronoun is commonly attracted into the gender of the predicate." [4] Frequent illustrations occur in classical Greek.

> ἐκεῖνος δ' ἐστὶν ἔλεγχος μέγιστος . . .
>
> Lysias XVI, 6

> νομίζοντες καὶ τῆς πόλεως ταύτην ἱκανωτάτην εἶναι σωτηρίαν καὶ τῶν ἐχθρῶν μεγίστην τιμωρίαν.
>
> Lysias XXV, 23

> ταύτην γὰρ τέχνην ἔχει.
>
> Lysias 1, 16

> αὕτη ἐστὶν ἀνδρὸς ἀρετή, ἱκανὸν εἶναι τὰ τῆς πόλεως πράττειν . . .
>
> Plato, *Meno,* 71 e

> οὗτοι δὴ 'Αθηναῖοί γε, ὦ Εὐθύφρον, δίκην αὐτὴν καλοῦσιν, ἀλλὰ γραφήν.
>
> Plato, *Euthyphro,* 2 a

> ὡς ταύτης οὔσης φύσεως ψυχῆς (τὸ αὐτὸ ἑαυτὸ κινοῦν) . . .
>
> Plato, *Phaedrus,* 245 e

> εἰ δὲ μή, καὶ παρὰ τῶν προγεγενημένων μανθάνετε· αὕτη γὰρ ἀρίστη διδασκαλία.
>
> Xenophon, *Cyr.,* VIII, 7, 24

> κίνησις γὰρ αὕτη μεγίστη . . . ἐγένετο.
>
> Thucydides I, 1, 2

> 'Ηροδότου 'Αλικαρνησσέος ἱστορίης ἀπόδεξις ἥδε . . .
>
> Herodotus I, 1

> ἀκτὴ μὲν ἥδε . . . Λήμνου.
>
> Sophocles, *Ph.,* 1—2

> αἰδὼς μὲν νῦν ἥδε . . . Ἴλιον εἰσαναβῆναι . . .
>
> Homer, *Iliad,* XVII, 336—337

In the light of this evidence it is clear that C. P. Krauth momentarily forgot a point of grammar of the classical languages when he wrote the statements cited above on the gender of τοῦτο in the text, "This is My body." Nor had he read the New Testament in Greek with a sufficiently discerning eye. For then he could not have declared so dogmatically: "Not one instance can be

[3] Cf. Cicero, *Tusc.,* I, 23, 53—54.

[4] *Syntax of Classical Greek,* B. L. Gildersleeve (American Book Company: Part I, 1900; Part II, 1911), p. 58.

found from Genesis to Malachi, in the Septuagint, or from Matthew to Revelation, in the New Testament, in which such a conjunction must be made as that of *touto neuter* with *artos masculine,* in order to reach the full sense of a passage." [5] "Such a conjunction" is easily explained and even expected on the basis of the grammatical rule that demonstrative pronouns are commonly attracted into the gender of the predicate nominative; and this rule obtains also in the New Testament. Several examples are the following:

> τὸ δὲ εἰς τὰς ἀκάνθας πεσόν, οὗτοί εἰσιν οἱ ἀκούσαντες . . .
>
> **Luke 8:14**
>
> τὸ δὲ ἐν τῇ καλῇ γῇ, οὗτοί εἰσιν οἵτινες ἐν καρδίᾳ καλῇ καὶ ἀγαθῇ ἀκούσαντες . . .
>
> **Luke 8:15**
>
> πάντα οὖν ὅσα ἐὰν θέλητε ἵνα ποιῶσιν ὑμῖν οἱ ἄνθρωποι, οὕτως καὶ ὑμεῖς ποιεῖτε αὐτοῖς· οὗτος γάρ ἐστιν ὁ νόμος καὶ οἱ προφῆται.
>
> **Matthew 7:12**
>
> καὶ αὕτη αὐτοῖς ἡ παρ' ἐμοῦ διαθήκη, ὅταν ἀφέλωμαι τὰς ἁμαρτίας αὐτῶν.
>
> **Romans 11:27**
>
> ἐγένετο δὲ ἐν ταῖς ἡμέραις ἐκείναις ἐξῆλθεν δόγμα παρὰ Καίσαρος Αὐγούστου ἀπογράφεσθαι πᾶσαν τὴν οἰκουμένην. αὕτη ἀπογραφὴ πρώτη ἐγένετο ἡγεμονεύοντος τῆς Συρίας Κυρηνίου.
>
> **Luke 2:1-2**
>
> αὕτη γάρ ἐστιν ἡ ἀγάπη τοῦ θεοῦ, ἵνα τὰς ἐντολὰς αὐτοῦ τηρῶμεν . . .
>
> **1 John 5:3**
>
> αὕτη ἐστὶν ἡ μαρτυρία τοῦ θεοῦ, ὅτι μεμαρτύρηκεν περὶ τοῦ υἱοῦ αὐτοῦ.
>
> **1 John 5:9**
>
> καὶ αὕτη ἐστὶν ἡ μαρτυρία, ὅτι ζωὴν αἰώνιον ἔδωκεν ὁ θεὸς ἡμῖν . . .
>
> **1 John 5:11**
>
> καὶ αὕτη ἐστὶν ἡ παρρησία ἣν ἔχομεν πρὸς αὐτόν, ὅτι ἐάν τι αἰτώμεθα κατὰ τὸ θέλημα αὐτοῦ ἀκούει ἡμῶν.
>
> **1 John 5:14** [6]

It is, therefore, to put it mildly, disconcerting to read that "the accepted view of the *Lutheran* theologians is that *touto* cannot refer grammatically to *artos.* This is especially illustrated among those we have examined by Gerhard, Quenstedt, Calovius, Carpzov, Oliarius, Scherzer, Bengel, and the best of our earlier and later commentators." [7] The preceding evidence clearly demonstrates that τοῦτο, although neuter, can refer grammatically to ἄρτος, in view of the gender of σῶμα, the predicate nominative.

Attraction of the demonstrative pronoun, however, to the

---

[5] *Op. cit.,* p. 669.

[6] Cf. Luke 8:11; 22:53; John 1:19; 1 Corinthians 9:3; Matthew 22:38; John 2:11.

[7] Krauth, *op. cit.,* p. 671.

gender of the predicate nominative does not always occur in Latin, classical Greek, and the New Testament.[8] In such cases the construction according to sense rather than the grammatical gender may prevail, or the demonstrative may retain the gender of its antecedent and not become assimilated to the predicate nominative in gender. The question, then, arises whether there is any difference in meaning between those instances in which the demonstrative pronoun assimilates itself to the predicate nominative and those in which it retains agreement with its antecedent. The difference appears to be one of slight emphasis. Attraction to the predicate nominative may stress to a degree the predicate nominative, while agreement with the antecedent (rather than assimilation to the predicate nominative) would place the emphasis on the antecedent.

The accent of τοῦτό ἐστιν is worthy of note, distinguishing it from the phrase τοῦτ' ἔστιν. The latter is the equivalent of "that is," *"id est"* and *"hoc est."* It appears in the New Testament without any regard for number, case, and gender of either the antecedent or the predicate nominative.[9] The accent on the penult of the verb stresses the idea of existence.

The article in the predicate shows that the sentence expresses a convertible proposition — the subject and predicate are identical and interchangeable.[10] The presence of the article, therefore, is natural in the text; for τὸ σῶμά μου is the only way of expressing "My body." The absence of the article would imply "a body of mine."

Summary

The statement τοῦτό ἐστιν τὸ σῶμά μου is correctly translated: "This is My body." The gender of the demonstrative pronoun is natural, being attracted into the gender of the predicate nominative, τὸ σῶμά μου; the reference may very well be to ἄρτος although it is masculine. The only grammatical implication in the attraction of the demonstrative pronoun to the gender of the predicate nominative is that the predicate nominative may have a slight stress instead of the antecedent. That is, the emphasis may be "This is My *body*" rather than "*This* is My body." The accent of the verb argues against the translation "This *is* My body." The presence of the article in the predicate reveals that "This is a body of Mine" would also be an incorrect rendering of Christ's declaration.

Fulton, Missouri

---

[8] Vergil, Aeneid, III, 173; Lysias III, 28; Plato, *Gorgias,* 478 c, 492 c, 492 e; Plato, *Phaedrus,* 245 c; Xenophon, *Cyropaedeia,* I, 3, 10; Acts 8:10; 9:15; 2 Peter 2:17; Revelation 11:4; 1 Peter 2:19-20; Philippians 3:7; 1 Corinthians 6:11; 10:6.

[9] Cf. 1 Peter 3:20; Romans 7:18; Mark 7:2; Acts 19:4; Hebrews 13:15; 9:11; 11:16; 7:5; 2:14; Philemon 12; Matthew 27:46.

[10] Gildersleeve, *op. cit.,* pp. 324—328. *A Grammar of the Greek New Testament in the Light of Historical Research,* A. T. Robertson (Harper and Brothers, 1931), pp. 767—769. *Greek Grammar,* W. W. Goodwin and C. B. Gulick (Ginn and Company, 1930), paragraph 954.

The Problems in John 8:25

The edition of Eberhard and Erwin Nestle (Stuttgart) contains the following reading for St. John 8:25, 26: ἔλεγον οὖν αὐτῷ· σὺ τίς εἶ; εἶπεν αὐτοῖς ὁ 'Ιησοῦς· τὴν ἀρχὴν ὅ τι καὶ λαλῶ ὑμῖν; πολλὰ ἔχω περὶ ὑμῶν λαλεῖν καὶ κρίνειν· ἀλλ' ὁ πέμψας με ἀληθής ἐστιν, κἀγὼ ἃ ἤκουσα παρ' αὐτοῦ, ταῦτα λαλῶ εἰς τὸν κόσμον. The Oxford text, edited by Alexander Souter, presents one basic variation; the conclusion of verse 25 is a statement instead of a question: Τὴν ἀρχὴν ὅ τι καὶ λαλῶ ὑμῖν.

The challenge which the conclusion of verse 25 presents to translators is evident from the various versions:

"Even the same that I said unto you from the beginning." (King James)

"Why should I talk to you at all?" (Moffatt)

"Why do I even talk to you at all?" (Goodspeed)

"Even what I have told you from the beginning." A footnote gives the variation: "Why do I talk to you at all?" (Revised Standard Version)

"Principium, quia et loquor vobis." (Vulgate, ed. of Wordsworth and White; Oxford)

"Erstlich der, der ich mit euch rede." (Luther)

"Ce que je vous dis dès le commencement." (Segond; Oxford)

"Ο, τι σᾶς λέγω ἀπ' ἀρχῆς. (Modern Greek; British Bible Society)

Some of the difficulties involved in the passage are noted by A. T. Robertson in *A Grammar of the Greek New Testament in the Light of Historical Research:* "In John 8:25 both Westcott-Hort and Nestle print as a question, Τὴν ἀρχὴν ὅ τι καὶ λαλῶ ὑμῖν; The Latin versions have *quod* or *quia.* It is a very difficult passage at best. Τὴν ἀρχὴν ὅ τι may be taken to mean 'Why do I speak to you at all?' (Τὴν ἀρχήν = ὅλως.) But there may be ellipsis, 'Why do you reproach me that (ὅτι) I speak to you at all?' If necessary to the sense, ὅ τι may be taken here as interrogative. Moulton admits the New Testament use of ὅστις in a direct question. Recitative ὅτι is even suggested in Winer-Schmiedel, but the occasional interrogative use of ὅ τι is sufficient explanation. But the passage in John 8:25 is more than doubtful. Chrysostom takes ὅ τι there as relative, Cyril as causal" (p. 730).

The variation in the Greek text, the various translations, and the remarks of Robertson point to three problems in the passage. First, should the sentence end with a period (Souter) or question mark (Nestle and Westcott-Hort)? Secondly, is ὅ τι to be taken as relative or interrogative? The reading of ὅτι as a conjunction is possible, but not accepted in the better editions. Thirdly, the translation of the phrase τὴν ἀρχήν. There is also a fourth problem: λαλῶ may be indicative or subjunctive.

The first and second problems are interdependent. If ὅ τι is relative, the sentence should end with a period; if ὅ τι is interrogative, a question mark should be the final punctuation. Although ὅ τι, the neuter of ὅστις, is more frequently used as a relative indefinite pronoun, in the context of John 8:25 there is no antecedent for it. The translators, furthermore, who imply or supply an unexpressed antecedent are inclined to translate λαλῶ as having the significance of a past tense, as in the King James and Revised Standard versions. It appears better, then, to regard ὅ τι as interrogative. There is no need to resort to the recitative or causal conjunction ὅτι. The indirect interrogative use of ὅστις is common throughout Greek literature beginning with Homer (*Iliad* 3.192; 14.509; *Odyssey* 8.28; 10.110). One example in the New Testament is Acts 9:6. Also the direct interrogative function is found in passages containing dialogue:

(Charon) . . . οὗτος τί ποιεῖς;
(Dionysus) ὅ τι ποιῶ; (Aristophanes, *Frogs* 198)
(Lamachus) ἀλλὰ τίς γὰρ εἶ;
(Dicaeopolis) ὅστις; (Aristophanes, *Acharnians* 594, 595)
(Poverty) τί δ' ἂν ὑμεῖς ἀγαθὸν ἐξεύροιθ';
(Chremylus) ὅ τι; (Aristophanes, *Wealth* 462)
(Euthyphro) . . . ἀλλὰ δὴ τίνα γραφήν σε γέγραπται;
(Socrates) Ἥντινα; (Plato, *Euthyphro* 2c).

In John 8:25, then, we may interpret ὅ τι as interrogative and conclude the sentence with a question mark.

The third problem, the interpretation of τὴν ἀρχήν, has confused the translators. Some render it "from the beginning," as if the text were ἐξ ἀρχῆς; others regard it as equivalent to ὅλως and translate "at all"—not to mention the Latin edition by Wordsworth and White. The confusion seems odd, since the phrase by itself should not be difficult; perhaps the other problems in the passage have caused the translators to stretch the point on τὴν ἀρχήν. The term is interpreted best as an adverbial accusative meaning "to begin with," "at first," "in the first place," or "first of all." Both ἀρχήν and τὴν ἀρχήν have this signification throughout Greek literature. Examples of ἀρχήν are:

ἀρχὴν γὰρ ἐγὼ μηχανήσομαι οὕτω ὥστε μηδὲ μαθεῖν μιν ὀφθεῖσαν ὑπὸ σεῦ. (Herodotus 1.9)

Ταῦτα μέν νυν ἔστω ὡς ἔστι τε καὶ ὡς ἀρχὴν ἐγένετο. (Herodotus 2.28)

ἀρχὴν δὲ θηρᾶν οὐ πρέπει τἀμήχανα· (Sophocles, *Antigone* 92)

ἀρχὴν κλύειν ἂν οὐδ' ἅπαξ ἐβουλόμην. (Sophocles, *Philoctetes* 1239)

ἀρχὴν δ' ἄν, εἰ μὴ τλημονεστάτη γυνὴ πασῶν έβλαστε, τάσδε δυσμενεῖς χοὰς οὐκ ἄν ποθ' ὃν γ' ἔκτεινε τῷδ', ἐπέστρεφε. (Sophocles, *Electra* 439—441)

Examples of τὴν ἀρχήν are as follows:

Τὴν ἀρχὴν γὰρ ἐξῆν αὐτῷ μὴ γράφειν . . . (Demosthenes, *Against Aristocrates* 93)

. . . ὃς ἔφη ἢ τὴν ἀρχὴν οὐ δεῖν ἐμὲ δεῦρο εἰσελθεῖν . . . (Plato, *Apology* 29c)

Πῶς οὖν οἱ ἀγαθοὶ τοῖς ἀγαθοῖς ἡμῖν φίλοι ἔσονται τὴν ἀρχήν, οἳ μήτε ἀπόντες ποθεινοὶ ἀλλήλοις . . . (Plato, *Lysis* 215b)

The reading of Herodotus 4.25 is given either with the article or without it: τοῦτο δὲ οὐκ ἐνδέκομαι (τὴν) ἀρχήν. Plato's *Gorgias* (478c) contains a query of Socrates using ἀρχήν, followed by τὴν ἀρχήν in Socrates' next statement:

(Socrates) Ἆρ' οὖν οὕτως ἂν περὶ σῶμα εὐδαιμονέστατος ἄνθρωπος εἴη, ἰατρευόμενος, ἢ μηδὲ κάμνων ἀρχήν;

(Polus) Δῆλον ὅτι μηδὲ κάμνων.

(Socrates) Οὐ γὰρ τοῦτ' ἦν εὐδαιμονία, ὡς ἔοικε, κακοῦ ἀπαλλαγή, ἀλλὰ τὴν ἀρχὴν μηδὲ κτῆσις.

The fourth question, the interpretation of λαλῶ, apparently has not impressed the translators as presenting any problem. The verb has been taken as unquestionably present indicative. Yet some scholars have translated it as if it were a past tense, perhaps because they have interpreted ὅ τι as relative and have rendered τὴν ἀρχήν as "from the beginning." The verb, λαλῶ, however, may be the present subjunctive employed in a deliberative question. Such an interpretation harmonizes with the interrogative use of ὅ τι and the question mark as a final punctuation. The deliberative subjunctive, furthermore, is not foreign to the New Testament, which presents among others the following instances:

τί ποιῶμεν ἵνα ἐργαζώμεθα τὰ ἔργα τοῦ θεοῦ; (John 6:28)

τὸ ποτήριον ὃ δέδωκέν μοι ὁ πατήρ, οὐ μὴ πίω αὐτό; (John 18:11) ἔξεστιν δοῦναι κῆνσον Καίσαρι ἢ οὔ; δῶμεν ἢ μὴ δῶμεν; (Mark 12:14)

Καὶ ἐπηρώτων αὐτὸν οἱ ὄχλοι λέγοντες· τί οὖν ποιήσωμεν; (Luke 3:10)

μὴ οὖν μεριμνήσητε λέγοντες· τί φάγωμεν; ἤ· τί πίωμεν; ἤ· τί περιβαλώμεθα; (Matthew 6:31)

Καὶ τί ἔτι λέγω; (Hebrews 11:32)

According to our solutions of the problems present in the conclusion of John 8:25, we may translate the passage: "What (or, Just what) shall I say to you in the first place (or, to begin with; or, first of all)?" The adverbial use of καί (meaning "just") for emphasis is common in Greek literature; in interrogatives it frequently implies emphasis in intonation. (Cf. Euripides, *Andromache* 906; Plato, *Theaetetus* 166d; *Gorgias* 456a; Aeschylus, *Agamemnon* 278; Euripides, *Alcestis* 834; Plato, *Euthyphro* 6b; Demosthenes, *Against Philipp I* 46.) The verb λαλῶ as equivalent to λέγω is a characteristic of later writers and occurs in Acts 3:22; 9:6; Matthew 9:33; John 8:30.

The context, which is a primary test, substantiates the solutions and translation presented above. John 8:25, 26 would read: "Then they said to Him, 'Who are You?' Jesus said to them, 'What shall I say to you in the first place? I have many things to say and to judge concerning you. He who has sent Me is true; and what I have heard from Him I speak to the world.' "

Galatians 2:1-10 and the Acts of the Apostles

No doubt the chief crux in the comparison of Paul's Epistle to the Galatians with the Acts of the Apostles is the relating of Gal. 2:1-10 to the account of Acts. To equate Gal. 2:1-10 with Acts 15 raises such serious difficulties in the judgment of many scholars that they have proposed various explanations. The essential difficulties of course would be: (1) Paul in Galatians, although concerned about every connection with Jerusalem in order to prove that his Gospel did not come from men, would be omitting the visit at the time of the famine recorded in Acts 11:27-30 and 12:25 and thus would be exposing himself to the charge of deceiving his readers. (2) It would seem strange, to say the least, that Paul in Galatians would fail to refer to the decree of the Council of Jerusalem, which could be one of his weightiest arguments for the thesis he develops in that epistle. (3) Several inconsistencies would appear between Gal. 2:1-10 and Acts 15 — e. g., the private nature of the conference between Paul and James, Peter, and John in Galatians as against the public council described in Acts 15; the provision to abstain from certain foods in Acts (15:20, 28 f.; 21:25) as against Paul's claim in Galatians (2:6 ff.) that the leaders in Jerusalem imposed on his work of converting the Gentiles no obligations concerning the Jewish Law; the strangeness of the incident with Peter at Antioch reported in Gal. 2:11-14 both concerning Peter, if his defection occurred after the decree of the council, and concerning Paul, since he fails to cite the decree, which again could be his weightiest argument before Peter.

Some of the attempts to explain the difficulties between Acts 15 and Gal. 2:1-10 may be cited briefly: (1) Paul does not refer to the decree and letter of Acts 15 because he had nothing to do with their composition.[1] (2) Galatians 2:1-10 describes merely a private conference at Jerusalem on the "eve" of the council.[2] (3) Paul ignores the visit of Acts 11 because he saw only the "elders" at Jerusalem at the time of the famine, for the apostles were absent at that time as a result of the persecution of Herod Agrippa I.[3] (4) The council took place later than Acts 15 — possibly at the visit of Paul to Jerusalem mentioned in Acts 18:22.[4] (5) Acts omits the visit of Gal. 2:1-10, which really occurred before Paul and Barnabas departed for Cyprus and Asia Minor.[5] (6) Acts 11:27-30 and 15:2 ff. are in reality one visit, but the author made two visits out of

---

[1] H. Windisch, *Beginnings of Christianity*, ed. Foakes-Jackson and Lake (London, 1922), II, 328; H. Lietzmann, *The Beginnings of the Christian Church* (London, 1949), pp. 108 ff.; O. Cullmann, *Peter: Disciple, Apostle, Martyr* (London, 1953), pp. 42 ff.

[2] J. B. Lightfoot, *Galatians* (London, 1890), pp. 125 f.; H. N. Ridderbos, *Galatians* (Grand Rapids, 1953), pp. 78 ff.

[3] J. B. Lightfoot, p. 127.

[4] John Knox, *Chapters in a Life of Paul* (Nashville, 1950), pp. 64 ff.; D. T. Rowlingson, "The Jerusalem Conference and Jesus' Nazareth Visit" in *Journal of Biblical Literature*, LXXI (1952), 69 ff.

[5] T. W. Manson, "The Problem of the Epistle to the Galatians" in *Bulletin of the John Rylands Library*, XXIV (1940), 59 ff.

one because he drew from two sources.[6] (7) The dislocation of the text of Acts has caused the apparent inaccuracy, the original order being 11:25 f.; 13:1—15:2; 11:27-30; 15:3-33 (?34); 12:25; 12:1-24; 15:35-41.[7]

The failure of the attempts to parallel Acts 15 with Gal. 2:1-10 raises the question of the advisability of equating Gal. 2:1-10 with the visit at the time of the famine recorded in Acts 11:27-30. Such a thesis is not new. Ramsay is cited frequently as the first to suggest it (1895), but John Calvin made the identification in his commentary on Galatians (1548). A number of scholars in the 20th century have held this thesis,[8] usually, however, offering only one or several arguments and treating only a few of the points involved.[9] We may attempt, therefore, to examine anew the evidence available, since the problem is not only a chief crux in the comparison of Galatians with Acts but also has wide implications in such questions as the reliability of Acts, the date of Galatians, the Northern or Southern Galatian theories, and the portrayal of the personal convictions of Paul.

Since Paul in Galatians is concerned particularly with each of his visits to Jerusalem, in order to prove his point on the source of his message (1:1, 11, 12), the more logical parallelism between Galatians and Acts would be:

Galatians 1:18-24 coincides with Acts 9:26-29.[10]

Galatians 2:1-10 coincides with Acts 11:27-30.

The equation of Gal. 2:1-10 and Acts 15, on the other hand, both involves the serious difficulties and necessitates one or two of the various explanations referred to above.

In Gal. 2:2 Paul states that a "revelation" prompted his visit to Jerusalem. Acts 11:27-30 describes Paul's visit to Jerusalem as a result of Agabus' prophecy concerning the famine, while in Acts 15:1, 2 Paul's visit stemmed from dissension with Judaizers.

The same verse in Galatians states that Paul conferred *privately* with the prom-

---

6 J. Wellhausen in *Nachrichten d. kgl. Gesellschaft d. Wissenschaften zu Göttingen* (1907), pp. 1 ff.; E. Schwartz, ibid., pp. 263 ff.; K. Lake, *Beginnings of Christianity* (London, 1933), V, 199 ff.; H. Windisch, ibid., II, 322; H. W. Beyer, *Die Apostelgeschichte* (Göttingen, 1951), *ad loc.*

7 R. Eisler, *The Enigma of the Fourth Gospel* (London, 1938), p. 80.

8 K. Lake, *Earlier Epistles of Paul* (London, 1911), pp. 297 ff. (a view he changes in *Beginnings of Christianity*); V. Weber, *Die Abfassung des Galaterbriefs vor dem Apostelkonzil* (Ravensburg, 1900); D. Round, *The Date of St. Paul's Epistle to the Galatians* (Cambridge, 1906); W. M. Ramsay, *Teaching of Paul* (London, 1913), pp. 372 ff., and *St. Paul the Traveller* (London, 1920), pp. xxii, xxxi; C. W. Emmet, *Galatians* (London, 1912), pp. xiv ff., and in *Beginnings of Christianity*, II, pp. 269 ff.; A. W. F. Blunt, *Acts* (Oxford, 1922), pp. 182 ff., and *Galatians* (1925), pp. 22 ff., 77 ff.; F. C. Burkitt, *Christian Beginnings* (London, 1924), pp. 116 ff.; H. N. Bate, *A Guide to the Epistles of St. Paul* (London, 1926), pp. 45 ff.; G. S. Duncan, *Galatians* (London, 1934), pp. xxiiff.; W. L. Knox, *The Acts of the Apostles* (Cambridge, 1948), pp. 40 ff.; R. Heard, *Introduction to the New Testament* (London, 1950), p. 183; H. F. D. Sparks, *The Formation of the New Testament* (London, 1952), pp. 60 f.

9 Emmet, for example, in *Beginnings of Christianity*, II 265—297, omits any treatment of the date and addressees of Galatians, because "a full discussion . . . obviously belongs to a commentary on that Epistle" (p. 282).

10 That Gal. 1:18-24 and Acts 9:26-29 are parallel seems to be the consensus of opinion among students of the New Testament. That some minor differences, either apparent or real, exist is another problem and has no essential bearing on the topic at hand.

inent men. Acts 11:27-30, it is true, does not mention such a conference, but there is nothing in the passage to exclude it, while Acts 15 definitely describes a *public* meeting of the church in Jerusalem.

Gal. 2:10 refers to only one condition between Paul (and Barnabas) and the prominent leaders in Jerusalem. A close observation of the tenses in Greek reveals that the condition was "that we continue to remember the poor — the very matter I was careful to do."[11] Charitable relief was the chief purpose of the visit of Acts 11:27-30, while Acts 15 makes no mention of any charity. Thus the condition placed upon Paul and Barnabas suits well the fact that they just had brought a gift to Jerusalem.

The defection of Peter related in Gal. 2:11-14 raises a serious difficulty if Gal. 2:1-10 were paralleled with Acts 15; for it then would have to be placed after the full agreement of the council at Jerusalem, or Paul would be relating events out of chronological order, either solution entailing manifest objections. If Gal. 2:1-10, however, equates Acts 11:27-30, Peter's defection may be placed easily before the council, probably at Antioch during the description of Acts 15:1. In fact ἐλθεῖν τινας ἀπὸ Ἰακώβου (Gal. 2:12) tallies very closely with Καί τινες κατελθόντες ἀπὸ τῆς Ἰουδαίας (Acts 15:1).

Gal. 2:6 implies that the leaders in Jerusalem imposed no restrictions concerning the Jewish Law on Paul's activity in converting the Gentiles. Acts 15:20, 28,[12] however, definitely gives restrictive clauses concerning certain foods, while the silence of Acts 11:27-30 does not present the same problem.

According to Gal. 1:6, the trouble in Galatia with the Judaizers occurred "so soon," or "so quickly," that Paul is "surprised" at the attitude of the Galatians. Paul is not specific, it is true, whether he means "so soon" after the conversion of the Galatians or after his last visit to them. But if Gal. 2:1-10 refers to the council, would the threatening defection of the Galatians be so soon as to cause surprise, since the Judaizers had been active in Jerusalem and Antioch already several years previously? If, however, Gal. 2:1-10 is parallel to Acts 11:27-30, the threatening defection of the Galatians could be placed soon after their conversion on Paul's first journey — the suddenness of which naturally would cause Paul to be surprised.

---

[11] Or "— the very matter I was making every effort to do"; or "— the very matter I was hastening to do." The present tense of the subjunctive for "remember" is missed by most translations; but cf. A. T. Robertson, *A Grammar of the Greek New Testament in the Light of Historical Research* (New York, 1931), p. 933. For the tense of "careful" (or "making every effort," or "hastening") cf. Moulton, *A Grammar of New Testament Greek* (London, 1908), I, 148: ". . . and the aorist which simply states that the event happened is generally quite enough to describe what we should like to define more exactly as preceding the time of the main verb."

[12] Cf. Acts 21:25 for another reference to the restrictive clauses concerning certain foods. This passage gives no basis, however, for arguing that Paul was not at the council, because James seems to be informing him of the restrictive clauses as though Paul had never heard them. The statement of James does not represent necessarily new information given to Paul, but may recall information Paul already knew. Or the author of Acts may have included the statement mainly for the benefit of the readers, in lieu of the use of a footnote, which ancient authors did not employ, and somewhat to the confusion of modern critics. For arguments that the decree was a food law, cf. *Beginnings of Christianity* (London, 1922), II, 324—325.

The implication of Gal. 4:20 is that Paul at the time of writing to the Galatians is anxious to revisit them, is temporarily hindered, but will appear in person in the not too distant future. Of course a number of occasions might fit such a situation. But in connection with the point of the previous paragraph it would suit remarkably well to place the composition of Galatians at Antioch just prior to his visit to Jerusalem for the council. Paul then not only would be surprised at the suddenness of the trouble with the Judaizers but also would feel it extremely important to attend the council at Jerusalem, even if it meant the postponement of another urgent matter — the trouble in the Galatian churches — a matter which he could try to deal with in a letter, necessarily composed with some haste and anger, as the undertone of the epistle clearly implies.

The last two points broach two problems closely related to the topic of the present study — the addressees of Galatians and the date of that epistle. We may begin by summarizing the complicated historical data on the territory involved in the possible addressees of Galatians.

In 278 B.C., when a tribe of Gauls invaded Asia Minor, King Attalus of Pergamum confined them to the north central portion of Asia Minor. This area became known as GALATIA, with the leading towns of Ancyra, Pessinus, and Tavium. During the reign of the Gaulish King Amyntas the Roman Emperor Augustus allowed him to control a large dominion called the Kingdom of Galatia, which included GALATIA, part of Phrygia, Lycaonia, Pisidia, Pamphylia, and western Cilicia. After the death of Amyntas (25 B.C.), when the Romans took over this "kingdom," Pamphylia became a Roman province, western Cilicia and part of Lycaonia became "the Kingdom of Attalus" by the time of Paul's first journey, and the remaining territory formed a Roman province called *Galatia,* which included such cities in the south as Antioch, Lystra, Derbe, and Iconium, as well as northern GALATIA. After approximately three centuries the wider meaning of *Galatia* was abandoned, and the term reverted merely to the northern part of the area (referred to in these paragraphs for convenience and clarity as GALATIA). The research of William Ramsay, who discovered the wider use of the term (referred to in the present study as *Galatia*), raised the question of the addressees of Paul's Epistle to the Galatians — the northern GALATIANS or the southern *Galatians.* There are a number of points which may throw light on this question.

There was a considerable Jewish population in south *Galatia,* and the Judaizers, therefore, in all likelihood would have caused there the trouble which Paul combats in his letter. This point, however, is not too strong, since there were some Jews also in north GALATIA, and the opposition of the Judaizers conceivably could have arisen in north GALATIA.

On the southern theory we have an extant letter of Paul to the churches he visited at least on his first and second journeys. On the basis of the northern theory there would be extant no letter to these congregations. Again, this point is not decisive, but it should be taken into account in discussing the evidence as a whole.

Does Acts refer to any work of Paul in northern GALATIA? Three passages are cited by those who favor the northern theory: (a) "And they went through the region of Phrygia and Galatia, having been forbidden by the Holy Spirit to speak the word in Asia" (Acts 16:6); (b) "After spending some time there [i. e., Antioch in Syria] he departed and went from place to place through the region of Galatia and Phrygia, strengthening all the disciples" (Acts 18:23); (c) "While Apollos was at Corinth, Paul passed through the upper country and came to Ephesus. There he found some disciples" (Acts 19:1). Each of these verses merits closer study in the original.

Acts 16:6 employs the phrase τὴν Φρυγίαν καὶ Γαλατικὴν χώραν. The single article and the position of χώραν favors the view that one district is indicated, "the region which is Phrygia and Galatia." For evidence on the adjectival use of Φρυγία, apparently questioned by some commentators, one needs to consult merely the lexicon of Liddell-Scott-Jones and Aeschylus' *Suppliants* (547, 548): δὶ αἴας . . . Φρυγίας.[13] The parallel phrase in Luke 3:1, τῆς Ἰτουραίας καὶ Τραχωνίτιδος χώρας, is also a case in point, for Ἰτουραία appears to be used as an adjective, although elsewhere it is a substantive. According to Ramsay, part of the old Kingdom of Phrygia belonged to the province of Galatia and part to the province of Asia, known respectively as *regio Phrygia Galatia* and *regio Phrygia Asia.*[14]

Acts 18:23 contains the phrase τὴν Γαλατικὴν χώραν καὶ Φρυγίαν. The position of χώραν here favors the substantive use of Φρυγία and the translation "through the region of Galatia and through Phrygia." The difference in the order of the words as compared with Acts 16:6 probably denotes a different route. In Acts 18:23, because he received no warning to the contrary, Paul passed through the region of Galatia (i. e., Galatic Lycaonia, so called to distinguish it from eastern Lycaonia, which lay in the territory of King Antiochus) and through Phrygia — including both the part which lay in Galatia and the section which was in Asia — or continuing west instead of going north as in Acts 16:6.

In Acts 19:1 the phrase τὰ ἀνωτερικὰ μέρη, "the upper country," probably denotes that Paul traveled across the high ground west of Pisidian Antioch instead of along the lower main road through Colossae and Laodicea. Or as Ramsay states, Paul took "the higher-lying and more direct route, not the regular trade route on the lower level down the Lycus and Maeander valleys."[15] Acts 19:1 apparently continues the description of Acts 18:23, and the part of Asian Phrygia through which Paul traveled was known as Upper Phrygia. According to Col. 2:1, Paul was a stranger to the people in the Lycus valley.

Thus there appears to be in Acts no clear reference to any work of Paul in northern GALATIA. The interpretation presented in the previous paragraphs on the three passages of Acts is the view of such scholars as William Ramsay and W. M. Calder. K. Lake held to the view in *The*

---

13 Liddell-Scott-Jones, *A Greek-English Lexicon* (Oxford, 1940). Doubt seems to be cast on the adjectival use of the word by F. F. Bruce, *The Acts of the Apostles* (Grand Rapids, 1953), p. 310, and by K. Lake, *Beginnings of Christianity* (London, 1953), V, 231. It is also confusing that the word is listed only as a noun by W. F. Arndt and F. W. Gingrich, *A Greek-English Lexicon of the New Testament and Other Early Christian Literature* (Chicago and Cambridge, 1957).

14 *The Church in the Roman Empire before A. D. 170* (London, 1893), pp. 59—111.

15 *St. Paul the Traveller* (London, 1920), p. 265.

Earlier Epistles of St. Paul (1911), but later in *Beginnings of Christianity* (V, 231 to 237) he proposed that the ethnic sense of Galatia may be preferable and that the phrase "the region of Phrygia and Galatia" possibly means "the territory in which sometimes Phrygian and sometimes Gaulish was the language of the villagers." According to a recent study of this subject, however, that view seems to be impossible.[16]

In Gal. 2:1 and 2:9 Paul mentions Barnabas, apparently as a person known to the readers. Now Barnabas definitely was with Paul on the first journey when they established congregations in southern *Galatia,* but there is no record of Barnabas accompanying Paul on the other journeys. In fact, the separation of the two missionaries Acts records before the beginning of the second journey. (Acts 15:36-41)

In 1 Cor. 16:1-5 (written from Ephesus on the third journey) Paul refers to his instructions to "the churches of Galatia" concerning the contribution to those in Jerusalem and speaks of possible delegates to accompany him. He no doubt has in mind southern *Galatia,* for in Acts 20:1-4 (which traces Paul's steps from Ephesus to Corinth on the same journey) there is a list of delegates accompanying Paul — there is no delegate from northern GALATIA, but two delegates from cities in southern *Galatia* are present: "Gaius of Derbe and Timothy," who of course was from Lystra. (Acts 16:1)

According to Gal. 4:14, the addressees received Paul when he first came to them "as an angel of God" — or as the Greek text might be translated, "as a messenger of a god." The reference seems to point to the reception at Lystra in southern *Galatia,* where the people called Barnabas Zeus and Paul Hermes, who of course was the messenger of Zeus in Greek mythology.

Gal. 4:13 states that Paul first preached to the addressees because of a physical ailment. The southern theory offers a reasonable reconstruction of events by deducing that Paul left the swampy lands of the Mediterranean coast and traveled north to the mountains of south *Galatia.* North GALATIA, however, does not have swamps and mountains so close together.

According to Acts 16:1-5, the Judaizers, about whom Paul is writing in Galatians, were active in south *Galatia.* There is no evidence in Acts that Judaizers went to northern GALATIA.

The Gauls of northern GALATIA, according to Jerome, seem to have spoken their native tongue as late as A. D. 400. Some critics question whether the inhabitants of northern GALATIA at the time of Paul understood Greek — the language in which he wrote the Epistle to the Galatians.[17]

Does Paul employ (ever or usually) geographical names in their ethnic sense or with their official Roman significance? We might note in passing that 1 Peter 1:1 and Rev. 1:4 (cf. 1:11) appear to use "Asia" in its official sense. The lexicon of Arndt-Gingrich, furthermore, raises no question concerning "Achaia," "Asia," and "Mace-

---

[16] "The Boundary of Galatic Phrygia" by W. M. Calder in *Proceedings of the Orientalist Congress* (Istanbul, 1951) as cited by F. F. Bruce, *The Book of the Acts* (Grand Rapids, 1956), p. 326.

[17] The statement of Jerome, however, in his Preface to Book II of his *Commentary on Galatians* reads: "While the Galatians, in common with the whole East, speak Greek, their own language is almost identical with that of the Treviri"; cf. *The Nicene and Post-Nicene Fathers* (Grand Rapids, 1954), VI, 497.

donia," merely equating these names with the respective Roman provinces. Whether "Galatia," however, is to be taken as ethnic or official, the disagreement among scholars is very manifest. Von Dobschütz, Jülicher, M. Dibelius, Feine, H. Lietzmann, J. Moffatt, Goguel, Sickenberger, Lagrange, Meinertz, Oepke, A. Steinmann, and Mommsen favor the ethnic sense. Zahn, Ramsay, E. Meyer, E. D. Burton, G. S. Duncan, and V. Weber conclude that Paul meant "Galatia" in the official sense. Such disagreement would be unlikely if Paul's use of geographical names in general were decisive; nor would the disagreement of scholars be possible if it could be proved that the official Roman significance of "Galatia" is not tenable. Scholars, therefore, must base their conclusions regarding the meaning of "Galatia" ultimately on the other points presented in the previous paragraphs. To me it seems that on the basis of the previous points the official sense of "Galatia" is more probable — particularly in view of 1 Cor. 16:1-5 (which speaks of "Galatia" and probable delegates) compared with Acts 20:1-4 (which lists two delegates from southern *Galatia* but none from northern GALATIA).

If the addressees of Galatians can be the churches in southern *Galatia,* the date of the epistle — the second of the two problems closely related to the topic of the present study — could be earlier than on the basis of the northern theory. The chief passage for study is Gal. 4:13, particularly the implication of τὸ πρότερον. Does the comparative degree necessarily imply two former visits? After Homer the neuter frequently was used as an adverb meaning "before," "earlier," both with and without the article. Three examples from classical Greek, one from the Apostolic Fathers, and three from the New Testament may be cited.

'Αλλ' ἄρα μουσικὴ ὅσην τὸ πρότερον διήλθομεν; — Plato, *Republic* 522a

'Αριστίππου δὲ ἐπιχειροῦντος ἐλέγχειν τὸν Σωκράτην, ὥσπερ αὐτὸς ὑπ' ἐκείνου τὸ πρότερον ἠλέγχετο . . . — Xenophon, *Memorabilia* 3.8.1

ὅσοι δὲ ὅτε τὸ πρότερον ἀπῆσαν τὰς οἰκίας ἐνέπρησαν ὑπὸ ἀτασθαλίας, δίκην ἐδίδοσαν κακῶς σκηνοῦντες. — Xenophon, *Anabasis* 4.4.14

Εἶπά σοι, φησίν, καὶ τὸ πρότερον, καὶ ἐκζητεῖς ἐπιμελῶς. — Hermas, *Visions* 3.3.5

ἐὰν οὖν θεωρῆτε τὸν υἱὸν τοῦ ἀνθρώπου ἀναβαίνοντα ὅπου ἦν τὸ πρότερον; — John 6.62

Οἱ οὖν γείτονες καὶ οἱ θεωροῦντες αὐτὸν τὸ πρότερον, ὅτι προσαίτης ἦν, ἔλεγον . . . — John 9.8

Χάριν ἔχω τῷ ἐνδυναμώσαντί με Χριστῷ 'Ιησοῦ τῷ κυρίῳ ἡμῶν, ὅτι πιστόν με ἡγήσατο θέμενος εἰς διακονίαν, τὸ πρότερον ὄντα βλάσφημον καὶ διώκτην καὶ ὑβριστήν . . . — 1 Timothy 1.12, 13

One need not, therefore, on the basis of lexicography, explain the comparative degree to τὸ πρότερον as referring to the two visits of Paul to each city (except Derbe) in southern *Galatia* on his first journey. (Cf. John 7:50; 2 Cor. 1:15; Eph. 4:22; Heb. 4:6; 7:27; 10:32; 1 Peter 1:14)

An early date for Galatians has a definite advantage. Its composition shortly before the council at Jerusalem implies that the great controversy over circumcision broke out and was settled once and for all. A later date, however, must presume that the controversy, supposedly settled by the Jerusalem council, broke out anew to be settled by Paul in Galatians — a premise which, while possible, is not equally probable. Peter's defection of Gal. 2:11-14, as stated above, is more logical before the council at Jerusalem.

Several minor objections have been raised to the equating of Gal. 2:1-10 with Acts 11:27-30. Each apparent difficulty seems to vanish, however, on closer investigation.

Since Gal. 2:1-10 speaks of James, Cephas, and John as being in Jerusalem, while Acts 11:27-30 mentions only the presbyters, some have assumed that the apostles at the time of Acts 11:27-30 had left Jerusalem as a result of Herod's persecution. But the reception of the relief fund by the presbyters is merely in line with Acts 6, which states that it was not the task of the apostles to "serve tables," and there is no necessary implication that the apostles were not present in Jerusalem. There is no reason, furthermore, to assume the absence of the apostles if Acts is taken chronologically, for then Paul and Barnabas reach Jerusalem before the persecution by Herod. But the order of events in Acts is no doubt not chronological. After relating the events at Antioch to the famine (A. D. 46), the author resumes the story at Jerusalem with chapter 12, leading up to the death of Herod (A. D. 44). Also, one must admit, Acts does not suggest that all the apostles fled from Jerusalem to escape persecution in A. D. 44; nor does Acts necessarily state that Peter left Jerusalem — ἕτερος τόπος (Acts 12:17) may mean "another house," not "another city" (cf. Acts 4:31). Even on the assumption that Peter and the other apostles left Jerusalem in A. D. 44, they easily could have returned by A. D. 46—47, because the persecution ceased at the death of Herod.

The difficulty of chronology concerning Paul, which some have assumed, disappears merely by taking "after 14 years" of Gal. 2:1 to mean 14 years after Paul's conversion, as the phrase "after three years" of Gal. 1:18 no doubt means. Even if the 14 years is to be calculated from the first visit to Jerusalem (Gal. 1:18), one must bear in mind two idiosyncrasies of calculation among the ancients: (a) inclusive calculation as, for example, in expressing Roman days of the month — three days before the Kalends (first) of February would be January 30; (b) fractions of a year referred to as a while year —

"after three years" could be $a + 1$ yr. $+ b$;

"after fourteen years" could be $c + 12$ yrs. $+ d$;

thus, taking *a, b, c,* and *d* as an unknown number of months, the total could be approximately 14 years. Another possible but not too probable explanation is to assume a corruption in the text of Gal. 2:1 — the corruption of "4" to "14" by the addition of a single *iota*.[18] The first explanation — "14 years" means after Paul's conversion — seems the most logical because of its simplicity and the parallelism with Gal. 1:18.

Romans and Galatians (and to a certain extent 1 and 2 Corinthians) are so close in language, subject, and style, some say, that they must belong to the same period. But the argument from similarity of style to identity of date is quite misleading. Galatians, moreover, is a hasty sketch, written with clear traces of anger under the pressure of an immediate crisis, while the Epistle to the Romans is a mature, philosophical treatment, composed at a time when the most pressing danger had passed

[18] Cf. K. Lake, "The Date of Herod's Marriage with Herodias" in *Expositor* (November 1912), 462—477; cf. p. 473.

away. Nor does Galatians mention the later collection for Jerusalem.

The silence of Acts, likewise, concerning the defection of the Galatians offers no serious objection. Acts is silent also about the troubles in Corinth — a fact even more significant. All scholars recognize omissions in Acts, moreover, of numerous matters which readers of today might wish had been included — compare, for example, 2 Cor. 11:23-27 with Acts; and also the paucity of information which Acts relates concerning Paul's three years at Ephesus (Acts 19:1-20). The same objection, furthermore, would remain regardless of the date and addressees of the Epistle to the Galatians. It seems, then, that Acts records the beginning (Cornelius' incident) and the end (Jerusalem council) of the movement toward Gentile Christianity, but omits the intermediate stages which led to no decisive result and possibly could arouse painful memories.

The circumcision of Timothy (Acts 16:3), according to some, is inconceivable after the writing of Galatians. Special circumstances, however, attended the case of Timothy, as Acts informs us. Nor is the meaning of Gal. 2:3 clear as to whether Titus was circumcised or not. In neither case did Paul yield to the pressure of the Judaizers. Thus the circumcision of Timothy could have occurred after the writing of Galatians as well as after the decision of the council in Acts 15.

If Gal. 2:1-10 equates Acts 11:27-30, why, some ask, were fresh negotiations necessary in Acts 15? There are good reasons for the Judaizers' rejection of the decision of the leaders in Gal. 2:1-10 if it occurred during the famine visit. Peter's defection in Gal. 2:11-14, which then also would be before the council met, reveals that the decision of the leaders (Gal. 2:1-10) failed to produce a final settlement. Also, the decision of Gal. 2:1-10 occurred when Paul's missionary work was limited to a relatively small area in Syria and Cilicia — regions close enough to Jerusalem that the influence of the Jewish Christians might be hoped to counteract that of the smaller number of Gentile Christians. After Paul's first journey, however, the greater number of Gentiles and their greater distance from Jerusalem would make it extremely more difficult for them to be absorbed into the church without a serious danger to the Jewish standard of morality. In the face of this danger the Judaizers no doubt renewed their perfectly sincere attempt to save Christianity from the danger of Gentile vices — not to mention the racial prejudice which no doubt was also active.

An extremely pertinent point, and in the final analysis one of the best tests, is the possible development of events on the basis of the equation of Gal. 2:1-10 with Acts 11:27-30. We may consider, then, a possible and even probable, though not the only possible, reconstruction of events, to see whether the account of Acts easily dovetails with Galatians on the basis of the equation proposed.

The church at Jerusalem sends Barnabas to Antioch to investigate the news concerning the preaching of the Gospel to Gentiles on a relatively large scale (Acts 11:20-22). Barnabas, recognizing the grace of God in the new movement, fetches Paul from Tarsus and both work with the church at Antioch for a whole year (Acts 11:23-26). During this time Agabus, also from Jerusalem, comes to Antioch and predicts a famine, which causes the Christians at Antioch to collect a purse and send it to Jerusalem through Barnabas and Paul (Acts 11:27-30). At Jerusalem Barnabas and Paul both deliver the purse and report privately and informally on the Gentile movement around Antioch — Acts records the relief fund (Acts 11:30) to show that the center of gravity is shifting to the Gentile churches, while Paul recalls the private and informal discussion because it suits his purpose (Gal. 2:1-10). Acts is silent about the private conference because its importance is dwarfed by the later Jerusalem council. Accompanied by Barnabas, a most respected representative of Hellenistic Christianity, Paul no doubt receives a recognition at Jerusalem, which he had not enjoyed formerly; he and Barnabas might have discussed even their projected tour to south *Galatia.* (Gal.2:9)

Returning to Antioch with John Mark (Acts 12:25), Paul and Barnabas set out on the first journey (Acts 13:1-3), which occupied one or two years (Acts 13, 14), returning again to Antioch, relating their successes among the Gentiles in south *Galatia* and remaining at Antioch "no little time" (Acts 14:26-28). The vigorous Gentile mission in *Galatia* brings to a head two related problems: (a) Some ultra-Judaizers come from Jerusalem and insist on the circumcision of Gentile converts (Acts 15:1,2), observing apparently that the Gentile Christians soon (if they had not done so already) would outnumber the Jewish Christians. The Judaistic propaganda, that Baptism is not a complete substitution for circumcision, spreads to the newly founded church of *Galatia.* (b) Social intercourse between Jewish and Gentile Christians — a related problem — arises about the same time at Antioch, possibly brought to a head by the inconsistency of Peter himself (Acts 2:11-14). It also is a serious problem because it involves either division or unity at the common meals of the churches with combined membership of Jews and Gentiles. Since unity could come only if the Gentiles observe Jewish customs on "clean" and "unclean" foods, Paul can say that the Jews were compelling the Gentiles to live as Jews (Gal. 2:14). Both problems are closely related and both problems are so important that a meeting at Jerusalem seems imperative; but before leaving Antioch, Paul in haste and with anger writes to the churches of south *Galatia,* not being able to visit them immediately because of the coming council.

Paul and Barnabas, together with others, go again to Jerusalem for the council (Acts 15:2-5), which decides both of these important and related problems. Although the problem of circumcision had been discussed and decided privately in Gal. 2:1-10, it now is raised in more acute form as a result of the implications of Paul's first journey. The decree of the council concerns both problems: (a) "Not to trouble those of the Gentiles who turn to God" (Acts 15:19) decides the first problem against the Judaizers, in line with the informal discussion of some previous years (Gal. 2:1-10). The second problem results in a compromise, with the Gentiles urged to concede to the conscience of the Jews who are loyal to the Law of Moses (Acts 15: 20,21,28,29).[19]

---

[19] Paul in 1 Cor. is silent about the decree because the question there is different. In 1 Cor. the problem is the relation between the Gentile Christians and pagan society, while the decree of Acts 15 concerns the imposition of Jewish obligations on Gentile Christians.

The Decree of Claudius in Acts 18:2

According to the Acts of the Apostles Paul met at Corinth Aquila and his wife Priscilla, who recently (προσφάτως) had come from Italy διὰ τὸ διατεταχέναι Κλαύδιον χωρίζεσθαι πάντας τοὺς Ἰουδαίους ἀπὸ τῆς Ῥώμης . . . (18:2). Although the bibliography on the passage is extensive, the treatment by New Testament critics frequently fails to discuss all the ramifications of the problem. We shall attempt, therefore, to evaluate the pertinent primary evidence.

Six ancient authors must be considered at the outset.

1. Iudaeos impulsore Chresto assidue tumultuantes Roma expulit — Suetonius, *Claudius* 25.4

2. τούς τε Ἰουδαίους πλεονάσαντας αὖθις, ὥστε χαλεπῶς ἂν ἄνευ ταραχῆς ἀπὸ τοῦ ὄχλου σφῶν τῆς πόλεως εἰρχθῆναι, οὐκ ἐξήλασε μέν, τῷ δὲ δὴ πατρίῳ βίῳ χρωμένους ἐκέλευσε μὴ συναθροίζεσθαι — Dio Cassius, *Historia Romana* 60.6.6

3. Anno eius nono expulsos per Claudium urbe Iudaeos Josephus refert, sed me magis Suetonius movet qui ait hoc modo: Claudius Iudaeos impulsore Christo adsidue tumultuantes Roma expulit, quod, utrum contra Christum tumultuantes Iudaeos coerceri et comprimi iusserat, an etiam Christianos simul velut cognatae religionis homines voluerit expelli, nequaquam discernitur — Orosius, *Historia contra Paganos* 7.6.15-16

4. Κατὰ δὲ τούσδε τοὺς χρόνους Παύλου τὴν ἀπὸ Ἱερουσαλὴμ καὶ κύκλῳ πορείαν μέχρι τοῦ Ἰλλυρικοῦ διανύοντος, Ἰουδαίους Ῥώμης ἀπελαύνει Κλαύδιος, ὅτε Ἀκύλας καί Πρίσκιλλα μετὰ τῶν ἄλλων Ἰουδαίων τῆς Ῥώμης ἀπαλλαγέντες ἐπὶ τὴν Ἀσίαν καταίρουσιν, ἐνταῦθά τε Παύλῳ τῷ ἀποστόλῳ συνδιατρίβουσιν, τοὺς αὐτόθι τῶν ἐκκλησιῶν ἄρτι πρὸς αὐτοῦ καταβληθέντας θεμελίους ἐπιστηρίζοντι. διδάσκαλος καὶ τούτων ἡ ἱερά τῶν Πράξεων γραφή — Eusebius, *Historia Ecclesiastica* 2.18.9

5. No reference in Josephus, *Antiquitates Judaicae*

6. No reference in Tacitus, *Annales*

On comparing Suetonius with Acts 18:2, it appears that Claudius, who ruled from 41—54 A. D., expelled from Rome *all* Jews as a result of constant rioting. Although the ablative absolute *impulsore Chresto* has produced much controversy, we may assume that heated discussions in the Jewish community at Rome concerned the acceptance of Jesus as the Christ, and we may conjecture that Suetonius, misinterpreting his source, as he seems to do not infrequently, thought Christus (or Chrestus, as the name was often spelled, with the pronunciation no doubt being the same in the Greek of the day) was present in person to stir up trouble. Suetonius, who lived ca. 75—160 A. D., serving for a brief period as secretary to the emperor Hadrian (117—138 A. D.), is of no help in establishing the date of the "expulsion"; for each biography in the *Lives of the Twelve Caesars* (Julius Caesar to Domitian) follows a fixed pattern: the family and birth of the emperor; his life to his principate, the events of his rule arranged by subjects rather than by chronology, his character and personal appearance, and his death.

Dio Cassius (ca. 155—230 A. D.), however, seems not only to disagree with Suetonius, but even to be refuting deliberately some statement that Claudius had expelled the Jews. Dio's *Roman History* covered originally in eighty Books the period from the supposed landing of Aeneas in Italy to his own time. The extant portions are Books 34—60, which cover 70 B.C. to 46 A.D.; Books 78 and 79; and the Paris fragments, which include the events of the years 207 to 200 B.C. Also extant are some excerpts and quotations made by later writers, and especially the epitome of Books 1—30 made by Zonaras in the twelfth century, and the epitome of Books 61—80 made by Xiphilinus toward the end of the eleventh century. Since Dio Cassius is far superior as a historian to Suetonius, following as closely as he can his great exemplar Thucydides, his remarks are not to be taken lightly. Although his work originally bridged approximately one thousand years, for the early Empire (or from Julius Caesar to Marcus Aurelius) he apparently relied on such official accounts as the emperors allowed to be published.

The disagreement betwen Dio Cassius and Suetonius has led some scholars to conclude that their respective remarks do not refer to the same occasion.[1] The statement of Dio, it is true, occurs in his discussion of the events of 41 A.D., the first year of Claudius' reign; while Orosius (loc. cit.; cf. supra) defintely dates an expulsion in the ninth year of Claudius (49 A.D.). Claudius' pro-Jewish edict[2] of the year 42 A.D., however, seems inconsistent with the early date implied by Dio Cassius. Orosius, moreover, cites Josephus as his source for the date, although there is no reference in the extant works of Josephus to such an expulsion of the Jews by Claudius. Orosius, furthermore, who died ca. 418 A.D., as presbyter in Africa, is frequently referred to as notoriously inaccurate. Also the silence of Tacitus, whose extant writings cover the second part of Claudius' reign, must be explained in any discussion of the later date (49 A.D.).[3] The statement of Eusebius is of little assistance, since Acts is apparently his only source. Nor can the adverb προσφάτως (Acts 18:2) be decisive on the date; for while "recently" seems inclined to the later date (49 A.D.), the adverb in Greek as well as in English is relative. Aristotle employs the cognate πρόσφατος in referring to Homer (*Meteorologica* 351b35).

In spite of the difficulties involved, and assuming that Suetonius and Cassius are referring to the same incident, with some reservation the date usually is placed at approximately 49 A.D.[4] Orosius, it is true, may have mistaken his authority as Josephus (unless he is citing a work of Josephus no longer extant, which assumption appears not too likely), but upon some authority he dates the incident in the ninth year of Claudius, which would be from Jan. 25, 49, to Jan. 25, 50 A.D. This date fits well the Pauline chronology of Acts (18:1) as enlightened by the Gallio inscriptions,[5] and would permit the preferable interpretation of προσφάτως (Acts 18:2). The main difficulty to the late date (49 A.D.) seems to be Dio Cassius. The extant portions of his *Roman History,* as noted above, present Claudius' reign to 46 A.D. Whether he made further mention of Claudius' decree in the

---

[1] Cf. Sherman Johnson, *Anglican Theological Review,* XXIII (1941), 175; M. Shepherd, "The Source Analysis of Acts" in *Munera Studiosa,* ed. Shepherd and Johnson (Cambridge, Mass.: Episcopal Theological School, 1946), p. 96.

[2] Josephus, *Antiquitates Judaicae* 19.5.2-3.

[3] Tacitus' *Annales* originally covered the years 14—68 A.D. (Tiberius through Nero) in 16 books. Extant are Books 1—4; parts of Book 5 and of Book 6; and Books 11—15 with part of Book 16—covering respectively the reign of Tiberius (14—37); the second part of Claudius' rule; and the reign of Nero (54—68) except the last years.

[4] Ramsay would prefer 50 A.D., since in one instance Orosius is off a year according to Tacitus; but one instançe gives little authority for assuming that all of Orosius' dates are incorrect by a year. Cf. *St. Paul the Traveller and Roman Citizen* (1927), pp. 68, 254, 459.

[5] Cf. *Beginnings of Christianity,* ed. Foakes-Jackson and Lake (1933), V, pp. 460—464.

section no longer extant, unfortunately, cannot be determined. But since Dio's remark is general, without citing any date, he may not have intended to define the incident with the year 41 A.D.

Of more serious implication, again assuming with some reservation that Suetonius and Dio are referring to the same incident, is the nature of the decree. Dio's apparently deliberate refutation of a general expulsion of the Jews, as seemingly implied by Suetonius, no doubt has had more influence than any probable disagreement on dates in deducing that each refers to a separate incident.[6] But must Suetonius be thus interpreted? The Latin of Suetonius may mean that Claudius' action concerned only those Jews who "were constantly rioting," not a general expulsion of all Jews from Rome. In view of Dio Cassius such an interpretation of Suetonius seems preferable. Also the silence of Tacitus, provided the incident occurred in 49 A.D., and of Josephus, seems to agree with the suggested interpretation of Suetonius. Any edict concerning the banishment of the entire Jewish population from Rome appears to be so drastic that mention of it would be expected in Tacitus and Josephus; a "police action" involving a limited number of individuals who were regarded as troublemakers in the community, however, might have been omitted much more easily by Josephus and Tacitus. By deducing, then, that in addition to a probable forbidding of Jewish assemblies only the "ringleaders" suffered banishment, the remarks of Suetonius and Dio Cassius appear to agree as to the nature of Claudius' action.

But Acts states: διὰ τὸ διατεταχέναι Κλαύδιον χωρίζεσθαι πάντας τοὺς Ἰουδαίους ἀπὸ τῆς Ῥώμης. How much stress should be placed on πάντας? To assist in answering the query, let us examine several other passages in Acts.

> Ἦσαν δὲ εἰς Ἰερουσαλὴμ κατοικοῦντες Ἰουδαῖοι, ἄνδρες εὐλαβεῖς ἀπὸ παντὸς ἔθνους τῶν ὑπὸ τὸν οὐρανόν (2:5)

Was *every* nation in the world represented at Pentecost?

> ὁ δὲ θεὸς ἃ προκατήγγειλεν διὰ στόματος πάντων τῶν προφητῶν, παθεῖν τὸν χριστὸν αὐτοῦ, ἐπλήρωσεν οὕτως (3:18)

Did *all* the Old Testament prophets proclaim the suffering of Christ?

> Ἐγένετο δε ἐν ἐκείνῃ τῇ ἡμέρᾳ διωγμὸς μέγας ἐπὶ τὴν ἐκκλησίαν τὴν ἐν Ἱεροσολύμοις· πάντες διεσπάρησαν κατὰ τὰς χώρας τῆς Ἰουδαίας καὶ Σαμαρείας πλὴν τῶν ἀποστόλων (8:1)

Did *all* the Christians leave Jerusalem except only the twelve apostles?

> καὶ εἶδαν αὐτὸν πάντες οἱ κατοικοῦντες Λύδδα καὶ τὸν Σαρῶνα, οἵτινες ἐπέστρεψαν ἐπὶ τὸν κύριον (9:35)

Were *all* the inhabitants of Lydda and Sharon converted?

> τοῦτο δὲ ἐγένετο ἐπὶ ἔτη δύο, ὥστε πάντας τοὺς κατοικοῦντας τὴν Ἀσίαν ἀκοῦσαι τὸν λόγον τοῦ κυρίου, Ἰουδαίους τε καὶ Ἕλληνας (19:10)

Did the Gospel reach *all* the inhabitants of the Roman province Asia during the two to three years Paul labored at Ephesus? It appears that Acts in the cases cited is employing the figure hyperbole and that the literal

[6] Kirsopp Lake oversimplifies the differences between Dio and Suetonius: "Dio Cassius confirms the evidence of Suetonius, but adds that the difficulty of expelling so many persons led to a revision of the decree, in which Claudius contented himself with forbidding Jewish assemblies" (*Beginnings of Christianity,* V, 459). Some would compare the reversal of Tiberius concerning the astrologers (Suetonius, *Tiberius* 36), but a revision of a decree concerning the expulsion of astrologers by Tiberius is hardly parallel; for the astrologers would not have been nearly so numerous as the Jewish population in Rome, and Tiberius revoked his decree only after the astrologers promised to renounce their profession.

meaning of πάντας in 18:2 should not be stressed.

Nor is the hyperbolic use of πᾶς peculiar to Acts. One example each from Matthew, Mark, and John will suffice.

> Τότε ἐξεπορεύετο πρὸς αὐτὸν Ἱεροσόλυμα καὶ πᾶσα ἡ Ἰουδαία καὶ πᾶσα ἡ περίχωρος τοῦ Ἰορδάνου, καί ἐβαπτίζοντο ἐν τῷ Ἰορδάνῃ ποταμῷ ὑπ' αὐτοῦ ἐξομολογούμενοι τὰς ἁμαρτίας αὐτῶν (Matt. 3:5-6)
>
> καί κατεδίωξεν αὐτὸν Σίμων καὶ οἱ μετ' αὐτοῦ, καὶ εὗρον αὐτὸν καὶ λέγουσιν αὐτῷ ὅτι πάντες ζητοῦσίν σε (Mark 1:36-37)
>
> καὶ ἦλθον πρὸς τὸν Ἰωάννην καὶ εἶπαν αὐτῷ· ῥαββί, ὃς ἦν μετὰ σοῦ πέραν τοῦ Ἰορδάνου, ᾧ σὺ μεμαρτύρηκας, ἴδε οὗτος βαπτίζει καὶ πάντες ἔρχονται πρὸς αὐτόν (John 3:26)

In addition to the figure hyperbole in the New Testament, several other aspects of πᾶς should be considered before insisting on taking πάντας in its literal sense in Acts 18:2. Xenophon of Ephesus in the second century A. D. writes (2.13.4):

> πάντας ἀπέκτεινεν, ὀλίγους δὲ καὶ ζῶντας ἔλαβε. μόνος δὲ ὁ Ἱππόθοος ἠδυνήθη διαφυγεῖν

The most stress πάντας can bear here is "many," "very many," or "nearly all." In Plato's *Republic* the context indicates that πᾶς implies "composed wholly of," "nothing but," or "only" (579b):

> Ἔτι ἄν, ἔφη, οἶμαι, μᾶλλον ἐν παντὶ κακοῦ εἴη, κύκλῳ φρουρούμενος ὑπὸ πάντων πολεμίων

The *Corpus Hermeticum* (13.2) contains another example of this use of πᾶς.[7] Although πᾶς frequently denotes "every," it also may imply merely "any"—cf. Demosthenes, *First Olynthiac* 16, *Against Meidias* 2, *On the Crown* 5; Plato, *Ion* 532e, *First Alcibiades* 129a, *Apology* 39a, *Phaedo* 114c; Sophocles, *Antigone* 175, *Oedipus Colonus* 761; Herodotus 4.162.4, 4.195.2; Lysias, *Against Eratosthenes* 84, *For the Soldier* 16; Xenophon, *Hellenica* 7.4.21; Matt. 13:19; Luke 1:37; Gal. 2:16.[8]

The predicate position of πάντας in Acts 18:2, furthermore, deserves consideration. It is the attributive position of πᾶς which stresses totality. Several examples from Classical Greek and from the New Testament will be sufficient.

> καὶ γὰρ οὐδὲν πλείων ὁ πᾶς χρόνος φαίνεται οὕτω δὴ εἶναι ἢ μία νύξ

"For in that case eternity appears to be no greater than a single night" (Plato, *Apology* 40e)

> μόνος οὗτος τῶν πάντων ἀνθρώπων

"He alone of all men" (Lycurgus 131)

> τούτων δὲ κατεχομένων οὐδ' ἂν οἱ πάντες ἄνθρωποι δύναιντ' ἂν διελθεῖν

"With these [mountain peaks] occupied, neither could absolutely all the men pass through" (Xenophon, *Anabasis* 5.6.7)

> τοὺς σὺν αὐτοῖς πάντας ἁγίους

"all the saints with them" (Rom. 16:15)

> οἱ σὺν ἐμοὶ πάντες ἀδελφοί

"all the brethren with me" (Gal. 1:2)

> ἤμεθα δὲ αἱ πᾶσαι ψυχαὶ ἐν τῷ πλοίῳ διακόσιαι ἑβδομήκοντα ἕξ

"We in the boat were in all 276 persons" (Acts 27:37). An attributive position of πάντας in Acts 18:2, therefore, would stress totality, but the predicate position appears to permit the interpretation that only the "ringleaders" suffered banishment.

According to Dio Cassius, furthermore, the great number of the Jews in Rome at

---

[7] Cf. Sophocles, *Electra* 301, *Philoctetes* 622 and 927.

[8] Perhaps we should note in passing the adverbial phrase παντὸς μᾶλλον, denoting "more than anything" (Plato, *Crito* 49b, *Protagoras* 344b, *Gorgias* 527b, *Phaedrus* 228d), and equating "quite so" in answers (Plato, *Phaedo* 67b).

that time would have made it difficult for Claudius to have expelled the entire Jewish population. Other primary evidence seems to corroborate Dio. As early as Cicero's *Pro Flacco,*[9] delivered in 59 B.C., the Jews in Rome who possessed citizenship were numerous enough to influence the political assemblies and the jury courts of the Romans, and the amount of gold sent yearly to Jerusalem from Italy and the provinces caused alarm to some statesmen of Rome. In 4 A.D., it is believed, more than 30,000 Jews lived in Rome, for above 8,000 joined a deputation from Jerusalem.[10] The number of Jews at Rome under Tiberius no doubt was even larger, for he was able to draft 4,000 Jews from Rome for military service.[11] Scholars, therefore, estimate that the Jewish population at Rome at the time of Claudius may have been as high as 50,000 — a rather large group to be expelled.

The usual policy of Rome, likewise, seems to have been the banishment only of the leading Jewish propagandists. Already in 139 B.C. an aggressive spirit of proselytism led to such action.[12] Also under Tiberius the legislation appears to have been leveled against those who were highly suspected, or convicted of guilt, or overzealous in making converts among the native Romans.[13] Thus Claudius' decree concerned perhaps only those Jews who took active part in the disorders and were the chief protagonists; for while his charter of liberties for the Jews, cited by Josephus (*Antiquitates Judaicae* 19.5.3), granted religious privileges to the Jews, it also limited their activities by forbidding wholesale propaganda. In spite of Orosius' doubt (7.16.15-16; cf. supra) the Christians who engaged in the heated discussions no doubt suffered banishment as well as the Jews. Claudius' action, referred to in Acts 18:2, may have been a part of his general "antioriental" policy, stressed from 47 to 54 A.D.,[14] although his measure seems to have been aimed primarily at removing civil disorders, with little, if any, theological ramifications.

---

9 28.66—69.

10 Cf. Josephus, *Antiquitates Judaicae* 17.11.1, *Bellum Judaicum* 2.6.1.

11 Cf. Josephus, *Antiquitates Judaicae* 18.3.5; Tacitus, *Annales* 2.85; Suetonius, *Tiberius* 36.

12 Cf. Valerius Maximus, *Epitome* 1.3.3.

13 Philo states (*Legatio ad Gaium* 24.161) καὶ τοῖς πανταχόσε χειροτονουμένοις ὑπάρχοις ἐπέσκηψε (i.e., Tiberius) παρηγορῆσαι μὲν τοὺς κατὰ πόλεις τῶν ἀπὸ τοῦ ἔθνους, ὡς οὐκ εἰς πάντας προβάσης τῆς ἐπεξελεύσεως, ἀλλ' ἐπὶ μόνους τοὺς αἰτίους — ὀλίγοι δὲ ἦσαν. Dio Cassius remarks (57.18.5): τῶν τε Ἰουδαίων πολλῶν ἐς τὴν Ῥώμην συνελθόντων καὶ συχνοὺς τῶν ἐπιχωρίων ἐς τὰ σφέτερα ἔθη μεθιστάντων, τοὺς πλείονας ἐξήλασεν.

"God Be Merciful To Me A Sinner" A Note on Luke 18:13

"God be merciful to me a sinner" is the KJV rendition of the Greek text in Luke 18:13: ὁ θεός, ἱλάσθητί μοι τῷ ἁμαρτωλῷ. More recent translators have attempted to improve the reading as follows:

O God, be reconciled to me, sinner that I am (Weymouth, 1903);
O God, be merciful to me, the sinner (Ferrar Fenton, 1905);
O God, have mercy on me for my sins (Moffatt, 1913);
God be merciful to me, the sinner (Ballantine, 1923);
O God, have mercy on a sinner like me (Goodspeed, 1923);
O God, be merciful to me, the sinner (Spencer, 1937, and the Roman Catholic Version of 1941);
O God, have mercy on me, sinner that I am (New English Bible, 1961).[1]

One minor alteration which most of the modern translators have adopted is the rendering of ὁ θεός as "O God," with a comma before the verb. The intention apparently has been to emphasize the fact that the imperative is in the second person, not in the third. A more fundamental change, however, is the attempt to stress the article before the adjective by translating "the sinner," "sinner that I am," "for my sins," or "a sinner like me." The attempt to emphasize the article raises an interesting point of Greek grammar and merits consideration.

Some of the New Testament grammarians are emphatic in their remarks on the article before ἁμαρτωλῷ· A. T. Robertson, for example, states: "But the Canterbury Revisers cannot be absolved from all blame, for they ignore the article in Lu. 18:13, τῷ ἁμαρτωλῷ."[2] He no doubt would translate the publican's prayer as follows: "God be merciful to me, the sinner." In another volume Robertson declares concerning this phrase: "The sinner, not a sinner. It is curious how modern scholars ignore this Greek article. The main point in the contrast lies in this article. The Pharisee thought of others as sinners. The publican thinks of himself as the sinner, not of others at all."[3] H. P. V. Nunn expresses similar disagreement with the usual translation of this text: "Many of the mistakes made by the translators of the *Authorized Version* were due to their misunderstanding or neglecting the use of the Definite Article. Compare the translations in the A. V. and the R. V. of such passages as 1 Tim. vi. 5, 10. See how greatly the force of the passage is altered by the omission of the Definite Article in Jn. iv. 27 in the R. V. and by its insertion in the marginal reading in Lk. xviii. 13."[4] Nunn apparently would insist on the use of the definite article in translating Luke 18:13.

Agreeing with the opinion of these two grammarians are the statements of most of the New Testament commentators: "'Be merciful (Dan. ix. 19) to me *the* sinner.' *He* also places himself in a class by himself; but he makes no comparisons. Consciousness of his own sin is supreme; *de nemine alio*

---

[1] The RSV (1946 and 1953) has retained basically the reading of the KJV, merely altering the punctuation: "God, be merciful to me a sinner!"

[2] *A Grammar of the Greek New Testament in the Light of Historical Research* (New York, 1931), p. 756.

[3] *Word Pictures in the New Testament* (New York, 1930), II, 233, 234.

[4] *A Short Syntax of New Testament Greek* (Cambridge, 1938), p. 56.

homine cogitat (Beng.)."[5] "The Publican did not lift his eyes to heaven. His prayer was more than asking for mercy. It means literally translated 'God be propitiated towards me, the sinner.'"[6] "His prayer is one shuddering sigh: God, be merciful to me, the sinner! In his eyes there is only one sinner worth mentioning, only one whose sins he can see; and that is himself. Cp. 1 Tim. 1:15."[7] "It is right to lay emphasis on the τῷ ἁμαρτωλῷ. He accounts himself a sinner, κατ' ἐξοχήν, as Paul names himself, 1 Tim. 1, 15, the chief of sinners, and all for which he prays is comprehended in the single word 'Grace.'"[8] "A sinner (τῷ ἁμαρτωλῷ). With the definite article, '*the* sinner.' 'He thinks about no other man' (Bengel)."[9] ". . . God, let Thyself be propitiated in regard to me, the open sinner! . . . he calls himself ὁ ἁμαρτωλός, 'the open and notorious sinner,' . . . R[obertson], *W{ord} P{ictures}* scores a point in pointing out that the article is so often overlooked. The main point lies in the article. The Pharisee thought of others as sinners; the publican thinks of himself alone as the sinner, not of others . . . '*the* sinner.'"[10] "τῷ ἁμαρτωλῷ, the sinner; he thinks of himself only and of himself as *the* sinner, well known as such, the one fact worth mentioning about him, as one might speak about the drunkard of the village."[11] "μοι τῷ ἁμαρτ. Observe the article. Bengel rightly says: '*de nemine alio homine cogitat.*' 'he thinks about no other man.'"[12] ". . . God, be merciful to me a sinner. The original has the definite article, '*the* sinner,' as if there were no other: and so his view of himself and representations of himself before God is just the opposite of that of the Pharisee above. 'To the Pharisee all are sinners and he is righteous; to the publican all are righteous and he only *the sinner*' (Westermeier)."[13] "Gott, sei mir [dem] Sünder (κατ' ἐξοχήν, d. i., dem vornehmsten unter allen 1 Tim. 1, 15) gnädig."[14] "Saying, God be merciful to me a sinner; properly *the* sinner. The American Bible Union Version and Dr. S. Davidson give the article conformably to the Greek, and the Revision allows it as the alternative."[15] ". . . to me a sinner . . . literally 'to me the sinner'; as if he should say, 'If ever there was a sinner, I am he.'"[16]

The citations exemplify the general consensus of opinion among the New Testament commentators and their agreement with several New Testament grammarians and translators on the interpretation of the article in

---

[5] A. Plummer, *The International Critical Commentary: The Gospel According to Luke* (New York, 1906), p. 419.

[6] A. C. Gaebelein, *The Annotated Bible: The New Testament* (New York, 1913), I, 162.

[7] P. E. Kretzmann, *Popular Commentary of the Bible: The New Testament* (St. Louis, 1921), I, 363.

[8] J. P. Lange and P. Schaff, *A Commentary on the Holy Scriptures: The Gospel According to Luke* (New York, 1873), p. 274; cf. J. P. Lange, *Bibelwerk: Das Evangelium nach Lukas* (Leipzig, 1867), p. 278.

[9] M. R. Vincent, *Word Studies in the New Testament* (New York, 1905), I, 406.

[10] R. C. H. Lenski, *The Interpretation of St. Mark's and St. Luke's Gospels* (Columbus, Ohio, 1934), pp. 1041, 1042.

[11] W. R. Nicoll, *The Expositor's Greek Testament* (London, n. d.), I, 599.

[12] H. A. W. Meyer, *Critical and Exegetical Handbook to the Gospels of Mark and Luke* (New York, 1884), 503; cf. H. A. W. Meyer, *Handbuch über die Evangelien des Markus und Lukas* (Göttingen, 1885), p. 559.

[13] H. L. Baugher, *The Lutheran Commentary* (New York, 1896), IV, 333, 334.

[14] A. Daechsel, *Die Bibel* (Leipzig, n. d.), V, 825.

[15] W. N. Clarke, *American Commentary on the New Testament* (Philadelphia, n. d.), II, 270.

[16] Jamieson-Fausset-Brown, *A Commentary, Critical, Experimental, and Practical, on the Old and New Testaments* (Philadelphia, n. d.), V, 303.

Luke 18:13.[17] Their remarks give the impression in no uncertain terms that the translation of the KJV is incorrect because it reads "a sinner" rather than "the sinner," "the well-known sinner," or "the open and notorious sinner." Such general agreement would be gratifying if the remarks of these commentators, translators, and grammarians were substantiated by Greek grammar. Their emphatic stress, however, of the Greek article in this verse is grammatically incorrect. It should be of interest and benefit, therefore, to clarify the point of grammar which so frequently has been overlooked.

According to the idiom of the Greek language, Luke should have written τῷ ἁμαρτωλῷ ἐκείνῳ to indicate the well-known or famous sinner.[18] The article alone does not generally imply such a connotation.[19] On the contrary, the article in Greek is natural and customary with words in apposition to personal pronouns, without implying any emphasis of the appositive. Under the heading ARTICLE WITH APPOSITIONS OF PERSONAL PRONOUNS, Professor Gildersleeve states: "Appositions with the personal pronoun take the article, even when the pronoun is involved in the verb. Omission occurs in poetry, rarely in prose." [20]

The following are several examples from classical Greek in which words in apposition to personal pronouns take the article and in this respect are parallel to the phrase μοι τῷ ἁμαρτωλῷ in Luke 18:13:

ἀλλ' ἤτοι κεῖνόν γε τὸν ταῦτα βουλεύσαντα δεῖ ἀπόλλυσθαι ἢ σὲ τὸν ἐμὲ γυμνὴν θεησάμενον καὶ ποιήσαντα οὐ νομιζόμενα. Herodotus 1.11.3;

καὶ ὑμῖν ἔστω τι τεκμήριον ἃ πρὸς ἡμᾶς τοὺς ξυγγενεῖς δρῶσιν . . . Thucydides 1.34.3;

τούτων δὲ πάντων ἀπορώτατον τό τε μὴ οἷόν τε εἶναι ταῦτα ἐμοὶ κωλῦσαι τῷ στρατηγῷ . . . Thucydides 7.14.2;

ὑμῶν δὲ τῶν Ἑλλήνων καὶ στέφανον ἑκάστῳ χρυσοῦν δώσω. Xenophon, *Anabasis* 1.7.7;

χαίρω γὰρ ἀκούων ὑμῶν τῶν σοφῶν. Plato, *Ion* 532d;

ἀλλὰ μήν, ὦ ξένε, τήν γε περὶ Σαλαμῖνα ναυμαχίαν τῶν Ἑλλήνων πρὸς τοὺς βαρβάρους γενομένην ἡμεῖς γε οἱ Κρῆτες τὴν Ἑλλάδα φαμὲν σῶσαι. Plato, *Laws* 707b;

. . . οὗτος ὑμῖν, Αἰσχίνη, τοῖς προδιδοῦσι καί μισθαρνοῦσιν τὸ ἔχειν ἐφ' ὅτῳ δωροκήσετε περιποιεῖ . . . Demosthenes, *De Corona* 49;

. . . καὶ μετάσχοιεν ὧν ὑμεῖς οἱ τὰ βέλτιστα βουλόμενοι τοὺς θεοὺς αἰτεῖτε . . . Demosthenes, *De Corona* 89.[21]

The New Testament also contains illustrations of the rule that words in apposition to a personal pronoun have the definite article:

Πλὴν οὐαὶ ὑμῖν τοῖς πλουσίοις . . . Luke 6.24;

'Αλλὰ ὑμῖν λέγω τοῖς ἀκούουσιν . . . Luke 6.27;

νῦν ὑμεῖς οἱ Φαρισαῖοι . . . Luke 11.39;

ἀλλὰ οὐαὶ ὑμῖν τοῖς Φαρισαίοις . . . Luke 11.42;

οὐαὶ ὑμὶν τοῖς Φαρισαίοις . . . Luke 11.43;

καὶ ὑμῖν τοῖς νομικοῖς οὐαί . . . Luke 11.46;

---

[17] In checking the commentaries we noticed only two which did not stress the article in Luke 18:13: *The Greek Testament* by H. Alford, and *The Greek Testament with English Notes* by S. T. Bloomfield.

[18] Cf. Plato, *Protagoras,* 361c.

[19] Cf. Robert G. Hoerber, *A Grammatical Study of Romans 16:17* (Milwaukee, 1947), pp. 24, 25. The context alone may imply an emphasis of the article; the context of Luke 18:13, however, contains no such implication.

[20] B. L. Gildersleeve, *Syntax of Classical Greek from Homer to Demosthenes* (New York, 1911), II, 279.

[21] Cf. Homer, *Odyssey* 7.223, 248; Sophocles, *Antigone* 922, 923; *Electra* 303, 304; Euripides, *Andromache* 391, 392; Aristophanes, *Knights* 458, 1359; Thucydides 3.57.1; Xenophon, *Anabasis* 5.7.20, 6.6.14; Plato, *Laws* 680c; Demosthenes, *De Corona* 94.

οὐαὶ ὑμῖν τοῖς νομικοῖς . . . Luke 11.52;

καλῶς ἐπροφήτευσεν Ἠσαΐας περὶ ὑμῶν τῶν ὑποκριτῶν . . . Mark 7.6;

ὅσοι δὲ ἔλαβον αὐτόν, ἔδωκεν αὐτοῖς ἐξουσίαν τέκνα θεοῦ γενέσθαι, τοῖς πιστεύουσιν εἰς τὸ ὄνομα αὐτοῦ . . . John 1.12;

Ἄγουσιν αὐτὸν πρὸς τοὺς Φαρισαίους, τόν ποτε τυφλόν. John 9.13;

. . . ἵνα γινώσκωσιν σὲ τὸν μόνον ἀληθινὸν θεόν . . . John 17.3;

δοκῶ γάρ, ὁ θεὸς ἡμᾶς τοὺς ἀποστόλους ἐσχάτους ἀπέδειξεν ὡς ἐπιθανατίους . . . 1 Corinthians 4.9.

The article, according to the previous passages, is employed with attributive appositives of personal pronouns. An attributive appositive may be (1) a participle, (2) an adjective, or (3) a noun designating character, relation, or dignity. If a personal pronoun, however, is modified by (1) a participle, (2) an adjective, or (3) a noun denoting character, relation, or dignity and the article is not present, there is implied a difference in meaning — the modifying word would be in the predicate of its clause instead of being in apposition to the personal pronoun. Examples of the predicate function of the three types of modifiers also occur in the New Testament:

1. Participle

ἰδοὺ ἡμεῖς ἀφέντες τὰ ἴδια ἠκολουθήσαμέν σοι. Luke 18.28;

προσκαλεσάμενοι δὲ οἱ δώδεκα τὸ πλῆθος τῶν μαθητῶν εἶπαν· οὐκ ἀρεστόν ἐστιν ἡμᾶς καταλείψαντας τὸν λόγον τοῦ θεοῦ διακονεῖν τραπέζαις. Acts 6.2;

2. Adjective

κύριε, οὐ μέλει σοι ὅτι ἡ ἀδελφή μου μόνην με κατέλειπεν διακονεῖν; Luke 10.40;

. . . θέλω δὲ ὑμᾶς σοφοὺς εἶναι εἰς τὸ ἀγαθόν, ἀκεραίους δὲ εἰς τὸ κακόν. Romans 16.19;

3. Noun

ὑπάγετε· ἰδοὺ ἀποστέλλω ὑμᾶς ὡς ἄρνας ἐν μέσῳ λύκων. Luke 10.3;

. . . καθὼς γέγραπται ὅτι πατέρα πολλῶν ἐθνῶν τέθεικά σε . . . Romans 4.17.

The evidence, then, clearly substantiates the translation of Luke 18:13 found in the KJV, the RSV, and others.[22] The translations of Weymouth, Moffatt, Goodspeed, and the New English Bible are acceptable, although their circumlocutions are unnecessary. Contrary to the idiom of the Greek language, however, are the renderings of Fenton, Ballantine, Spencer, and the Roman Catholic Version of 1941, as well as the remarks of Robertson, Nunn, and most of the commentators. Their emphatic stress of the definite article, which denotes merely apposition, is more zealous than wise.

---

22 "O God, be merciful to me, a sinner" (Andrews Norton, 1855); "O God, have mercy on me, a sinner" (Twentieth Century, 1904); "God, have mercy on me, a sinner" (The New Testament in Basic English, 1941).

New Wine In Old Bottles

After thirty years of teaching and publishing in the area of the Greek classics, and recently privileged to transfer his attentions to New Testament studies, the author is reminded of the phrase of our Lord, "new wine in old bottles" (Matt. 9:17)—the "new wine being the newer subject of Biblical exegesis, and the "old bottles" representing the older methods of classical scholarship, especially in the nineteenth century. The further I delve into New Testament studies, the more I become aware of the similarity between these two periods of alleged scholarship—nineteenth-century classical scholarship and much of twentieth-century Biblical studies. Please do not misunderstand. The author is *for* scholarship—true, genuine, scientific scholarship. Not everything put in print, however, even in professional journals and books, under the threat of "publish or perish," represents true scholarship. Genuine scholarship is rare. Much of what passed for "scholarship" in the Greek classics in the nineteenth century was based largely on subjective opinion, not objective logical conclusion. The same may be said for much of the alleged "scholarship" in Biblical studies of the twentieth century. One prime difference is that classicists have tried and tested the subjective premises of the nineteenth century and have found many of them wanting, while Biblical exegesis to a large extent is still under the influence of assumptions formerly followed by classicists, but now discarded. To be specific, let us look more closely at an example of ninteenth-century "scholarship."

PLATO'S DIALOGUES AND SUBJECTIVE OPINION

The approach to the dialogues of Plato furnish an excellent example of nineteenth-century *subjective* "scholarship." Since the thirty-five dialogues seemed to some students of Plato to contain discrepancies, varying approaches to similar topics, and differences in style, two questions assumed prime importance in interpreting Plato. First, the genuine dialogues had to be separated from spurious treatises. Second, the genuine writings had to be placed in the chronological order in which they had been written. Only then could authentic statements be placed into a sequential order, to determine the evolution of Plato's thought, variations, and mental development. The logic behind such an approach appeared so scholarly that practically all Platonic scholars of the nineteenth century concentrated on the two questions of the authenticity and of the chronological order of the dialogues.

Robert Hoerber is professor of New Testament at Concordia Seminary, St. Louis, and was formerly professor of classics at

Westminster College, Fulton, Missouri. This essay was prepared as a lecture to the students of Concordia Theological Seminary, Springfield, Illinois.

That the criteria by which these students of Plato judged the question of authenticity were their subjective opinions rather than scholarly evidence is clear from the results of their varying conclusions. No major disagreement on the genuineness of the Platonic canon appeared before the nineteenth century, when Kant's philosophy gave impetus to the speculative mind. Friedrich Ast, for example, accepted only fourteen of the thirty-five dialogues as genuine, presumptuously regarding as spurious, among other dialogues, such compositions as the *Laws*, *Apology*, *Crito*, *Meno*, *Laches*, *Charmides*, and *Lysis*. Socher, by contrast, accepted as authentic twenty-four treatises, including several rejected by Ast (e.g., *Laws*, *Aplogy*, *Crito*, and *Meno*), but rejected such basic dialogues as the *Parmenides*, *Sophist*, and *Statesman* (which had been accepted by Ast). K. F. Hermann and Stallbaum concluded that there were twenty-eight genuine compositions of Plato, while Susenich asserted that only twenty-four were authentic. Munk put his stamp of approval on twenty-three, and Ueberweg accepted only twenty-two of the thirty-five compositions, rejecting the *Parmenides*.

Subjective judgment was the primary standard on which these scholars based their varying conclusions. They studied Plato, his tenets, his approach to questions and his manner of treatment in a few dialogues, expecting all genuine compositions to have the same characteristics and to betray signs of a mental development. The dialogues which did not in their estimation measure up to these characteristics, or did not fit into a previously conceived plan of Platonic development, they were prone to pronounce spurious. It is only natural that such subjective judgment should produce numerous contradictory views on the genuineness and chronological sequence of basic Platonic works and should lead to the rejection by some scholars of such dialogues as the *Laws*, *Apology*, *Crito*, *Parmenides*, and *Statesman*.

PLATO'S DIALOGUES, STYLOMETRY, AND LOGIC

The extremely subjective criteria of nineteenth-century Platonic scholarship have happily been replaced in part by more objective attempts to arrange in sequence the dialogues which are assumed to be authentic. Two basic criteria have been stylometry and the alleged development of Plato's logic. Aristotle states that the *Laws* was Plato's last work; scholars have noted numerous peculiarities of style in this and the other dialogues. Those dialogues which contain stylistic traits most similar to the *Laws*, Plato's last composition, are placed toward the end of his life, while the treatises which differ greatly in stylistic characteristics are put early in Plato's career as an author. Likewise, it is assumed that Plato's principles of logic grew and developed during his career. Some dialogues contain faint, undeveloped, poor, and even fallacious reasoning, while others exhibit logical arguments which are sound, good, much improved, and equal to a philosopher. The former treatises then must belong to Plato's early career, and the latter are supposedly specimens of Plato's thought after more mature development in the study of logic.

Although the criteria of stylometry and logic are more objective than subjective opinion, yet it must be noted that even these criteria are based on two presuppositions—namely, that Plato was not aware of erroneous reasonings in composing early treatises, and that stylistic peculiarities in dialogues have the same implication as in narrative. Both presuppositions fail to recognize that Plato wrote dramatic dialogues in *fact* as well as in *form*. That is, Plato purposely could have varied his style and his logic to suit the characters participating in each dialogue. When Socrates, for example, in the *Meno* discourses with a neophyte in philosophy who has been exposed merely to a few lectures by a skeptical sophist, Gorgias, the style and logic of that dialogue are suited to the personality of the dialogist. Any loose logical arguments on the part of Socrates serve to portray the mental deficiencies of Meno, not the embryonic logic of Plato. Also, stylistic peculiarities could depict purposely the variations in the style of the speakers, rather than a development in the writing ability of the author. Striking evidence is the difference in style, approach, and arguments in the *Republic*, *Laws*, and *Menexenus*, the genuineness of each of which Aristotle substantiates.

PAUL'S EPISTLES AND THE TÜBINGEN SCHOOL

Having glanced briefly at some examples of the "old bottles"—the subjective opinions and presuppositions of previous classical scholarship—let us recall that we are not to put "new wine" in these "old bottles"—that is, we are not to employ secular presuppositions in our approach to Biblical studies. If subjective opinion and untested assumptions have been discarded by classical scholars, we are to be wary, lest we be misled by similar suppositions in our study of the Holy Scriptures.

One of the most glaring examples of subjective opinion in Biblical studies was the acceptance by the Tübingen school of only four of Paul's Epistles as genuine—namely, Romans, 1 Corinthians, 2 Corinthians, and Galatians—rejecting the remaining nine as spurious. These scholars of the nineteenth century based their judgment merely on subjective opinion. They formulate in their minds certain ideas—based on their study of Romans, 1 Corinthians, 2 Corinthians, and Galatians—ideas which they labelled Pauline. Since the other letters contained what they considered non-Pauline thoughts, these Epistles they termed spurious, not withstanding the solid evidence of early church tradition and of textual criticism. I mention the example of the Tübingen school, because the methods and conclusions of such an approach are rejected today by all reliable students of the Bible as most unscholarly, since the basis of their approach was subjective opinion pure and simple.

Or was the basis entirely subjective? If we look a little deeper, we may observe that behind subjective opinion was a basic philosophical assumption—the assumption of the nineteenth century that the key to the understanding of history, philosophy, and religion was development. The development in political theory, the development in scientific progress, the development in the industrial revolution of that time were immense. Hegel, furthermore, had taught that "the movement of human thought followed the dialectic pattern in which a position (thesis) was countered by an opposite position (antithesis) and from an interaction of these two emerged a new insight or aspect of reality (synthesis). Hegel saw in the history of religion the evolution of Spirit in its dialectical apprehension of the divine, from nature religions, through religions of spiritual individuality, to the Absolute Religion, which is Christianity." As the assumption of progressive development no doubt lay behind the attempt of the classicists to see a development in Plato's thought, logic, and style, so the same assumption of Hegelian dialectics influenced the approach to development in early Christianity. Paul, taking the position that the Christian is freed from the Law, represents the *thesis*. James and Peter, taking the opposite position that the Law was permanently valid and an essential element in Chrisitanity, represented the *antithesis*. Apostolic Christianity, therefore, so it was claimed, must be read as a conflict between Pauline and Petrine Christianity, from which conflict emerged in the second century the Old Catholic Church, which represented the *synthesis*, or a harmonization of thesis and antithesis, of Paulinism and Petrinism.

ACTS AND HEGELIAN ASSUMPTIONS

It was against the background of the Hegelian concept of thesis, antithesis, and synthesis that the Acts of the Apostles was viewed as a second-century document which bolstered the synthesis or harmonization of Paulinism and Petrinism. It is true that an impressive list may be drawn up of parallel Petrine and Pauline events in the Acts of the Apostles, which might seem to argue for the Hegelian approach. Both Peter and Paul healed the lame and the ill, both opposed magic, both raised the dead, both were imprisoned and released miraculously, both were beaten by authorities, both warded off attempts to be worshipped, both addressed the Council at Jerusalem, both were encouraged by visions to continue to preach, both observed Jewish ceremonies, both appeared before the Sanhedrin. But when more objective facts—rather than assumptions—are studied, the conclusion is established that the Acts of the Apostles is a first-century treatise—not a second-century document. I am referring, of course, to the work of Sir William Ramsay, who began his career under the assumption that the Acts of the Apostles was a more or less fictional account with an "axe to grind"—namely, to bolster the synthesis or harmonization of Petrine and Pauline factions. His archaeological research, however, soon convinced him that the objective facts of correct titles for provincial officials and geographical borders point definitely to an earlier composition of the Acts of the Apostles. Harnack is a good example of the influence of facts rather than assumption on the dating of the Acts of the Apostles. He also assumed at first that it was a second-century document, a view which he expressed in a volume dated 1887. Ten years later, however, he designated the period between 78 and 93 A.D. as the date of composition. After another nine years Harnack suggested the year 80 A.D., and finally in 1910 he concluded that the Acts of the Apostles was written before 64 A.D.

ACTS AND TODAY'S SCIENTIFIC AGE

So we see that not only can purely subjective opinion be misleading, but also assumptions derived from contemporary thought may be equally misleading. We again employ the dating of the Acts of the Apostles as case in point. Today we are living in a scientific age. Conclusions are drawn on the basis of the test-tube and the laboratory experiment. Natural laws of physics and chemistry must be adhered to. The assumption that all events must agree with the laws of nature and ordinary human experience has permeated much of current theological thought and Biblical scholarship. The power of predicting future events is, therefore, questioned. Passages in the Old Testament which predict future events, therefore, must have been composed after the event, merely giving a false impression that these events were predicted at an earlier time.

A similar argument is used by many today in dating the Acts of the Apostles. Acts is the second volume of a two-volume work, Luke-Acts. Acts no doubt was written after the Gospel of Luke. But Luke gives a vivid description of the fall of Jerusalem, which occurred in 70 A.D. The Gospel of Luke, therefore, must have been written after the event—that is, after 70 A.D.—and the second volume, the Acts of the Apostles, should not be dated before about 80-85 A.D. The argument is based on the current assumption that the two-volume work of Luke-Acts could not have been composed until after the fall of Jerusalem in 70 A.D., mainly because the power of supernatural prediction is denied to the authors of Scripture—and also is denied to our Lord and Savior, who foretold the destruction of Jerusalem in the Gospels.

We, of course, who accept Jesus as the Son of God, true God as well as true Man, as our Savior who possessed the supernatural power to heal, raise the dead, rise from death Himself—we have no problem in accepting in Jesus the ability to predict future events. But for the moment, let us examine the argument concerning the dating of the Acts of Apostles merely on the human level—even on the assumption that supernatural prediction of future events is impossible. I refer not to a theologian, but to a classicist who has no theological "axe to grind." The question is discussed by C. H. Rieu in the introduction to the Penguin translation of the Acts of the Apostles as follows:

> . . .The date of the writing of Luke's Gospel and the 'Acts' is still usually assessed as in the 80's A.D. The main argument for this late date hinges on the date of the Jewish war with Rome, 66-70, and the sack of Jerusalem by the Romans (70) which terminated it. The argument runs: Mark, the earliest Gospel, gives Jesus' prophecy of disasters in Judaea in general terms (chapter 13), but Luke is far more specific. In Luke 19:43 Jesus is recorded as saying 'Your enemies shall fix a palisade around you', and in 21:20f. 'When you see armies closing round Jerusalem, know that her desolation is at hand. . .Pagan feet will tread Jerusalem till pagan days are done'. Luke, it is argued, altered the version he found in Mark to make the prophecy fit the facts after the event. Therefore Luke wrote his Gospel after 70 A.D., and his second book the 'Acts', after that. The argument is not conclusive. The description of the siege and the sack are in general terms and could apply to almost any siege of any town. Jerusalem had been sacked and the Holy of Holies desecrated four times in the previous 500 years, and it did not need Jesus to prophesy that Jewish intransigence was leading to war with Rome, or who would win.

The same author continues:

> The evidence seems to point to the period of Paul's imprisonment in Rome, namely 60-62, for the composition of the 'Acts', and Luke's Gospel too. It is unlikely that Paul was kept in prison for more than two years, and likely that he was either set free or tried and acquitted. In 64 Nero began the dramatic persecution of the Christians for which he is chiefly famous. In 67, it is thought Peter and Paul were martyred. Can anyone who reads the last eight chapters of 'Acts', which describe Paul's capture,

preliminary trials, and journey to Rome for trial by the Emperor, believe that if Luke had known of Paul's trial or acquittal or condemnation he would not have mentioned it? Or that the 'Acts', with its cool defence of Christianity, its calm optimism about it, and its unfeigned approval of Roman rule and law, was written after Nero's lions had been let loose on the Christians? Or that Luke knew about the martyrdom of Peter and Paul when he was writing? Or that he would have refrained from mentioning or hinting at retribution to come on the Jews if he had known about the sack of Jerusalem? It may be taken as likely, then, that the 'Acts' was written when the reader imagines it was written, during the two years of Paul's imprisonment described in the final paragraph, and the date for that we can fix with some certainty as 60-62. And the material for the 'Acts' and the Gospel was probably collected in Judaea during Paul's captivity in Caesarea, 57-59.

THE GOSPELS AND MODERN ASSUMPTIONS

The assumptions of our current scientific age have affected also the approach to the accounts of the life of our Lord which constitute the Gospels. It is assumed by many twentieth-century students of the New Testament that historical reality must be understood only in terms of unbroken historical causality. All ideas of supernatural acts—not only the predictive power of Christ, but also His real incarnation, virgin birth, miracles, bodily resurrection, etc.—are *ipso facto* unhistorical, i.e., mythological. The Gospels, therefore, present a theological picture of Jesus that cannot be historical, but must be mythological. It is the function of the student of the New Testament to "demythologize" the Gospel accounts—to ascertain the theological truths by separating the mythological additons.

The argument of many current critics may be summarized briefly. The death of Christ occurred at approximately 30 A.D. The Gospels, which allude to the fall of Jerusalem in 70 A.D., must have been written some time after 70 A.D.—possibly as late as 80-85 A.D. During the intervening fifty years the historical Jesus became "mythologized." That is, the words and deeds of Christ were told and retold numerous times. In the retelling of these events the historical facts gradually became embellished, changed, and distorted. Additions were made to historical fact. The Gospels, therefore, represent the "mythologized" Christ. The Gospels are a portrayal not of the historical Jesus, but rather of the faith of the church about fifty years after the death of Jesus. The Gospels; then, include much of "myth," of non-historical additions—yet these additions contain theological truths.

Two accounts in the Gospels may serve as illustrations. At the baptism of Jesus the Gospels tell of the appearance of the Holy Spirit in the form of a dove and the sounding of a voice from heaven declaring: "This is my beloved Son". According to many current interpreters, the Gospels do not relate historical facts at this point, but additional embellishment by the early church. These interpreters would "demythologize" the Gospel accounts by asserting that the appearance of a dove and the voice from heaven are merely later distortions added through the telling and retelling of the event of Jesus' baptism. Yet, they would hasten to add, that the mythologized account is true in that it teaches a theological truth, although not historical facts. The theological truth taught in the embellished version of the baptism in the Gospels is that Jesus is the chosen One, the Anointed One, whom God has picked to reveal His will to man.

Another account of interest in this connection is the transfiguration. Our Gospels relate that Jesus took Peter, James, and John to a mountain and that there appeared to them Moses and Elijah. Again, numerous current interpreters of the New Testament claim that the Gospels do not present historical facts here; for the details in the account of the transfiguration as recorded in the Gospels do not square with the knowledge and assumptions of our scientific age. The appearance of Moses and Elijah, these moderns would claim, in an additional embellishment which resulted from the telling and re-telling of a historical incident. Yet, they would hasten to add, the mythological embellishment teaches a theological truth—namely, that Jesus is the fulfillment of the Old Testament Law, which is represented by Moses, and the fulfillment of the Old Testament prophets, which is symbolized by Elijah.

PLATO AND MYTH

This use of myth as a form of presenting truth, although not historical fact, goes back to Plato. Since Plato held to a dualistic world—a world of eternal, unchanging, perfect Forms or Ideas beyond and above the world of the senses—it is only natural that myth plays an extraordinary role in his dialogues. For Plato myths were symbolic of the reality existing beyond the perceptive world. Plato's myths are the product of great imaginative and inventive power, which both fuses traditional elements to create new philosophical and mythical statements, and also produces completely new mythical constructs as being the only adequate means to express true thoughts. Plato uses reason (*logos*) as the dialectical presentation of thought, and myth (*mythos*) as the illustration of the metaphysical. Myth, to Plato, carries the arguments of reason beyond the frontiers of conceptual knowledge. This distinctive union of reason and myth in Plato is linked with the fact that his philosophy is a doctrine of salvation—the destiny of the human soul. Plato, to be sure, presents *rational* arguments for the immortality of the soul in dialogues such as the *Phaedo.* But he also depends largely on myth—the myth of Er in the *Republic*, the myth of creation in the *Timaeus*, the myth of the tripartite soul in the *Phaedrus*—to illustrate philosophical truths which are beyond the realm of logical proof.

Plato's use of myth to carry the arguments of reason beyond the frontiers of conceptual knowledge may be seen, for example, in the myth of Er at the conclusion of the *Republic.* The soul of Er, a man who has been killed in battle, is transported to a meadow, where he sees a gap in the earth leading downward, and a corresponding gap in the heavens above. Souls of individuals lately deceased are departing through the two gaps, after judgment has been passed on them, to receive their respective punishments or rewards. There are also two similar gaps from which other souls are returning either from heaven or from Hades, after a period of rewards or punishments, to choose a type of life for their next existence on earth. Er observed these souls making their choice and then passing on to a new birth, to a juncture with a new physical body, before he is allowed to return to life and to report his experience. This myth is not meant to represent historical fact, as if there ever were a person Er, who had such an experience. Plato employs the technique of the myth to teach truths which are beyond the realm of conceptual knowledge—such as the immortality of the soul, rewards and punishments for the good and evil respectively after death, personal responsibility for human actions in contrast to any fatalistic determinism.

NEW TESTAMENT AND MYTH

Other ancient authors, in addition to Plato, employed myth in various ways. Myth was used by the Greek poets such as Homer and Hesiod—largely for the enhancement of their poems. It was used in the mystery religions to bolster the faith of the adherents. It was used for allegorical reinterpretation by some Stoics. There existed also cases of frivolous mockery, criticism, and rejection of the use of myth on ethical and rational grounds. But there is no fundamental repudiation on religious grounds until we come to the New Testament.

In the New Testament there are five occurrences of the noun *mythos*—four in the Pastoral Epistles and one in 2 Peter. In each case the term occurs in a negative statement, with complete repudiation of *mythos*. It is the means and mark of an alien proclamation, especially of errors combatted in the Pastoral Epistles. The *mythoi* are invented stories or fables destitute of truth. Here are the five passages:

1 Timothy 1:4, "Neither give heed to fables and endless genealogies, which minister questions, rather than godly edifying which is in faith."

1 Timothy 4:7, "But refuse profane and old wives' fables, and exercise thyself rather unto godliness."

2 Timothy 4:3-4, "For the time will come when they will not endure sound doctrine; but after their own lusts shall heap to themselves teachers, having itching ears; and they shall turn away their ears from the truth, and shall be turned unto fables."

Titus 1:14, "Not giving heed to Jewish fables, and commandments of men, that turn from the truth."

2 Peter 1:16, "For we have not followed cunningly devised fables, when we made known unto you the power and coming of our Lord Jesus Christ, but were eyewitnesses of his majesty."

Note the derogatory descriptions of myth—or, as translated in the King James' Version, fables—they are classified with endless genealogies, described as profane and old wives' fables, as opposed to sound doctrine and truth, as Jewish fables that turn from the truth, and as cunningly devised or invented.

It is highly probable that these myths or fables referred to in the Pastoral Epistles and in 2 Peter derived from an early form of Gnosticism which flourished on the soil of Hellenistic Jewish Christianity. Of fundamental significance is the antithesis between myth and truth. Also in Philo and in Origen myth is the direct opposite of truth. In general, there can be no doubt that the church in every age has insisted that there can be no relation between the *Logos* of the New Testament and myth. Myth as such has no place on Biblical soil, either as a direct impartation of religious truths or as symbol. Myth is not a form of religious communication. In the Bible we have from first to last the account and narration of facts, plus revealed interpretation of these facts. The essential theme is the same throughout, namely, what God says and what God does; neither of these things is myth, a symbol of truth. To Plato myth may be a symbol of eternal verities which are independent of all history. The central symbol of the Gospel, however, is the Cross, and this embodies a hard and unromantic historical reality. No myth can be interpreted into or imposed upon this symbol in any form, for the *logos* of the Cross would be made of no effect (1 Cor. 1:17). Nor can this symbol be separated from its personal representative or historical setting, for without Christ at Golgotha the cross is indeed *kenos mythos*, a meaningless symbol or pagan sign.

Is there another way to make myth at home in the Biblical world? This question has to be faced in view of the current situation in Biblical studies. In spite of the facts adduced above, there have been and are many attempts to introduce myth into Christian terminology as something opposed to historical truth and yet containing positive value. Even when myth is used positively it tends to imply merely human interpretation.

MYTH IN CURRENT CLASSICAL STUDY

The question remains as to why the term "myth" was chosen for a theory in New Testament studies, although this term is so fraught with anti-Biblical connotations both in the New Testament and in early church history. A ready answer might be Plato's use of myth as a description of eternal verities which are beyond the concepts and rational proof of the material world of perception. The parallelism between Plato's use of myth and Bultmann's contention of seeing theological truth, but not necessarily historical mundane fact, in the Gospels may have played a part—even a substantial part—in the selection of the terms "myth," "demythologizing," etc. But one wonders whether another element did not play an extremely large part in the use of the term "myth" in recent New Testament studies. I am referring to the use of the term "myth" among current students of Greek mythology.

Students of Greek mythology distinguish three general types of stories, largely according to their development. One type is labelled *saga*, from the Scandinavian word for "tale" or "story." These stories supposedly originated with historical events. They are the results of legends developed around a historical person or event. Aeolus, for example, became in Greek mythology a character who controlled the winds with the power to soothe or excite them according to his pleasure. The origin of Aeolus, according to students of mythology, was probably a historical character who understood the techniques of sailing and who could tell the changes of weather and winds from the signs of the atmosphere. Through the telling and re-telling of his unusual accomplishments, the historical character of ages past soon developed into a mythological character who controlled, and not merely foretold, the weather. Another example of *saga*, of legend growing up around a historical event, is the Trojan War. There did occur in history a conflict between the Greeks and a town on the Dardanelles. This conflict was apparently due to economic causes—the attempt by Troy to assess a tax or tribute on all Greek ships passing through the Dardanelles. Later romanticism, however, altered the economic cause of the war into a struggle over the return of a beautiful woman, Helen, the wife of Menelaus.

A second type of mythological story is labelled *märchen*, from the German word meaning "fairy tale." Its sole purpose is to amuse or entertain. It did not develop from any historical person or event. It is a story pure and simple and makes no pretense at being anything else. *Märchen* would be the imaginative accounts of giants, witches, dragons, nymphs, etc. that inhabit forests, seas, and rivers. Parallels in modern mythology would be the fairy tales of Baron von Münchhausen.

There is also a third type of mythological story, which is called *myth proper*. It attempts to *explain* a name, a custom, or to *teach* a philosophical truth. The account of Icarus, for example, who escaped from Crete through the use of wings supplied by his father Daedalus—and then unfortunately fell into a sea and drowned—explains and accounts for the late name of that sea—the Icarian Sea. Another example of *myth proper* is the story of Cronus, the father of Zeus. Cronus had dethroned his father, Ouranus, as king of the gods and was told that some day he would be dethroned by one of his offspring. To avoid such a fate Cronus decided to devour each offspring of his at birth—and so he did devour, or swallow, each of his first five offspring—Hestia, Demeter, Hera, Hades, and Poseidon—until he was tricked at the birth of his sixth offspring Zeus. According to many current students of mythology, this story is a *myth proper* in that it serves to teach a truth—although the events are not historical truth. The name Cronus means time. So the story of Cronus devouring his offspring teaches the philosophical truth that time destroys whatever it brings into existence. It is this use of "myth," as an explanation or a mode of teaching truth, which is parallel to the use of the terms "myth" and "demythologizing" in New Testament studies—a form conveying a theological truth, but not necessarily historical fact.

NEW WINE IN NEW BOTTLES

"New wine in old bottles"—our Savior advises against this combination, whether the "old bottles" are subjective opinions, or assumptions of scholarship supposedly based on contemporary scientific and rational premises. Nor are we to equate Biblical accounts with myth, whether myth is based on Plato's use of the term as beyond the *logos* of logical human narrative, or derives from the use of the term by current students of Greek mythology as a mode of teaching truth, but not historical fact. For, while Plato views *mythos* as on a higher plane than *logos*, many contemporary New Testament scholars regard *mythos* as a *distortion* of the *Logos*, the Word that became flesh. Jesus advises, not "new wine in old bottles," but "new wine in new bottles." For we have a new *Logos*—a Savior who, in addition to His work as our Redeemer, prepared His disciples to carry on the work of the kingdom of God, and who in His high-priestly prayer thought of all future generations in God's kingdom—including us of the late twentieth century—when He said: "Neither pray I for these alone, but for them who shall believe on me through their *logos*," i.e., their word (John 17:20). The *Logos*, Christ, has given us the *logos* of the apostles and prophets, their written word, our Scriptures, which is inspired truth—not merely containing truth, or teaching truth through myth. "*All* Scripture is given by inspiration of God" (2 Timothy 3:16). The new *Logos*, Christ, is comprehended and comprehensible only through the Biblical *logos*, inspired Scripture, which contains fact, not mythological fiction, and which harmonizes with true, genuine, unbiased scholarship.

The basic ingredient of "new wine in new bottles" —the reverent approach to Scripture as God's holy Word—is and must remain the Biblical teaching of inspiration. But inspiration, critics will maintain, is a matter of faith and not of history. These critics wish to place faith and history in opposite categories. Whatever, for example, in the Gospels speaks to Christian faith, they claim cannot be historically true, but must represent merely the faith of the church a generation after Jesus' death when the synoptic Gospels were composed. This assumption, however, does not stand the test of genuine scholarship. Let us in conclusion bring out several points of genuine scholarship as applied to the accounts of the synoptic Gospels.

CONCLUSION

The idea that faith and history are antithetical is a false assumption alien to true historiography. True history is not a mere chronicle of facts, dates, events, and persons. Most historians today admit that all good history is *interpreted* history. History always tries to understand the meaning of the events. The fact that a writer has a viewpoint does not mean that he is a poor historian and distorts the facts to support his interpretation. An unbeliever could not have written a gospel. He could report Jesus' words and deeds, but he would do so in a context of doubt and scepticism that would view Jesus either as a charlatan or as a deranged person. Only a believer could write a gospel which presents the good news of what God has done in Jesus. So the current trend to place faith and history in opposite categories is a false assumption, not substantiated by genuine scholarship.

Another false assumption of many current critics is that the Gospels represent a fourth stage in development—not (1) the historical Jesus, not (2) the early Jewish church, not (3) the

Hellenistic Jewish church, but (4) the Hellenistic Gentile church. Again, these alleged stages do not emerge clearly from our historical sources, but are the result of a methodology based on a set of presuppositions as to how history must have unfolded. This methodology does not take into account the fact that the Gospel tradition throughout its entire life was under the control of eyewitnesses who had seen and heard Jesus (1 Cor. 15:6). The Gospels assumed written form within about a generation after Jesus' death, when eyewitnesses were still in the church. The controlling influence of eyewitnesses is a fact of genuine scholarship that is too often ignored by many current critics.

As can be substantiated by genuine scholarship, the Gospels contain many evidences that the tradition was not completely recast by the faith of the early church, but does embody sound historical truth. Although in the early church, for example, the title "Christ" soon became a proper name for Jesus, in the synoptic Gospels Jesus avoided the title "Messiah" or "Christ." His favorite designation for himself was "the Son of Man," a title which apparently was not picked up by the early church. Again, while the early church called Jesus "the Son of God," in the synoptic Gospels Jesus does not attribute this title to Himself, but only the veiled term, "the Son." Also, Jesus was called the "Servant" (*pais*) in the early church (Acts 3:13, 26; 4:25, 30), but this usage was not read back into the synoptic Gospels. Other evidence in addition to the varied terms for Jesus likewise substantiates the view that the Gospel tradition is historically sound and not the creation of early Christian theology. I refer to the fact that the synoptic Gospels have little to say about the meaning of Jesus' death, although the redemptive meaning of Jesus' death was a central theological tenet in the early church. I refer to the fact that the Lord's Prayer in both Matthew and Luke contains no word that is uniquely Christian. I refer to the fact that the Sermon on the Mount has not a word about the grace of God. I refer to the fact that the synoptic Gospels do not attempt to answer one of the most pressing issues in the early church—the terms under which Gentiles might enter the church.

Genuine scholarship, based upon such facts, does not reject the Biblical portrait of Jesus in favor of a hypothetical historical Jesus; genuine scholarship rather substantiates the Gospel portrait as basically sound and in harmony with the Scriptural teaching of inspiration. Genuine scholarship merely substantiates, however; it does not prove. For we are dealing with "new wine in new bottles"—the reverent approach to

Scripture as God's holy Word. Our faith, while merely substantiated by genuine scholarship, is in the final analysis the divine work of the Holy Spirit. It can come only by hearing, and hearing by the Word of God (Rom. 10:17). The *Logos*, the Word that became flesh, is revealed to us through the *logos* of the apostles and prophets.

Terminology: Material and Format Principles

During recent interviews with members of our fourth-year class it became evident that some students had not been exposed in their previous theological education to the terms "material principle" and "formal principle." Several men stopped me in the corridor on the morning of their scheduled interview to request assistance on the distinction between these two terms. Others had checked written sources and had memorized the definitions with some comprehension. In most cases, I felt, it was primarily a matter of rote memory of words not previously in the students' functional vocabulary.

To be quite candid, while students in my generation learned to use the phrases "material principle" and "formal principle" with adequate comprehension, also we depended initially on rote memory, without any explanation of the origin of these terms in Western culture. The usual occurence of "material" is in contrast to "spiritual," while the word "formal" brings to mind the concept "informal." But, "material and formal"—what a strange combination! At least that is what many of us felt thirty years ago.

The purpose of the present brief comments is to clarify the origin of the terms "material" and "formal" in Western culture, with the hope that they may be employed with more complete comprehension, instead of a reliance primarily on rote memory.

So much of our Western culture begins with the Greeks. Also the concepts "material" and "formal" in a specialized sense have their origin with the Greeks—in this case with Aristotle (384-322 B.C.). Aristotle was a tremendous cataloger, analyzing problems with a pigeon-hole mind. Today, if alive, he no doubt would plan a perfect filing system, to be out-done only by computers—or he might be expected to construct a master computer.

When Aristotle discusses "causality" or "causation" (cf. *Metaphysics* A, 983 a 24-b 1; *Physics* II, 198 a 21-31) he concludes that there are four and only four "causes" or "causal determinants": 1. The *material* cause is the matter or material out of which a thing is constructed. 2. The *formal* cause refers to the form or shape which is imposed on the material. 3. The *efficient* cause becomes the agent that arranges the material in a particular form. (Cf. the Latin *efficio,* from *ex* and *facio,* "to bring about"—hence the name "efficient" cause). 4. The *final* cause denotes the purpose for which the agent imposes a particular form on certain material. (In Greek and Latin grammars published in England, "purpose" clauses frequently are called "final" causes—from the Latin *finis,* meaning "end" or "final goal.")

One example should clarify Aristotle's distinct use of these terms. Four "causes" were essential in the construction of the Ludwig Fuerbringer Library on our campus. First, the *material* determinant was the matter (*hyle* in Greek) out of which the building was built—the brick, steel, glass, wood, nails, etc. Without the material a structure could not have taken place. Secondly, this material had to be put into a certain *form (eidos),* or it would not become a library. The same material arranged in a different form might become a house, or a dormitory, or a church. Thirdly, it was necessary for agents, called the *efficient* "cause," to move (*to kinesan*) the matter into the proper form, in order for a library to come into being. In constructing the library, the agents (carpenters, bricklayers, etc.) followed the form which originated in the mind of the architect, who transferred his plan to blueprints. Fourthly, and most importantly, the Ludwig Fuerbringer Library was constructed because the Board of Control decided that a new building was needed to house books for the use of students and faculty—which was the purpose, or goal (*telos* in Greek), or *final* "cause" (*finis* in Latin) of the structure.

It is interesting to note that, from one point of view, the material cause and the formal cause may be grouped together, for they are *static* and in a sense *passive* determinants, while the efficient cause and the final cause are *dynamic* and *active* determinants. From another point of view, the material and formal causes are the two *internal* elements, whereas the efficient and final causes are the two *external* conditions. It is logical, therefore, that the first two causes be grouped together by our dogmaticians in describing Holy Scripture.

Concerning Holy Scripture, then, the *material* principle refers to the matter, the material, the chief message of Holy Writ—the doctrine of justification by faith alone (*sola fide*). The *formal* principle is Holy Scripture as the source and norm of all doctine (*sola Scriptura*). In the case of the Ludwig Fuerbringer Library, material and formal principles cannot be separated. One cannot have one without the other. Once the form is removed from the material, or the material removed from the form, a library no longer exists. So in the case of Holy Scripture, the message is the material of the Gospel or justification by faith alone. This message has been put in the form of Holy Scripture, which by inspiration is God's Word—unlike human documents produced by fallible individuals. The two principles should not be separated. God's Word in the sense of the material principle is the message of the Gospel (*sola fide*); in the sense of the formal principle God's Word is Holy Scripture (*sola Scriptura*). Removal of one principle affects the other. A message of salvation derived from an uninspired volume (e.g., *The Koran*) is unreliable.

Although the last two Aristotelian causes have not been applied by our dogmaticians to the doctrine of Holy Scripture, their application might also be appropriate. The *efficient* cause, the agent that placed the material principle (the Gospel) into the formal principle (Holy Scripture) is

God the Holy Spirit, who through inspiration guided the thoughts and words of the prophets and apostles in composing the Old and New Testaments (2 Tim. 3:16a and 2 Peter 1:21). The *final* cause, the purpose of Holy Scripture and the Gospel message, is "to make us wise unto Salvation"— which necessitates at times reproof and correction, as well as teaching and training, if the Gospel and Holy Scripture are not to degenerate into an emaciated emotionalism. (2 Tim. 3:16b and John 20:30-31)

It might be of interest to note that the terms "material principle" and "formal principle" of Holy Scripture are used in the new *Lutheran Cyclopedia* (CPH, 1975, pp. 523, 305), in F. E. Mayer's *The Religious Bodies of America* (CPH, 1958, pp. 142-5) and in *Popular Symbolics* (CPH, 1934, pp. 2, 3, 6). However, these two terms are not employed in the *Book of Concord* (1580), in J. T. Mueller's *Christian Dogmatics* (CPH, 1934) or in Pieper's three volumes on *Christliche Dogmatik* (CPH, vol. I, 1924, pp. 24, 29), although the terms do appear in the English edition (CPH, vol. I, 1950, pp. 23,28), the chief translator of which was Dr. Engelder.

Be that as it may, the tenets involved in the terms "material principle" and "formal principle" are clearly taught in our Confessions. For the "material principle" see Ap. IV, 1-2; A.C. XXVI, 4; S.A., II, 5; S.D., III, 6. For the "formal principle" see Ap. XII, 66; II, 50; S.A., II, 15; S.D., Preface, 3.

A Review of the Apostolic Council After 1925 Years

It is fitting that we review in 1976 the historical setting and issues of the first Church Conference, the Apostolic Council at Jerusalem in 49 A.D. The decisions derived by the apostles at this important juncture in the history of Christianity contain essential principles applicable for all ages, particularly on the 1925th anniversary of its occurrence.

Change in Outlook

The change and growth in the outlook of the apostles in less than twenty years become vividly apparent when we compare their attitude immediately after Pentecost to the decisions reached at the Jerusalem Conference. Soon after Peter's speech at Pentecost, he and John observe the hours of prayer at the temple in Jerusalem (Acts 3:1 ff.). They, as well as the other apostles, no doubt conceive of their mission rather narrowly—to convince primarily local Jews, and any others from the Dispersion who may be visiting Jerusalem, that Jesus of Nazareth is the predicted Messiah. By centering their activities at the temple in Jerusalem, any outreach beyond Judaea would be minimal. Contact with the Gentiles, including the "God-fearers" in the Dispersion, possibly would be almost nonexistent. Within less than twenty years, however, these same apostles face issues brought on by the fact that the Good News has permeated Gentile territory in Syria, Cilicia, Cyprus, and Southern Galatia—with the result that Gentile members probably outnumber Jewish followers by a fairly large percentage.

The early chapters of Acts, which relate the growth of Christianity during this period and the change in the outlook of the apostles, also inform us of the reasons for the development in the early Church. The Holy Spirit is at work in the Church. The Spirit allows internal dissension among the Christians at Jerusalem to bring to the foreground Stephen, "a man full of faith and of the Holy Ghost," whose grasp of the situation is much more comprehensive (Acts 6). Stephen's long address may seem

---

Dr. Hoerber is a member of the Exegetical Department of Concordia Seminary and also serves as Faculty Secretary and Marshal.

at first reading to ramble, but closer analysis shows that he is indicating the mistake of associating religion primarily with Jerusalem and with the temple (Acts 7). God also allows persecution by Saul (Paul) to force Christians of the Jerusalem congregation to spread the Good News throughout Judaea and Samaria (Acts 8). God then changes the prime persecutor into the main missionary of early Christianity when Jesus appears to Saul (Paul) on the road to Damascus (Acts 9). God, furthermore, changes the attitude of Peter regarding "clean" and "unclean" by a vision on the housetop, with the result that Peter the Jew proclaims the Gospel in the home of the Roman Centurion Cornelius at Caesarea (Acts 10). Peter's action represents such an extreme change in attitude, that he is constrained to explain at length to his fellow Jews at Jerusalem (Acts 11). This is in part also a literary device used by Luke to emphasize the importance of an event by retelling the incident, a technique which Luke also employs to underline the conversion of Saul (Paul) (Acts 22 and 26).

While the Spirit is at work in the Church, He allows time for attitudes to take root and for leaders to develop. Peter does not at once advocate wholesale preaching to Gentiles. Paul does not become a primary missionary to the Gentiles overnight. After a brief visit to Jerusalem of fifteen days, during which many are afraid of him, and understandably so, he goes to Syria and Cilicia, including his home town Tarsus (Acts 9:26-30; Gal. 1:18-24), where he spends a number of "silent years," growing in spiritual stature and being prepared by God for the great work as missionary which God has in store for him.

Historical Setting

While the Holy Spirit is at work preparing individual leaders in the early Church through influencing their outlook and providing for their spiritual growth, He also is preparing the Church as a whole for a crucial conference, whose decisions will determine the future of the Church doctrinally, ethnically, and geographically. Will the Gospel of salvation by grace alone through faith engendered by the Holy Spirit remain pure? Or, will synergism be allowed to take root in Christianity as it did in Judaism? Will the Gospel be actively spread among all nations in the Mediterranean world in keeping with Jesus' commission at the conclusion of Matthew? Or, will the main core of Christianity center around Jerusalem and Palestine, confining the Gospel primarily to people of Jewish descent? Will the Church make proper provision for the assimilation of Gentiles into the practices of the Church? Or, will a cleavage in nationality prevent a unity in the Church comprised of believers of various ethnic groups?

Let us review briefly the historical setting which leads to the Apostolic Council. Although the acceptance of the Good News by Samaritans through the initial work of Philip, one of the Seven, represents a sufficient change in policy that Peter and John arrive from Jerusalem to investigate the new movement (Acts 8:5-14), and although Peter's visit to the home of Cornelius the Roman Centurion demands an explanation when the apostles and brethren at Jerusalem hear that the Gentiles also are receiving the Good News (Act 11:1 ff.), the number of non-Jewish converts (Samaritan and Gentile) is relatively small. It is at Antioch in Syria that the Gospel is preached to Gentiles on a relatively large scale, so that Barnabas, sent by the apostles at Jerusalem, comes to Antioch to investigate (Acts 11:20-22).

Recognizing the grace of God in the new movement, and realizing the need for additional assistance, Barnabas brings Paul from Tarsus, and both work for an entire year with the congregation at Antioch in Syria, where the followers of Jesus are first called "Christians" (Acts 11:23-26). During this year Agabus comes to Antioch from Jerusalem and predicts a famine. The Christians at Antioch collect a purse and send it by Paul and Barnabas to Jerusalem (Acts 11:27-30). Paul and Barnabas not only deliver the purse to Jerusalem; they also report privately and informally to the leaders at Jerusalem concerning the great success of their preaching to the Gentiles around Antioch. Acts records the delivery of the relief fund (Acts 11:30). This indicates that the center of gravity is shifting to the Gentile congregations, which by now are sufficiently strong to assist the Jews in Jerusalem. In recalling this visit to Jerusalem Paul emphasizes the private and informal discussion with James, Peter, and John because it suits his purpose to inform his readers that he and the leaders at Jerusalem were in total agreement on the Gospel (Gal. 2:1-10). Acts is silent about the private conference because its importance is dwarfed by the later Apostolic Council. Paul, in the company of Barnabas, a person of some prestige with the apostles, unquestionably receives a recognition at Jerusalem which he has not enjoyed on his previous visit. He and Barnabas possibly discuss with the "pillars" at Jerusalem plans for their projected tour to Cyprus and Asia Minor (Gal. 2:9).

After they return to Antioch with John Mark (Acts 12:25), Paul and Barnabas begin the first missionary journey (Acts 13:1-3), which occupies about two years (Acts 13, 14), returning to the home-base Antioch in Syria, where they joyfully and thankfully relate their success among the Gentiles, remaining at Antioch "no little time" (Acts 14:26-28).

The vigorous mission of Paul's first journey, with its great success among Gentile converts, brings to a head two related problems: 1) Some Judaizers come from Jerusalem and insist on the circumcision of Gentile Christians (Acts 15:1-2), observing apparently that the Gentiles soon (if they had not done so already) would outnumber the Jews in the Christian Church. The propaganda of the Judaizers spreads to the newly founded congregations in Asia Minor. 2) Social intercourse between Jewish and Gentile Christians—a related problem—arises about the same time at Antioch, possibly brought to a head by the inconsistency of Peter himself (Gal. 2:11-14). It also is a serious problem, because it involves either division or unity at the common meals in congregations with membership of both Jews and Gentiles. Since unity could exist only if the Gentiles observe the customs of the Jews on "clean" and "unclean" foods, Paul is able to state that the Jews are compelling the Gentiles to live as Jews (Gal. 2:14).

Both problems are closely related and both problems are so important that a meeting in Jerusalem seems imperative. But before leaving Antioch (or, as soon as arriving in Jerusalem and before the Apostolic Council convenes) Paul with urgency and with extreme disappointment writes a letter to the congregations of Asia Minor, founded on his first journey, since he is not able to visit them immediately because of the impending meeting at Jerusalem of the leaders of the Church.

Paul and Barnabas in company with others depart for Jerusalem to attend and to take an active part in the Apostolic Council (Acts 15:2-5), which decides the two important and related problems. Although the question of circumcision has been discussed and decided privately in Galatians 2:1-10, it now is raised in more acute form as a result of the implications of Paul's first journey, which increased greatly the number of Gentile converts and which brought to the foreground the activity of some Pharisees, whose insistence on circumcision was similar to that of Judaizers (Acts 15:5). The decisions of the Apostolic Council concern both problems: 1) "Not to trouble those of the Gentiles who turn to God" (Acts 15:19) decides the first problem against the Judaizers, in line with the informal discussion some years previously (Gal. 2:1-10). 2) The decision on the second problem results in a compromise, with the Gentiles being urged to concede to the conscience of Jews who wish to be loyal to the Law of Moses (Acts 15:20-21, 28-29).

Issues Involved

Underlying the action of the Apostolic Council and basic to its solution of the two related problems is the fact, too often overlooked, that the decisions of the apostles were based on God's Word, not on the authority of an ecclesiastical hierarchy. On a superficial reading of Acts 15 it may appear that such "pillars" as Peter, Paul, Barnabas, and James dominate the assembly because of their position as leaders of the Church. On closer examination, however, it becomes apparent that the assembly first reviews the history of the Christian movement among the Gentiles in preparation for any decisions. Peter speaks first, naturally, since it was his contact with Cornelius, emphasized by a repetition of the incident in two successive chapters (Acts 10 and 11), that began the movement. Paul and Barnabas follow Peter in addressing the assembly, again naturally, for it was their work at Antioch in Syria for over a year and also their missionary journey to Cyprus and southern Asia Minor which gave great impetus to the Christian movement in Gentile territory. Their success leads to the crises, causing alarm among the Judaizers, who attempt to undermine the message of Paul and Barnabas in the congregations of Galatia.

After the brief review of the history of the Christian movement among the Gentiles, James, a most respected leader at Jerusalem, rises to speak. He realizes that any decision by the apostles on the question confronting the assembly—and this is the important fact so frequently overlooked—must be based on God's Word. The review of the history of the movement may assist in bringing the issues into proper focus, but decisions of the Church are to be Scriptural. By reminding the assembly that it was Peter's contact with Cornelius in which "God at the first did visit the Gentiles" (Acts 15:14), he is basically recalling that Peter's action was a direct result of a divine directive and that Peter visited Cornelius, the Roman Centurion, because of a specific and clear command from God. To remove all doubt that any decision of the apostles must be based on God's Word, James cites Scripture: "After this I will return, and will build again the tabernacle of David, which is fallen down; and I will build again the ruins thereof, and I will set it up: That the residue of men might seek after the Lord, and all the Gentiles, upon whom my name is called, saith the Lord . . ." (Acts 15:16-17). "Saith the Lord" is the only foundation and source on which a Scriptural solution to the questions confronting the Church must be based. James continues: "Wherefore" (*dio*—because God's Word has clearly spoken), "my sentence is . . ." (*ego krino*—it is my judgment). James once more makes it clear that his conclusion (and the conclusion of the assembly) must be based on Scripture.

Not only must decisions be based on God's Word, but Scripture also assists James and the assembly to distinguish between the two related problems: 1) How are Gentiles to be admitted to the Church? 2) How can unity be maintained in a Church comprised of both Jews and Gentiles? Again, on superficial reading of Acts 15, it may seem that the assembly attempts to reach a compromise by deciding the first question in favor of the Gentiles and the second question in favor of the Jews, thus attempting to keep peace in the Church by political strategy, hoping that each side will feel it has won a point. On closer examination, however, it is clear that James, and later the assembly, distinguish between doctrine and adiaphora — again on the basis of Scripture. The first question, on the admission of Gentiles to the Church, is a matter of doctine, and on such matters no compromise or yielding is possible, for God's Word expressly teaches that salvation comes to a person who is justified on the basis of faith in Christ's all-sufficient atonement alone through God's grace (cf. Romans 1:16-17 and Eph. 2:8-9 for Paul's later summary of the Gospel message). There can be no yielding to, or compromise with, the position of some Pharisees and the Judaizers (Acts 15:1, 5; Gal. 5:1-9), for their position undermines the "grace of Christ" (Gal. 1:6-9).

The second question, however, is an adiaphoron, a matter on which God's Word neither commands nor forbids. The new aeon, the period beginning with the Incarnation and Death of Christ and ending at Jesus' Second Coming, has abrogated the demands of the Old Testament ceremonial law, including the distinction between "clean" and "unclean" foods — as clearly indicated by the vision to Peter before his contact with Cornelius. Since no doctrine is involved in the second question, on the maintenance of unity in a Church composed of both Jews and Gentiles, compromise is possible and at times even advisable. So the Gentiles are requested to abstain from eating certain foods traditionally considered objectionable by Jews, thus removing voluntarily a hindrance to the unity of the Church at the "love-feasts" or meals attended by both Jews and Gentiles. Therefore, the distinction between a doctrine and an adiaphoron is Scriptural and is basic to an understanding of the decisions of the Apostolic Council.

But is not the practice of circumcision also a matter of the Old Testament ceremonial law and in a way an adiaphoron? Although circumcision was a sacramental rite by which a person became a member of God's people, the observance of circumcision in the New Testament era and the differentiation between "clean" and "unclean" foods may both be adiaphora in themselves. Now, to understand the distinction between the two matters made by the Apostolic Council, it will be helpful to review the principles involved in Christian liberty on adiaphora, as presented in 1 Corinthians 8. The matter at issue is whether a follower of Christ may in good conscience eat meat that has been offered at a temple of a heathen god — a matter which the second question confronting the Apostolic Council apparently also involved, as indicated by the phrases "pollutions of idols" (Acts 15:20) and "meats offered to idols" (Acts 15:29). St. Paul's first principle on adiaphora is that Christians have liberty in such matters. For "an idol is nothing" and "meat commendeth us not to God: for neither if we eat, are we the better; neither, if we eat not, are we the worse" (1 Cor. 8:4,8). According to the second principle on adiaphora, Christians at times should voluntarily forego their liberty in such matters, in order that they not cause a fellow Christian with a weak conscience to sin. "But take heed lest by any means this liberty of yours become a stumblingblock to them that are weak. . . . Wherefore, if meat cause my brother to offend, I will eat no flesh while the world standeth, lest I cause my brother to offend" (1 Cor. 8:9,13).

The third principle on adiaphora becomes evident in Paul's attitude toward circumcision. Even after the Apostolic Council, St. Paul, on taking Timothy as a companion for his second journey, has him circumcised "because of the Jews which were in those quarters: for they knew that his father was a Greek" (Acts 16:3). When Titus accompanied Paul to Jerusalem, no doubt on occasion of the famine visit some years previously, however, Titus was not compelled to be circumcised "because of false brethren unawares brought in, who came in privily to spy out our liberty which we have in Christ Jesus, that they might bring us into bondage; To whom we gave place by subjection, no, not for an hour; that the truth of the gospel might continue with you" (Gal. 2:4-5). In the case of Timothy Paul applies the second principle on adiaphora — a voluntary limiting of Christian liberty in consideration of the attitude of fellow Christians. In the case of Titus, as in the first question confronting the Apostolic Council, Paul indicates a third principle on adiaphora — a firm adherence to the Gospel when opponents are making propaganda, publicly or privately, for a teaching contrary to God's Word, for in no way may doctrine be compromised when God's eternal truth is being challenged.

The Apostolic Council, therefore, properly makes a distinction between two matters, both of which in the New Testament era are essentially adiaphora. The distinction is proper, since some Pharisees and Judaizers are making public propaganda on the necessity of circumcision for salvation. Their propaganda, at Antioch in Syria and at Jerusalem, as well as in the congregations addressed in Galatians, cause the matter of circumcision to become a threat to Christian doctrine, undermining and even destroying the Gospel of God's grace through faith, without any dependence on any actions of human individuals, such as being circumcised. Hence the first question, on the necessity of circumcision for Christians, is no longer an adiaphoron. No compromise is possible without sacrificing doctine. The second question concerns the eating or abstaining from certain foods traditionally objectionable to those of Jewish descent. Since no opponents are making public propaganda on this issue according to the account in Acts, the matter remains an adiaphoron. Compromise is possible and even advisable for the preservation of unity of the Church. Therefore, the Apostolic Council correctly makes a distinction between the two questions confronting the Church in 49 A.D.

Paul's Position

The implications of the Apostolic Council for the Church today need only to be summarized briefly. Decisions concerning issues on which God's Word speaks clearly must be based entirely on Scripture. At times a distinction must be made between doctrine and adiaphora. No compromise is possible on matters of doctine. On matters concerning which God's Word has neither command nor prohibition (adiaphora), compromise is not only possible, but is at times advisable out of loving consideration for fellow Christians. However, Scripture knows no distinction between doctrine and theology, as if doctrine concerns only the essentials of the Gospel (narrowly understood), with all other questions coming under the heading of "theology." Doctrine, according to Scripture, includes everything learned from Scripture.

Paul's position in regard to the events surrounding the Apostolic Council presents an important implication for leaders in the Church today. On the assumption that Paul wrote his Epistle to the Galatians before the Apostolic Council, it is most instructive to note that he could have waited a few days, or a few weeks at the most, before writing to the congregations in southern Galatia. Then he would have been able to cite the decisions of the Apostolic Council as prime proof that his position concerning the Judaizers was correct. He then would have had the backing of an official resolution of the Church. Also, if one prefers to date the Epistle to the Galatians after the Apostolic Council—even to the Christians in northern Galatia as possibly written on Paul's third journey—the fact that Paul does not cite the decisions of the Apostolic Council also is germane.

It is true that one of Paul's main points in his Epistle to the Galatians is that he received the Gospel he was preaching by revelation from God and did not depend on instruction from the apostles at Jerusalem. Most commentators conclude, therefore, that Paul's omission of the decisions of the Apostolic Council in his Letter to the Galatians—especially if written after the meeting of the Council—is in line with his personal argumentation. But is there not more involved in Paul's omission of the decisions reached by the Apostolic Council—especially if he wrote to southern Galatian congregations on the eve of the Council or at most a few weeks previously? Do we have an insight into Paul's attitude on doctine? Is doctrinal truth so important in his judgment that errors of false teachers have to be dealt with immediately? "A little leaven leaveneth the whole lump," he writes (Gal. 5:9). The leaven of false doctine quickly, "so soon" (Gal. 1:6), infiltrates the truth of God's Word, and so must be dealt with at once. It cannot be allowed to make deep inroads into the Church; it must be attacked at once. "A stitch in time saves nine," Paul would agree, also concerning the truths of Scripture.

But, even more important and instructive for leaders in the Church today is Paul's position throughout his Letter to the Galatians that doctrinal matters must be settled on the basis of God's Word. After setting the readers straight on his personal activities since his conversion, he bases the bulk of his argument on Scriptural authority. The decision of any future Apostolic Council (or of a previous Council, if Galatians is dated later) seems to be less important to Paul than what God's Word clearly states. He is confident of his doctrinal position because it is based on Scripture. If the forthcoming Council should show signs of wavering from the truth of Scripture, Paul no doubt would argue vehemently for Biblical decisions on matters confronting the assembly. Since he is convinced that his position is entirely Scriptural, he prefers to write his Epistle on the basis of God's Word instead of citing "Resolution No. —." Paul writes with conviction, because his convictions are based on God's truth as revealed to him from his careful study of God's Word. He needs no additional support from an Apostolic Council. His convictions are solid enough to challenge any decisions not based on Scripture. No wonder, humanly speaking, that Paul devotes the last thirty years of his life to the cause of Christ among the Gentiles, for a person with such convictions cannot do otherwise.

In summary, the situation surrounding the Apostolic Council, the issues involved, the decisions of the Apostles, and the position of Paul are of prime importance for the Church and her leaders today. The lessons learned from the Apostolic Council are as applicable in 1976 as they were 1925 years ago.

The Greek of the New Testament: Some Theological Implications

A number of English renditions of Holy Scripture are available today. In spite of—and also because of—the numerous translations presently available, the original Hebrew and Greek must remain the standard text for pastors and other professional students of the Bible. No rendering from one language to another, whether it is God's Word or a secular classic, can avoid losing something vital through translating.

In respect to the New Testament, scholars over the centuries have displayed various attitudes to the type of language utilized in the Greek text, particularly in regard to its place in the history of the Greek language. Several examples of different approaches should suffice to illustrate the basic importance of this subject in the interpretation and the serious exegesis of Scripture. Some of the theological implications will include the nature of Christ, an apparent redundancy in the stoning of Stephen, the meaning of Jesus' words to Mary about touching Him, and the authorship of Hebrews—to mention a few.

Holy Ghost Greek

One attitude, which may be commended for its reverential respect for Holy Writ but seriously questioned as a scholarly philological assumption, seems to have been that the Greek of the New Testament is explained best as Holy Ghost Greek, representing the type of Greek uttered by the Spirit through inspiration. Hence any divergence, apparent or real, from classical Greek either in the formation and meaning of words (etymology or accidence) or in the construction of sentences (grammar or syntax) may be expected and explained on the premise that the Holy Spirit employed a peculiar and individualistic type of Greek.

Dr. Robert G. Hoerber, Professor of Greek and Latin at various colleges for over thirty years, was Visiting Professor in the School of Graduate Studies at Concordia Seminary (1958-60) and currently is Associate Professor of Exegetical Theology.

While such an approach was seldom openly advocated, as it was in the seventeenth century, this attitude appears to have pervaded Jerome's rendition of the Greek New Testament into the Latin Vulgate. It seems that he had so great reverence for the Greek text as divine diction that, insofar as possible, he equated a Latin word for every Greek vocable and retained with relatively few exceptions the identical word order—which at times makes his Latin awkward and even ridiculous. That a translator must not attempt to equate every vocable and to retain the identical order of words becomes apparent when one renders "*Wie geht es Ihnen*?" as "How goes it to you?"

An analysis of Jerome's version of the temptation of Jesus by the devil in Luke 4:1-4 may serve as an illustration. Jerome substitutes a Latin word for each Greek vocable wherever possible—and in almost identical word order. The definite articles he has to omit since Latin has no article. He also must alter the participle "being tempted," because Latin has no present passive participle. For "in those days" Jerome employs the preposition *in*, as the Greek has the preposition *en*, although "time when" should not have a preposition in Latin. The clause, "and Jesus answered him," in the Greek uses a preposition plus the accusative case (*pros auton*), so Jerome matches it with a preposition and the accusative case in Latin (*ad illum*), in spite of the fact that the Latin construction denotes "place to which," not "indirect object." His version also has Jesus led "on the Spirit" or "in the Spirit," since he replaces the Greek *en* with the Latin *in*, even though the substitution changes the thought of the phrase. Because Jerome follows almost entirely the same order of the words, the position of the verbs frequently leaves much to be desired. But the most ridiculous example is Jerome's rendering of "man shall not live by bread alone." Jerome imitates the Greek preposition (and dative case) with a Latin preposition (and ablative case)—although *in* plus the ablative shows "place in/at which"—and the Latin may be paraphrased, "man shall not live in a lonely loaf of bread."

Semitic Greek

Another approach, employed especially by some scholars several generations ago, is that semitisms (the influence of Hebraic, Aramaic, or semitic constructions) are the sole determining factors in explaining the Greek of the New Testament. This assumption at first appears logical, since the apostles are predominantly Galileans whose native language is of the semitic variety. Although they write in Greek, their Greek is essentially of a semitic type. Hence, to comprehend the sentence structure of the New Testament, one must be thoroughly acquainted with semitic dialects. That semitisms occur in the Greek of the New Testament no scholar should deny. Nor do we intend to deny or demean the work of Matthew Black, particularly on the Gospels and Acts. But there is a danger of exaggerating semitic parallelisms, so that they become the principal key to the understanding of the Greek text. In the early part of this century professors at Yale (C. F. Burney and C. C. Torrey) used this approach to excess, but the faculty at the University of Chicago counteracted, showing that principles of Greek grammar account for numerous so-called semitisms. We recall a New Testament scholar of the latter part of the nineteenth century who desired his son also to become a specialist in the Greek New Testament and sent him to the University of Leipzig to earn a doctor's degree in Hebrew. Today, however, students of the New Testament do not exaggerate the semitisms as the prime criterion in judging the type of Greek found in the New Testament, especially in the Epistles of Saint Paul.

Papyri Greek

Another trend, popular a generation ago, seems to be the result of Adolf Deissmann's work, *Light from the Ancient East,* on the numerous remains of papyri (the papyrus plant was used as paper by ancient peoples) uncovered in the sands of Egypt after being preserved for two thousand years. These papyri represent to a large extent notes, letters, deeds, titles, and other items of daily life in the Greek culture of Egypt. The papyri remains are similar to a hypothetical situation in which Americans of the twentieth century would empty their wastebaskets in rubbish heaps in a location sufficiently dry to preserve them for two thousand years; then scholars would discover them and study such material, noticing particularly the type of English employed in the twentieth century. We dare surmise that the deductions of those scholars would give a narrow and warped picture of the linguistic ability and practice of twentieth-century Americans.

To be more specific, practically every age of Western civilization, particularly after the composing and recording of the Homeric epics, exhibits three basic levels of language: literary, conversational, and "vulgar" (in the sense of the idiomatic common usage of the uneducated). The extant compositions of ancient Greece and Rome are almost entirely on the literary level—and many of them, we trust, are the "cream of the crop" as a result of a sifting process. Aeschylus, Sophocles, and Euripides, for instance, are the authors of ninety to over one hundred Greek tragedies apiece. But their superior dramas, we hope, are extant through the vicissitudes of ancient library science (the change from capital letters to small letters in copying manuscripts, and the later substitution of pages for scrolls), bequeathing us only seven dramas of Aeschylus, seven of Sophocles, and eighteen (or nineteen, depending on the genuineness of the *Rhesus*) of Euripides. Also the bulk of other Greek and Latin authors in prose as well as poetry represents the literary level of language.

The conversational level—the type of language spoken and written by the educated people, grammatically correct, but not on the same high level as literary compositions—is represented in Latin literature by Cicero, both in his philosophical essays (e.g., *On Friendship* and *On Old Age*) and especially in his Letters, published by his secretary posthumously without any editing. The Latin is correct grammatically, but represents the freer sentence structure of oral speech with little employment of literary rhetorical figures and artistic construction of sentences.

Unique in classical Latin is *Trimalchio's Dinner,* an extant portion of an extensive novel, entitled *Satyricon,* composed during the reign of Nero (A.D. 54-68) by Petronius, the "Emily Post" of Nero's court. The scene is the home of Trimalchio, who suddenly becoming wealthy gives a banquet, to which he invites members of the current social register in Rome, in order to impress them with his new status and his recently-acquired art objects (although he himself exhibits profound ignorance of their meaning). Also present by invitation are his former associates or "old cronies" from a low level of society, also to be impressed by the rapid rise in his standard of living.

The unique characteristic of *Trimalchio's Dinner* is that it is the only example of "vulgar" Latin among the classical authors, and that it contains all three levels of language current in first-century Rome. The banter carried on between Trimalchio and his former associates and among themselves is ungrammatical. They confuse the indicative and subjunctive moods; they do not follow the correct use of cases; they show little sensitivity to the construction of a Latin sentence. Slang, not style, is their hallmark. In the same document, moreover, there are also examples both of the conversational style with correct grammar in the discussion among the invited guests from the social register of the day, and of the literary level of Latin in the narrative sections of the author, which describe the scenes and connect the comments and discussions of the various *personae*.

To return to Deissmann's work on the Greek papyri, the question arises whether the Greek of the New Testament is to be equated with the style of Greek found in the sands of Egypt, representing the level of language used, for example, by a young lad in military service, apparently with little or no formal education, writing a letter to his mother, or is the Greek of the New Testament to be explained on the basis of the literary, conversational, or common ("vulgar") level of language?

New Testament scholars today seem to agree that the Greek language experienced a decided change after the exploits of Alexander the Great (356-323 B.C.), who not only is a conqueror in battle from the coast of the Mediterranean Sea to the Indus river in India, but is also a founder in much of this territory of settlements (e.g., Alexandria in Egypt) for the fostering, promoting, and spreading of the Greek language and culture. In fact the change is so apparent that historians term the period after Alexander's career as Hellenistic Greece in distinction to the previous Hellenic Greece. The Greek language of the period following Alexander is usually called *koine* Greek, which means "common" Greek, in contrast to the classical Greek of previous writers.

Koine and Classical Greek

While all students of the New Testament are not ready to regard its style of Greek as parallel to the specimens of "vulgar" or "slang" Greek contained in some of the papyri, the assumption of most scholars of the New Testament is that a sharp distinction must be made between classical Greek and *koine* Greek. A frequent query to a teacher of elementary Greek, particularly if the students are preparing for the ministry, is whether he instructs such a class in classical or *koine* Greek, as if they are so different types of Greek that separate rules are applicable for each.

It is our contention that Greek is basically one language from Homer to Modern Greek, that the Greek language has fewer changes over three thousand years than English has since Chaucer (?1340-1400) or *Beowulf* (8th century), and that the so-called *koine* of the New Testament exhibits relatively few changes from classical Greek.

In previous years, before joining Concordia's faculty, it was the practice of the author in preparing students for reading the New Testament, to teach classical Greek for three semesters and then in the fourth semester to introduce the New Testament by listing the following six points of difference, which takes about ten minutes:

1. Disappearance of the dual. (If something does not appear, it surely should not trouble the student.)

2. The limited use of the optative mood, occurring only about sixty-seven times. (The infrequency of the optative should cause little concern. Most occurences are optative of wish, as "God forbid," in Paul, and in indirect discourse after an introductory verb in the past tense in Luke-Acts. Both of these uses plus others found in the New Testament are the same as in classical Greek.)

3. The extension of the meaning of *hina*. (The use of *hina* to introduce result and object clauses as well as purpose clauses is similar to the function of the conjunction "that" in English.)

4. The extension of the use of the negative *me*. (That *me* instead of *ou* appears with infinitives and participles also causes no trouble, since the students know that both words mean "not.")

5. The substitution of regular verb endings (*o,-eis, ei*, etc.) for some forms of *-mi* verbs. (Again there is no problem, as the students are thoroughly familiar with the regular endings of verbs.)

6. The simplication of sentence construction by the frequent use of *kai* ("and") and *de* ("but" or "and") to join clauses and sentences. (The paratactic sentence with "and" or "but" is much simpler than involved periodic sentences which employ all sorts of conjunctions as connectives.)

Our experience, tested for over thirty years, indicated that students should regard the Greek of the New Testament as very similar to the accidence and syntax of classical Greek, not as a different type of Greek with new rules. Experience also showed that with this approach students began to read (not necessarily translate) the New Testament at the rate of three pages of Nestle's text for a Gospel per class assignment and two pages of an Epistle of Paul each class period. In one semester they regularly read— again the emphasis is on *read*, not translate— one Gospel, 1 Corinthians, and two or three shorter letters of Paul (e.g., Galatians and Philippians plus Philemon). They soon developed a *Sprachgefühl* in the New Testament, considering its Greek as the same general type as classical Greek. In fact many of these students scored so high on the entrance examination at a seminary that they were given an assistantship to teach the class of beginning New Testament Greek while they were at the seminary as students.

Is the Greek of the New Testament really so similar to classical Greek? What is implied by the term "classical Greek"? "Ay, there's the rub." Most pupils and many teachers of Greek think of the forms and rules given in an elementary text such as Crosby and Schaeffer's *An Intro-*

duction to Greek as classical Greek. (Even on this assumption the six differences listed above are minimal.) But classical Greek is not limited to the fourth-century Attic orators, whose speeches form the basis for most elementary texts in classical Greek. Classical Greek includes, besides the fourth-century Attic orators, who compose according to very strict rules, also Plato, Aristotle, Thucydides, and Xenophon, not to mention Homer and the epic poets, Pindar and the lyric poets, as well as the authors of Greek tragedy and comedy. All these writers compose samples of classical Greek. While Plato, Aristotle, Thucydides, and Xenophon write in Attic Greek, they do not follow the stricter rules of the fourth-century Attic orators. Homer and Herodotus compose in an altogether different dialect, Ionic; yet their Greek is still classical Greek. Although Greek drama is in Doric Greek, another dialect, nevertheless it also is classical Greek.

The point is that classical Greek is much broader than the form and syntax presented in textbooks for beginning classical Greek. The more one reads in the various authors of classical Greek, the more one observes that many so-called differences between classical Greek and the language of the New Testament vanish. One difference mentioned above, for example, is that in the New Testament there is an extension of the meaning of *hina,* including result and object clauses as well as clauses of purpose. The fourth-century Attic orators, however, limited the function of *hina* to purpose clauses, so most elementary texts specify that *hina* is to be translated "in order that." But Xenophon, who did not have the advantage of studying Greek through a modern textbook under one of our current teachers, employs *hina* with the meaning "where"—and Xenophon, we repeat, writes classical Greek.

Crosby and Schaeffer's book presents strict rules for expressing purpose—e.g., a *hina* clause or a future participle—but does not mention the genitive of the articular infinitive, since the Attic orators of the fourth century do not use *tou* plus the infinitive to show purpose. When one observes that the New Testament frequently employs the genitive of the articular infinitive denoting purpose, one is likely to mark this construction as a peculiarity of the New Testament Greek. Thucydides, however, uses such construction to indicate purpose—and Thucydides is a classical Greek author, although he does not follow the same rules as do the fourth-century Attic orators.

Crosby and Schaeffer and the Attic orators of the fourth century consistently spell the verb meaning "become," "be born," "prove to be" *gignomai,* while the New Testament has *ginomai.* Also Aristotle—most assuredly a writer of classical Greek—always writes this verb as a form of *ginomai.* In texts of elementary classical Greek, furthermore, the second aorist active ending fo. the third person plural is *-on*, the same as for the first person singular, as in the works of the Attic orators. In the New Testament, however, the ending for the third person plural frequently is *-an,* apparently to distinguish it from the first person singular. Indeed we find the same distinction in Plato, who frequently has the third person plural aorist active end in *-an*—and Plato most definitely composes in classical Greek.

Implications

If our approach to the Greek of the New Testament is correct, the implications are numerous in New Testament exegesis. Our approach implies that the level of language in the New Testament should not be considered as *koine* in the sense of non-literary, "common," or "vulgar" Greek, parallel to the syntax of much of the papyri, in which some basic rules of classical Greek are not applied. New Testament Greek may be termed *koine* primarily in the sense that after the career of Alexander the Great the Greek language "common" in the Hellenistic world in countries near or bordering on the Mediterranean Sea becomes broader, including also forms and syntax employed by classical authors other than the Attic orators of the fourth century. The New Testament then should be studied as being on the level of literary and conversational Greek, in which many rules of classical syntax still apply, similar to Hellenistic Greek authors as Polybius, whose history of the rise of Rome in the Mediterranean represents a type of literary Greek written during the period of *koine* Greek, but quite similar to classical constructions in the broader sense of the term.

A few specific implications regarding some passages will suffice for the present. We shall limit our examples to implications, mainly theological, which involve basic rules of classical Greek on the use of the article, on the tenses of various moods, and on gender. These few samples, we trust, will illustrate the importance of our proposed approach to the exegesis of the Greek New Testament.

On the Article

According to our approach to the New Testament, the basic rules of Greek concerning the use of the definite article are applicable. In John 1:1, for example, we translate *kai theos en ho logos* "and the Word was God," rather than "and God was the Word," because the article with "Word" (and not with "God") determines the subject of the clause—according to a rule of classical Greek that when subject and predicate are joined by a linking verb (e.g., "to be") and only one nominative has the article, the noun with the article is the subject regardless of the order of the words in Greek.

The Greek of Acts 1:8 has only one article with "Judaea and Samaria," denoting according to classical Greek that the two proper nouns are to be taken together as one group. Thus the implication is that the document has three basic divisions geographically: Jerusalem, Judaea and Samaria, and the uttermost part of the earth. An absence of the article, or an article with Samaria as well as with Judaea, would suggest a fourfold division of Acts. Acts, therefore, may be divided geographically as follows: chapters 1-7 on Jerusalem, 8-12 concerning Judaea and Samaria, 13-28 unto the uttermost part of the earth. There is, of course, another possible outline on the basis of six summary statements (6:7; 9:31; 12:24; 16:5; 19:20; 28:31), the first five alternating between a stress on "word" and "church."

According to the same grammatical principle, the question arises whether the single article with "pastors and teachers" in Ephesians 4:11 would imply that Saint Paul is referring to four (not five) functions among the leaders of the early church: apostles, prophets, evangelists, and pastors and teachers (as one function).

On Tense and Mood

Equally important as the definite article in our approach to the Greek of the New Testament is the implication concerning the finer points of tense and mood. In Acts 7:58-59, for example, the *King James Version* reads "stoned" twice in successive verses concerning Stephen, as if translating the aorist tense. But the Greek has in each instance the imperfect tense of the indicative mood, which in classical Greek refers to a continuous, customary, usual, attempted, or beginning action in past time (not to simple completed past action). In the *King James* the repeated use of "stoned" in successive sentences seems superfluous and might be interpreted as supporting Harnack's thesis that Acts is based on two duplicate sources (A and B). The implication of the Greek, however, according to principles of classical Greek removes the apparent redundancy by rendering the first imperfect tense as "they began to stone" and the second occurrence as "they continued to stone."

Also the comparison of Jesus' words to Mary on the day of His resurrection with His invitation to Thomas a week later may appear puzzling until one applies the basic rules of classical Greek regarding the tenses of the imperative mood. On the basis of English versions it seems that Jesus prohibited Mary from touching Him "not yet ascended to the Father" (John 20:17), while a week later He instructs Thomas to thrust his hand into His side (John 20:27), which certainly involves touching. Some readers might explain the presumed puzzle by suggesting an ascension of Jesus during the intervening week. But an application of the syntax of classical Greek provides a simpler, sounder, and more realistic interpretation. To Mary Jesus speaks in the present tense of the imperative mood, which means "do not continue to touch, or hang on, Me"—that is to say, "we have work to do and we have no time for your clinging to Me." Mary is already touching Jesus when He speaks these words. If Mary were not touching Him, the Greek should have the aorist subjunctive with the negative *me*, implying "do not begin to touch Me." In His instruction to Thomas, however, Jesus employs the aorist imperative, as He does to all the disciples in Luke 24:39: "handle Me." Mary, as well as Thomas and the other disciples, is not prevented from touching Jesus, but is advised not to continue to cling to the risen Savior.

On Gender

Gender too in the New Testament has implications, both historical and theological, on the basis of the rules of classical Greek. Two instances, usually overlooked by commentators, may be cited. The one with historical implication involves the minor moot question of the author of Hebrews. Almost every conceivable candidate is suggested by New Testament scholars, including Harnack's proposal of Priscilla, also favorably regarded by J. Rendel Harris, on the basis of detailed internal evidence. But basic Greek syntax on gender seems to eliminate Priscilla in Hebrews 11:32: "And what shall I more say? For time would fail me to tell . . ." The Greek for the latter clause is *epileipsei me gar diegoumenon*. If Priscilla were the author, the participle should be feminine, *diegoumenen*, not masculine.

The instance of gender with theological implication involves a finer point of classical Greek syntax, occurring in Jesus' high-priestly prayer. In John 17 Jesus twice refers to Himself and the Father as being "one" (vv. 11, 22). The Greek text has the neuter *hen*, although the words for Jesus and Father in Greek are both masculine. To explain a point of Greek grammar—that the masculine gender for males refers to identity in interrogative sentences, while the neuter gender may indicate quality or essence or substance—we might illustrate with two hypothetical questions introduced by the interrogative pronoun. "*Tis* [masculine] is Socrates?" indicates that the speaker sees a group of men in ancient Athens and wishes to know which one is Socrates by asking: "Who is Socrates?" "*Ti* [neuter] is Socrates?" denotes that the speaker is inquiring: "What kind of a fellow is Socrates?" If this fine point of classical Greek distinction is applied to the passages cited, the neuter for "one" seems to specify that Jesus and the Father are one in essence or substance, although two separate persons, substantiating the theme of John's Gospel (20:30-31) that "Jesus is the Christ, the Son of God."

These few examples on the article, moods and tenses, and gender are sufficient to show that a good case can be made for approaching the Greek of the New Testament not as a unique type of Greek employed by the Holy Spirit, nor as essentially to be explained by semitic parallelisms, nor as ungrammatically "common" or "vulgar" language similar to papyri specimens from the uneducated, nor as documents composed in a type of Greek which varies greatly from classical authors, but rather as compositions of literary and grammatical quality, many of whose presumed variations are similar to the Greek of classical authors in a wider sense of the term than that of the orators in fourth-century Attica.

The frequent use by Saint Paul and others of rhetorical figures of speech found in classical authors also substantiates in no insignificant way our proposed approach to the Greek of the New Testament; but this topic must await a separate treatment.

Immortality and Resurrection: A Critical Exegetical Study

In a recent issue of *Dialog* Professor Robert L. Wilken writes:

> It has become fashionable in the last several generations, especially among Protestant theologians, to attack the Christian belief in the immortality of the soul. Somewhat crudely, theologians pose the question: immortality of the soul or resurrection of the body? This question usually assumes that the immortality of the soul is a philosophical conception derived from the Greeks and that it rests on a fundamental misunderstanding of the Bible; whereas resurrection is a Biblical idea and therefore authentically Christian. . . . the opposition between immortality of the soul and resurrection of the body has been woefully, and often mindlessly, overstressed![1]

A statement in Lutheran literature of some years ago is relevant: "Recent studies indicate that the traditional division of man into body and soul is not possible Biblically any more than it is medically."[2] Further inquiry reveals that "recent studies" stem from a paper by Professor Oscar Cullmann, "Immortality of the Soul and the Resurrection of the Dead: The Witness of the New Testament."[3]

In the preface of the Macmillan edition Cullmann writes:

> No other publication of mine has provoked such enthusiasm or such violent hostility. . . .
>
> My critics belong to the most varied camps. The contrast, which out of concern for the truth I have found it necessary to draw between the courageous and joyful primitive Christian

---

Dr. Hoerber is Associate Professor of Exegetical Theology. His revised and expanded version of an article in Christian News *(vol. 6, no. 32, August 6, 1973, pp. 5-8) is printed by permission of* CN.

hope of the resurrection of the dead and the serene philosophical expectation of the survival of the immortal soul, has displeased not only many sincere Christians in all Communions and of all theological outlooks, but also those whose convictions, while not outwardly alienated from Christianity, are more strongly moulded by philosophical considerations. So far, no critic of either kind has attempted to refute me by exegesis, that being the basis of our study. . . .

The attacks provoked by my work would impress me more if they were based on exegetical arguments.[4]

Since Professor Cullmann begins his argument with an exegesis of the *Phaedo* of Plato, whose dialogues have been the basis of many of my professional publications, and since he clearly invites an exegetical refutation of his thesis, I shall obligingly accept the challenge, endeavoring the same scholarly, scientific, and exegetical approach that I try to employ in my critique of others whose premises appear more unique than sound, whether it is an attempt to view Paul as an original Epicurean, [5] or an interpretation of Plato's theory of Forms primarily as a promotion of prose in the place of oral poetry.[6] For the benefit of those who do not have ready access to either English text of Professor Cullmann's study, I shall begin by summarizing the arguments of his four sections, or four chapters in the Macmillan edition, as briefly, candidly, and impartially as I am able.

Summary of Cullmann's Argument

In his first chapter,[7] or section,[8] Cullmann compares the *Phaedo* of Plato with Mark 14:33-37, 15:34-37, and Hebrews 5:7, to show "the radical difference between the Greek doctrine of the immortality of the soul and the Christian doctrine of the Resurrection."[9] Since Jesus trembled, was distressed, and was troubled even to death, "He was really afraid. Here is nothing of the composure of Socrates, who met death peacefully as a friend."[10] "Like Jesus, Socrates has his disciples about him on the day of his death; but he discourses serenely with them on immortality. Jesus, a few hours before His death, trembles and begs His disciples not to leave Him alone."[11] Applying Hebrews 5:7 to Gethsemane, Cullmann concludes: "There is Socrates, calmly and composedly speaking of the immortality of the soul; here Jesus, weeping and crying."[12] Cullmann portrays, on the basis of Plato's *Phaedo*, the picture of all Greeks regarding death as a friend because it releases the immortal soul from its temporary prison of the body, and depicts the Evangelists and the Jews as viewing death with horror since it means the death of both body and soul.

The second chapter,[13] or section,[14] attempts on the basis of Plato's Idealism to widen the gap between Greek thought and the teachings of the New Testament, particularly by substituting "inner and outer man" for soul and body, and by narrowing the meaning of flesh (*sarx*) and spirit (*pneuma*) in Pauline theology. "The Jewish and Christian interpretation of creation exclude the whole Greek dualism of body and soul."[15] "Behind the corporeal presence Plato senses the incorporeal, transcendent, pure Idea. Behind the corrupted creation, under sentence of death, the Christian sees the future creation brought into being by the resurrection, just as God willed it. The contrast, for the Christian, is not between the body and the soul, not between outward form and Idea, but rather between the creation delivered over to death by sin and new creation; between the corruptible, fleshly body and the incorruptible resurrection body."[16] "The New Testament certainly knows the difference between body and soul, or more precisely, between the inner and the outer man. This distinction does not, however, imply opposition, as if the one were by nature good, the other by nature bad."[17] ". . . flesh and spirit in the New Testament are two *transcendent* powers which can enter into man from without; but *neither is given with human existence as such.*"[18] " 'Flesh' is the power of sin or the power of death. It seizes the outer and the inner man *together*. *Spirit* (*pneuma*) is its great antagonist: the power of creation. It also seizes the outer and inner man *together*. Flesh and spirit are active powers, and as such they work within us."[19] ". . . deliverance consists not in a release of soul from body but in a release of both from flesh."[20] ". . . we hear Jesus saying in Matthew 10:28 that the soul can be killed. The soul is not immortal."[21] "The Christian hope relates not only to my individual fate, but to the entire creation."[22] "Not eternal Ideas, but concrete objects will then rise anew, in the new, incorruptible life-substance of the Holy Spirit; and among these objects belongs our body as well."[23] "Therefore the Christian belief in the resurrection, as distinct from the Greek belief in immortality, is tied to a *divine total process* implying deliverance."[24] Professor Cullmann seemingly regards a human being as a union of inner and outer man, into which whole man flesh (i.e., the power of death) entered with the sin of Adam, leading to decay and finally death; spirit, likewise, takes possession of the whole man, inner and outer, leading to "resurrection of the body, whose substance will no longer be that of the flesh, but that of the Holy Spirit. . . ."[25]

A very brief chapter,[26] or section,[27] tries to describe the meaning of Easter for the first Christians and their subsequent problem. "Christ is risen: that is, we stand in the new era in which death is conquered, in which corruptibility is no more. For if there is really *one* spiritual body (not an immortal soul, but a spiritual body) which has emerged from a fleshly body, then indeed the power of death is broken. Believers, according to the conviction of the first Christians, should no longer die: this was certainly their expectation in the earliest days. It must have been a problem when they discovered that Christians continued to die. . . ."[28] "In 1 Corinthians 11:30 Paul writes that basically death and sickness should no longer occur."[29] ". . . Paul writes . . .: if this Lord's Supper were partaken of by all members of the community in a completely worthy manner, then the union with Jesus' Resurrection Body would be so effective in our own bodies that even now there would be no more sickness or death (1 Corinthians 11:28-30)—a singularly bold assertion."[30] Yet men continued to die as before. Cullmann correctly explains: "Our body remains mortal and subject to sickness. Its transformation into the spiritual body does not take place until the whole creation is formed anew by God."[31] He objects, however, to the ancient Greek texts of the Apostles' Creed as ". . . quite certainly not biblical: 'I believe in the resurrection of the flesh!' Paul could not say that. Flesh and blood cannot inherit the Kingdom. Paul believes in the resurrection of the *body,* not of the *flesh.*"[32] According to Cullmann, apparently, St. Paul would never equate body and flesh.

In the fourth chapter,[33] or section,[34] Professor Cullmann discusses the "interim condition" of the dead, the time between their demise and their resurrection. Mentioning the passages which usually come to mind (Philippians 1:23; Luke 23:43; Luke 16:22-23; Revelation 6:9-11), Cullmann assumes merely figurative language: "They are 'with Christ' or 'in paradise' or 'in Abraham's bosom' or according to Revelation 6:9 'under the altar.' All these are various images of special nearness to God. But the most usual image for Paul is: 'They are asleep.' "[35] Cullmann speaks of "this intermediate state in which the inner man, stripped indeed of its fleshly body but deprived of the spiritual body exists with the Holy Spirit."[36] Seemingly sensing a striking similarity between the "inner man" and the traditional view of soul, Professor Cullmann summarizes his thesis thus:

> One could ask whether in this fashion we have not been led back again, in the last analysis, to the Greek doctrine of immortality, whether the New Testament does not assume, for the time after Easter, a continuity of the "inner Man" of converted people before and after death, so that here, too, death is presented for all practical purposes only as a natural "transition." There is a sense in which a kind of approximation to the Greek teaching does actually take place, to the extent that the inner man, who has already been transformed by the Spirit (Romans 6:3ff.), and consequently made alive, continues to live with Christ in this transformed state, in the condition of sleep. This continuity is emphasized especially strongly in the Gospel of John (3:36, 4:14, 6:54, and frequently). Here we observe at least a certain analogy to the "immortality of the soul," but the distinction remains none the less radical. Further, the condition of the dead in Christ is still imperfect, a state of "nakedness," as Paul says, of "sleep," of waiting for the resurrection of the whole creation, for the resurrection of the body. On the other hand, death in the New Testament continues to be the enemy, albeit a defeated enemy, who must yet be destroyed. The fact that even in this state the dead are already living with Christ does not correspond to the natural essence of the soul. Rather it is the result of a divine intervention from outside, through the Holy Spirit, who must already have quickened the inner man in earthly life by His miraculous power.[37]

Cullmann repeats his position in the last paragraph of his two-page Conclusion: "The answer to the question, 'Immortality of the soul or resurrection of the dead in the New Testament,' is unequivocal."[38]

Critique of Cullmann's Comments on the Greeks

Since Professor Cullmann begins his argument with a contrast between Greek philosophy and the tenets of the New Testament, let us look more closely into his exegesis of the teachings of the Greeks. Cullmann depicts two opposing positions: 1) the Greeks, believing in an immortal soul temporarily housed in an evil body, undergo death with calm and composure because death releases the soul from its material prison; 2) the Jews and Christians, particularly before Easter, without a belief in an immortal soul, fear death as an enemy, for death will put an end both to the body, which is a good creation of God, and to its life-giving power. Let us discuss first Cullmann's exegesis of the position of the Greeks.

Throughout the chapters, or sections, Cullman equates the non-New Testament position with the Idealism of Plato, referring to "the incorporeal, transcendent, pure Idea,"[39] "outward form and Ideas,"[40] "eternal Ideas,"[41] and "the Greek sense of bodiless Idea,"[42] as if Plato's doctrine of perfect, changeless, eternal Ideas or Forms were the accepted belief of the Greeks. A scientific investigation of the facts, however, reveals that such a doctrine was a unique teaching of Plato instead of one generally accepted by the Greeks or by the non-New Testament clientele. According to some Platonic scholars[43] the theory of Ideas was a tenet of Socrates, not of Plato, whose teachings must be gleaned from Aristotle. Other Platonists[44] regard the theory of Ideas in its usual connotation as a doctrine of Plato's early life, but later replaced by a theory of "mathematical numbers." Granting that Plato was the originator of the theory of Ideas and that he held to this teaching throughout his life, as I prefer to accept on the basis of the investigation of Professor Harold Cherniss,[45] it is a well-established fact that Plato's tenets were not accepted in general by the Greeks. In fact Plato's immediate successors as head of the Academy rejected the theory of Ideas as taught in the dialogues; viz., Speusippus, who succeeded Plato as head of the Academy and taught there for eight years after Plato's death in 347 B.C., and Xenocrates, the next successive head of the Academy, who taught for an additional twenty-five years.[46] Nor did Aristotle, who was associated with Plato at the Academy for twenty years (when Aristotle's age was seventeen through thirty-seven), adopt Plato's doctrine of Ideas.[47] To equate Greek philosophy with Plato's Idealism, therefore, is overstating the case.

It is also a generalization to equate Plato's teaching concerning an immortal soul with all of Greek philosophy, as if there were two clear-cut opposing positions: one accepted by all the Greeks and the other taught in the New Testament. Again Plato was one Greek who held to the immortality of the soul. While other Greeks agreed with Plato concerning the immortality of the soul, if not concerning its preexistence, many contemporaries of Plato and numerous subsequent Greeks did not believe the soul was immortal. Even in the *Phaedo,* in which treatise Plato presents most of his arguments in favor of the soul's immortality we read:

> Most of what you have been saying, Socrates, seems to me excellent, but your view about the soul is one that people find it very hard to accept; they suspect that, when it has left the body, it no longer exists anywhere; on the day when a man dies his soul is destroyed and annihilated; immediately upon its departure, its exit, it is dispersed like breath or smoke, vanishing into thin air, and thereafter not existing anywhere at all.[48]

After fourteen Stephanus pages of various arguments in behalf of the soul's immortality, Cebes and Simmias are still not convinced and proceed to raise specific objections (84c-88b), with Simmias still expressing doubt at the end of the discussion.[49] Instead of all Greeks agreeing with Plato on the immortality of the soul, the picture Plato portrays in the *Phaedo* is that "people" find it difficult to believe in the soul's immortality, while even Simmias and Cebes, disciples and friends of Socrates, see some weaknesses in the arguments so far elaborated, with doubt still lingering in the mind of Simmias at the end of all of Plato's arguments.

Aristotle, Plato's famous pupil and associate in the Academy for twenty years, seems to have argued in favor of Platonic tenets on the soul in the lost *Eudemus* of his early years; but in the treatise of his maturity, *De Anima,* Aristotle concludes that soul "is not separable from the body, and therefore not immortal; but in connexion with the body it is the formulative principle of the organism."[50] Also Epicurus' denial of immortal souls is well known.

> Epicurus regarded the soul as a mixture of four constituents: fire, air, pneuma and an unnameable. At death the soul-atoms are scattered, since they are no longer held together by the body. This was a great consolation to Epicurus, for only the conviction that after death we cease to exist can free us from the fear of the horrors of Hades.[51]

Since Epicureanism had extended far and wide by the time of the Apostles,[52] it is difficult to guess how many contemporaries of the Apostles in the Graeco-Roman world denied the immortality of the soul. That numerous Greeks and Romans did deny the soul's immortality is attested by Lucretius' *De Rerum Natura* and Cicero's philosophical works.[53] Cullmann's picture of a unified belief in immortal souls among the Greeks, therefore, is definitely distorted.

It is a further overstatement to imply that the Greeks, because they believed in the soul's immortality, faced death with calm and composure, while Jesus trembled, wept, and feared to be alone in the face of death. Again let us limit our remarks in this section to the case of the Greeks, to show that Cullmann's implication is a generalization. Plato in the *Phaedo,* it is true, depicts Socrates as meeting death with calm and composure, but in the same dialogue his companions do not share in his composure in the face of his death. Socrates' wife is led away crying loudly and beating her breasts,[54] while his companions weep and sob when they see Socrates drink the poison.[55] In the *Apology,* likewise, Plato implies that the usual scene in a Greek courtroom is quite emotional, with floods of tears and the parading of the infant children of the defendant to arouse the sympathy of the jury.[56] According to Epicurus, also, many Greeks feared death as the greatest of evils;[57] and it was such fear of death, which he found common among the Greeks, that Epicurus attempted to allay.

Cullmann should have realized, furthermore, that Plato's picture of Socrates' composure in the face of death is an idealized portrait. The *Phaedo* idealizes Socrates' last hours in much the same manner as Plato paints a superhuman picture of Socrates in the *Symposium* concerning the effects of alcohol. All of his companions fall asleep from excessive drinking; Socrates alone, after imbibing all night, remains completely sober and goes about his business the following day without any rest.[58] The portrayal of Socrates as a personification of "mind over matter," whether in the face of death or concerning alcohol, is an idealized portrait and furnishes no basis of sound exegesis to deduce that therefore all Greeks met death calmly or never suffered any ill effects from excessive use of alchohol. The facts reveal that Plato's Idealism was a unique theory, many Greeks denied the immortality of the soul, and their usual condition in the face of death was one of weeping and wailing instead of calm and composure.

So much for Cullmann's exaggeration concerning Plato and the Greeks; now let us turn to the New Testament to examine his exegesis, which centers on Paul's use of "flesh" and the experiences of the "soul" in the New Testament.

"Flesh" according to St. Paul

According to the thesis of Professor Cullmann "flesh" (*sarx*) usually does not have in the Epistles of St. Paul the same meaning as it has in secular Greek, but rather refers to the transcendent power of sin or death.[59] Cullmann warns in particular against being misled by the secular use of the Greek term. Let us check Cullmann's premise against Paul's use of *sarx* in Galatians. Since Cullmann invites an exegetical critique, the Greek text of Nestle will serve as the basis of the present study, with the pertinent Greek terms transliterated and inserted into the English rendering of the King James Version.

The first occurrence of *sarx* in Galatians is at 1:16: ". . . immediately I conferred not with flesh (*sarki*) and blood . . . ." The meaning of *sarx* clearly is "a human being" or "a human person." The same meaning obtains in the second occurrence of *sarx* in Galatians, at chapter 2 verse 16: ". . . a man is not justified by the works of the law . . . for by the works of the law shall no flesh (*sarx*) be justified." Here *sarx* is parallel to "man" or "a human being" or "a human person." The source of Paul's remark apparently is Psalm 143:2:[60] ". . . for in thy sight shall no man living (*pas zon*) be justified." Psalm 143:2 corroborates the meaning of *sarx* in Galatians 2:16 as "a human being" or "a human person" since Paul parallels *sarx* to *zon*, "a living person" or "a living human being." The third occurrence of *sarx* in Galatians is at chapter 2 verse 20: ". . . and the life which I now live in the flesh (*sarki*). . . ." St. Paul employs *sarx* as "human life" or "life in a human body" in the same sense in which he speaks in Philippians 1:22-24: "But if I live in the flesh (*sarki*) . . . to abide in the flesh (*sarki*) is more needful for you." Thus Paul's use of *sarx* in Galatians 2:20 as "human life" or "life in a human body" is close to his use of *sarx* in its first two occurrences in Galatians as "human being" or "human person." So far there is nothing in Galatians to equate *sarx* with a transcendent power of sin or death.

When Paul refers to his illness during his visit in Galatia, he employs *sarx* twice. Chapter 4 verse 13 reads: ". . . through infirmity of the flesh (*sarkos*) I preached the gospel to you at the first." Here the phrase "through infirmity of the flesh" clearly means "physical ailment" or "bodily illness." The term *sarx* is parallel to "body." Verse 14 continues: "And my temptation which was in my flesh (*sarki*) ye despised not nor rejected. . . ."[61] The meaning of *sarx* in verse 14, likewise, implies "the body." Similarly, speaking of circumcision in Galatians, Paul uses *sarx* twice. Chapter 6 verse 12 states: "As many as desire to make a fair show in the flesh (*sarki*), they constrain you to be circumcised. . . ." *Sarx* is "the body" or "the flesh, or material that covers the bones of the body." Verse 12 continues: " . . . but desire to have you circumcised that they may glory in your flesh (*sarki*)." Here the same meaning may obtain in view of the close context with verse 12, or *sarx* might be rendered as "human nature" or "human standard." At least in connection with circumcision the meaning of the "transcendent power of sin or death" cannot be read into *sarx*.

It is interesting to note the translation of the New English Bible in the seven passages from Galatians and two from Philippians which have been cited (italics added):

> When that happened, without consulting any *human being* . . . (Galatians 1:16).
>
> . . . no man is ever justified by doing what the law demands . . . for by such deeds, Scripture says, no *mortal man* shall be justified (Galatians 2:16).
>
> . . . and my present *bodily life* . . . (Galatians 2:20).
>
> . . . my living on in the *body* . . . (Philippians 1:22).
>
> . . . but for your sake there is greater need for me to stay on in the *body* (Philippians 1:24).
>
> . . . it was *bodily* illness that originally led to my bringing you the Gospel . . . (Galatians 4:13).
>
> . . . and you resisted any temptation to show scorn or disgust at the state of my poor *body* . . . (Galatians 4:14).
>
> It is all those who want to make a fair outward and *bodily* show who are trying to force circumcision upon you . . . (Galatians 6:12).
>
> . . . they only want you to be circumcised in order to boast of your *having submitted to that outward rite* (Galatians 6:13).

The New English Bible thus parallels *sarx* in these passages to "human being" or "man" or "body." Its rendering of *sarx* in Galatians 6:13 is unquestionably a paraphrase; but the close context with verse 12 makes its meaning clear.

In comparing the two sons of Abraham St. Paul employs the term *sarx* twice in Galatians. Chapter 4 verse 23 states: "But he who was of the bondswoman was born after the flesh (*sarka*). . . ." The meaning of *sarx* is "human nature" or "human means" or "natural means." Verse 29 of the same chapter reads: ". . . he that was born after the flesh (*sarka*). . . ." The New English Bible renders these two phrases, respectively, as follows (italics added): "The slave-woman's son was born in the course of *nature*" and "the *natural*-born son." The contrast between the birth of Ishmael and that of Isaac makes the meaning of *sarx* in these two passages indisputable. It definitely refers to a natural function of the human body, in contrast to the birth of Isaac when "it ceased to be with Sarah after the manner of women" (Genesis 18:11).

So far St. Paul in Galatians employs *sarx* as "body" or "human person" or "human bodily existence" or "flesh that covers a body" or "a natural function of the body." In Galatians 1:16 and 2:16 where I have translated *sarx* as "human being" or "human person," the use of *sarx* with a negative (as occurs in the Greek text) is similar to the English term "nobody"; the phrases could be rendered, respectively: "I conferred with nobody" and "nobody is justified by the works of the law . . . for by the works of the law shall nobody be justified." In Galatians St. Paul only once employs the term *soma* for "body" (6:17); *sarx* seems to be the usual equivalent in Galatians.

In Galatians 3:3 St. Paul queries: "Are ye so foolish? having begun in the Spirit, are ye now made perfect by the flesh (*sarki*)?" Paul contrasts *sarx* with "spirit." The immediate context of Galatians 3:1-5 makes clear the meaning of *sarx*. The New English Bible translates:

> You stupid Galatians! You must have been bewitched—you before whose eyes Jesus Christ was openly displayed upon His cross! Answer me one question: did you receive the Spirit by keeping the law, or by believing the gospel message? Can it be that you are so stupid? You started with the spiritual; do you now look to the material to make you perfect? Have all your great experiences been in vain—if vain indeed they should be? I ask then: when God gives you the Spirit and works miracles among you, why is this? Is it because you keep the law, or is it because you have faith in the gospel message? [62]

Paul is contrasting faith in the Gospel against the performance of the requirements of the ceremonial law; the former he parallels with "spirit," the latter with *sarx*, which therefore refers to "human deeds" or "bodily actions" or "human means." There is no implication of a transcendent power of sin or of death. Also the broader context of the preceding chapter and the rest of chapter three depict in no uncertain terms the contrast between "faith" and "deeds of the law." Galatians 2:15-21 states emphatically that no one is justified on the basis of his performance of the Law, but only by faith in Christ Jesus; chapter three continues with the illustration of Abraham to prove that salvation depends on "spiritual faith" and not on "bodily deeds." So St. Paul in Galatians 3:3 connotes by *sarx* "human actions" or "bodily observances" and not a transcendent power of sin or of death.

The last two chapters of Galatians employ *sarx* eight times;[63] the contrast between *sarx* and "spirit" is either stated or implied. In all of these occurrences the King James Version renders *sarx* as "flesh." The New English Bible, interpreting *sarx* as "lower nature," translates the passages as follows (italics added): "You, my friends, were called to be free men; only do not turn your freedom into licence for your *lower nature,* but be servants to one another in love" (5:13). "I mean this: if you are guided by the Spirit you will not fulfill the desires of your *lower nature. That nature* sets its desires against the Spirit, while the Spirit fights against it. They are in conflict with one another . . ." (5:16-17). "Anyone can see the kind of behavior that belongs to the *lower nature:* fornication, impurity, and indecency. . ." (5:19). "And those who belong to Christ Jesus have crucified the *lower nature* with its passions and desires" (5:24). "Make no mistake about this: God is not to be fooled; a man reaps what he sows. If he sows seed in the field of his *lower nature,* he will reap from it a harvest of corruption, but if he sows in the field of the Spirit, the Spirit will bring him a harvest of eternal life" (6:7-8).[64]

According to the traditional interpretation of scholars, *sarx* in these passages implies the "flesh (or body) as the instrument of sinful desires and passions" or "human nature as the seat of sin." Such is the implication particularly of "lust of the flesh" (5:16), "crucified the flesh with the affections and lusts" (5:24), "the works of the flesh . . . which are . . . adultery, fornication, uncleanness, lasciviousness, etc." (5:19-21). The translation of the New English Bible, cited previously, corroborates the traditional interpretation in these eight occurrences of *sarx*. Such is the meaning given to *sarx* in these passages by Walter Bauer's *Griechisch-Deutsches Wörterbuch zu den Schriften des Neuen Testaments und der übrigen urchristlichen Literatur,*[65] which is the leading lexicon of the New Testament. Also the standard reference work for classical Greek, *A Greek-English Lexicon,* compiled by H.G. Liddell and R. Scott, revised and augmented by H. S. Jones,[66] cites Galatians 5:19 under *sarx* as "the *flesh,* as the seat of the affections and lusts, *fleshly* nature." Note that Liddell-Scott-Jones refers to *sarx* as "the seat of the affections and lust," while Arndt-Gingrich's translation of Bauer speaks of *sarx* as the "willing instrument of sin"—the "seat" and the "instrument"; not, as Cullmann would have it, the transcendent power of sin or of death.

These passages complete the occurrences of *sarx* in Galatians, and in effect exhaust the meanings ascribed by Bauer to *sarx* in the entire New Testament as well as in Galatians.[67] A study of Liddell-Scott-Jones, furthermore, reveals that St. Paul's use of *sarx* coincides with its meaning in the classical Greek authors. Homer employs *sarx* as "flesh" in the story of the Cyclops who devours Odysseus' comrades (*Odyssey* 9.293) and in reference to Odysseus' wound in early life while hunting a boar (*Odyssey* 19.450). Similar instances of *sarx* as "flesh" occur in Hesiod, *Theogonia* 538; Aeschylus, *Agamemnon* 1097; Sophocles, *Philoctetes* 1157; Euripides, *Medea* 1200 and 1189, *Cyclops* 344, *Bacchae* 1136; Plato, *Phaedo* 96d and 98d, *Symposium* 207d and 211e, *Republic* 556d, and *Gorgias* 518c. Classical authors at times also use *sarx* to refer to the "whole body" as in Aeschylus, *Septem contra Thebas* 622, *Agamemnon* 72, and in Euripides, *Hippolytus* 1031, *Heracles Furens* 1269. The meaning of *sarx* as "the flesh, as the seat of the affections and lusts" occurs according to Liddell-Scott-Jones in Epicurus, *Sententiae* 18, *Gnomologium Vaticanum* 33, and in Plutarch, *Moralia* 2.107. There is no trace, then, of *sarx* as the transcendent power of sin or of death in Galatians, or according to Bauer in any New Testament literature, or according to Liddell-Scott-Jones in any of the classical Greek authors.

It is pertinent to compare Cullmann's premise with the tenets of Epicurus, since Epicurus is the particular classical author who employs *sarx* in the sense of "flesh (or body) as the willing instrument of sin" or "the seat of the affections and lusts" as St. Paul uses *sarx* in the last two chapters of Galatians. Diogenes Laertius preserves a collection of forty of the most important articles of faith in the Epicurean creed, that was famous in antiquity, consisting of extracts from the voluminous writings of Epicurus. Article twenty in the Loeb edition by R.D. Hicks reads:

> The flesh receives as unlimited the limits of pleasure; and to provide it requires unlimited time. But the mind, grasping in thought what the end and limit of flesh is, and banishing the terrors of futurity, procures a complete and perfect life, and has no longer any need of unlimited time. Nevertheless it does not shun pleasure, and even in the hour of death, when ushered out of existence by circumstances, the mind does not lack enjoyment of the best life.[68]

Cullmann attempts to portray all the Greeks as believing that the human body is evil and the soul immortal, while the New Testament teaches that the body is good with no separate immortal soul, but with *sarx* as the transcendent power of sin or of death. The tenets of Epicurus reveal the error of Cullmann's generalization. Epicurus, a Greek whose doctrines were widely spread in the New Testament world, denies an immortal soul and employs *sarx* in the same connotation as found in the last two chapters of Galatians and in many other passages of the New Testament. According to Cullmann a belief in the evil of the body is concomitant with a belief in the immortality of the soul — both tenets being characteristic of the Greeks. But Epicurus definitely denies the immortality of the soul, yet holds to the human body as the seat of sinful affections and lusts. Epicurus' use of *sarx* corroborates the traditional connotation placed on *sarx* in Galatians 5 and 6 and in numerous other New Testament passages, thus substantiating the two leading standard lexicons — Bauer and Liddell-Scott-Jones — and undermining Cullmann's premises.

As if *sarx* could never mean "body" in the New Testament, Cullmann states:

> The expression which stands in the ancient Greek texts of the Apostles' Creed is quite certainly not biblical: "I believe in the resurrection of the flesh!" Paul could not say that. Flesh and blood cannot inherit the Kingdom. Paul believes in the resurrection of the *body,* not of the *flesh.* The flesh is the power of death which must be destroyed. This error in the Greek creed made its entrance at a time when the biblical terminology had been misconstrued in the sense of Greek anthropology.[69]

Yet, as we have noted, St. Paul in Galatians does use *sarx* as equivalent to "body." Cullmann likewise should consider Colossians 1:22, which the New English Bible translates: "But now by Christ's death in his body of flesh (*sarkos*) and blood God has reconciled you to himself. . . ." Also pertinent is John 6:51-56 to show that *sarx* does have a meaning of "body" in the New Testament; the association of "eating Jesus' flesh" and "drinking Jesus' blood" makes the use of *sarx* in this passage indisputable. Ignatius, furthermore, whose death Eusebius in his *Chronicon* dates in 108 A.D., speaks of the *sarx* and *haima* ("flesh" or "body," and "blood") of Christ in his Epistles *To the Romans,*[70] *To the Philadelphians,*[71] *To the Smyrnaens,*[72] and *To the Trallians.*[73] According to Cullmann Christ conquered *sarx,* or the transcendent power of sin or of death, at Easter; according to Ignatius Christ was in the flesh even after the resurrection: "For I know and believe that he was in the flesh (*sarki*) even after the resurrection."[74] No doubt it was his anti-Docetic position rather than any influence of Greek philosophy that caused Ignatius to employ *sarx* in the sense of "body." Cullmann's premise concerning *sarx* simply does not stand up under scientific exegesis.[75]

"Killing" the "Soul"

Concerning the "soul" (*psyche*) Professor Cullmann contends for two premises: 1) the soul is not immortal since Jesus states in Matthew 10:28 that the soul can be killed;[76] in fact, in his judgment the term "soul" contains connotations of Greek philosophy, while the more correct Biblical term should be "inner man."[77] 2) the "inner man" experiences an interim state of sleep between death and the time of Christ's return.[78]

Cullmann's exegesis on the first premise, that the soul is not immortal, may be misleading. He asserts: ". . . we hear in Jesus' saying in Matthew 10:28 that the soul can be killed. The soul is not immortal."[79] Before studying Matthew 10:28 in more detail than Cullmann does, we should note that a few pages previous he claims that in Matthew 10:28 *psyche* means "life."[80] Perhaps the best explanation is that this contradiction is only apparent, and that Professor Cullmann had in mind Matthew 10:39 as the passage in which *psyche* refers to "life," since he cites also Mark 8:36 and Matthew 6:25 in the same sentence. In Matthew 10:28 the rendering of *psyche* as "life" would be ridiculous: And fear not them which kill the body, but are not able to kill the life. Cullmann himself translates the passage: "Fear not them that kill the body, but cannot kill the soul."[81] Also the Revised Standard Version, the New English Bible, Moffatt, and Goodspeed translate *psyche* as "soul" in Matthew 10:28.

Matthew 10:28 in the King James Version reads: "And fear not them which kill (*apoktennonton*) the body, but are not able to kill (*apokteinai*) the soul: but rather fear him which is able to destroy (*apolesai*) both soul and body in hell." One of the most obvious points of this passage is that the first portion uses forms of the verb *apokteino* (kill), while the latter part employs the verb *apollumi* (destroy or ruin). The distinction between *not* being able to *kill* the soul, but being able to *ruin* or *destroy* it is so manifest that all the major translations reflect it. The Revised Standard Version, the New English Bible, Goodspeed, and Moffatt agree with the King James Version in distinguishing between *kill* (*apokteino*) and *ruin* or *destroy* (*apollumi*) in Matthew 10:28. But Cullmann glosses over this distinction. He translates *apollumi* as either *kill* or *slay*, as if there were no distinction between *apollumi* and *apokteino*.[82]

The distinction between these two verbs is clearly maintained in the two leading lexicons. Arndt-Gingrich renders *apokteino* as *kill* or *put to death*, while specifying that *apollumi* in the active voice denotes basically *ruin, destroy* and in the middle voice *be destroyed, be ruined*.[83] Liddell-Scott-Jones gives *kill, slay* as the prime meaning of *apokteino* throughout Greek literature and *perish* as the implication of *apollumi* in the New Testament.[84]

Examples of *apollumi* in the New Testament, also cited by Liddell-Scott-Jones, are John 3:16 and 1 Corinthians 1:18. The King James Version of John 3:16 reads: "For God so loved the world, that he gave his only begotten Son, that whosoever believeth in him should not perish (*apoletai*), but have everlasting life." To translate *apoletai* as *die* or *be killed* instead of as *perish, be ruined*, or *be destroyed* would be ridiculous, since by the time the Gospel of St. John appeared many Christians had died. The clear teaching of the verse is that Christians will not perish eternally, but will enjoy eternal life after their physical death.

In 1 Corinthians 1:18 St. Paul asserts: "For the preaching of the cross is to them that perish (*apollumenois*) foolishness; but unto us which are saved (*soizomenois*) it is the power of God." The contrast between the two participles clearly manifests the basic connotation of *apollumi* by opposing it to *soizo*. Both Christians and non-Christians will *die*, but only non-Christians will be *ruined* or *destroyed* eternally. Likewise in 1 Corinthians 8:11 St. Paul warns against eating meat that has been offered to idols, lest such abuse of Christian liberty offend a fellow Christian: "And through thy knowledge shall thy weak brother perish (*apollutai*), for whom Christ died (*apethanen*)." The use of *apollumi* in contrast to *apothneisko* (*die*), once more reveals that *apollumi* basically denotes *ruin* or *destroy*, not necessarily physical death. Eating of meat offered previously to a heathen idol will not *kill* a weak Christian, but it may *ruin* or *destroy* his faith in Christ.

Returning to Matthew 10:28, let us note the translation in the Vulgate: "Et nolite timere eos qui occidunt corpus: animam autem non possunt occidere: sed potius eum timete, qui potest et animam et corpus perdere in gehennam." Again it is obvious that the prior part employs forms of *occido* to translate the Greek *apokteino*, but *perdo* to render *apollumi* in the latter section, making a definite distinction between *killing* the body and *destroying* the soul. To show that such a distinction between the two Latin verbs is basic we may cite a passage from Eutropius, a later Roman historian, summarizing the loss of Hannibal's brother, Hasdrubal, in Spain against the two Scipios during the Second Punic War: "Perdit in pugna XXXV milia hominum; ex his capiuntar X milia, occiduntur XXV milia."[85] In English the sentence would read: "He *loses* (*perdit*) in the battle 35,000 men, of whom 10,000 are captured and 25,000 are *killed* (*occiduntur*)." Eutropius distinguishes between the soldiers *killed* and the total *lost* or *destroyed* or *ruined* for further military use, employing the same two verbs that appear in the Latin Vulgate in Matthew

10:28 to differentiate between *killing* a body and *destroying, ruining,* or *losing* a soul.

It is not proper for Cullmann to pass over the distinction between *apollumi* and *apokteino* in Matthew 10:28, since all the major English translations, the leading lexicons, the pertinent parallel passages, and the Latin Vulgate indicate a definite difference in the basic meaning of these two Greek verbs. Professor Cullmann also omits several passages that indicate that the immortality of the soul is a concept taught in the New Testament as well as in Greek philosophy. Revelation 20:4 speaks of "souls (*psychas*) of them that were beheaded for the witness of Jesus" that "lived and reigned with Christ." Although this passage is from a book replete with figurative language, the reference to souls outliving bodies and being with Christ indicates that the immortality of the soul is a concept of the New Testament, as other non-figurative verses of the New Testament reveal. In James 5:20 we read: "Let him know, that he which converteth the sinner from the error of his way shall save a soul (*psychen*) from death, and shall hide a multitude of sins." Again the concept of an immortal soul is clearly manifest, as in an earlier chapter of James (1:21) that refers to the word "which is able to save your souls (*psychas*)." Also 1 Peter 1:9, speaking of "the end of your faith, even the salvation of your souls (*psychon*)," seemingly implies the concept of an immortal soul.

Two passages should be cited in full. Hebrews 10:39 presents an alternative for the soul: "But we are not of them who draw back unto perdition; but of them that believe to the saving of the soul." The alternative is either for the destruction (*apoleian*) or the salvation and preservation (*peripoiesin*) of the soul (*psyches*). Note that the soul either is *kept safe* (the basic meaning of *peripoiesis*) or is *ruined, lost, destroyed,* or *perishes* (the connotation of *apoleia*). Thus Hebrews apparently teaches the same concept of immortal souls that we find in Matthew 10:28. In fact, the use of *apoleia,* a cognate of *apollumi,* reinforces the deduction we make from Matthew 10:28 — the soul may be *ruined* or *destroyed,* but never *killed* or *slain.* The alternative for the soul is either to be *kept safe, saved,* or *preserved by faith* or to be *lost, ruined,* or *destroyed,* but never to be *killed* or *slain.*

The other passage to be cited in full is Acts 2:27: "Because thou wilt not leave my soul (*psychen*) in hell (*haden*), neither wilt thou suffer thine Holy One to see corruption." Both the Revised Standard Version and the New English Bible are closer to the original Greek in the first portion of the passage: "For thou wilt not abandon my soul to Hades." Thus Peter's speech on Pentecost reveals that the concept of an immortal soul is not foreign to the New Testament, since he proclaims such a tenet on the birthday of the New Testament Christian Church. Furthermore, the concept is not original even then, for Peter's statement is a quotation from the Old Testament (Psalm 16:10) and clearly indicates that the idea of a soul existing after the demise of a body is a concept familiar not only to the earliest Christians but also to previous generations who were acquainted with the Psalms.

Professor Cullmann's omission of any reference to the several passages that teach belief in the immortality of the soul[86] is similar to his failure to distinguish between *apollumi* and *apokteino* in Matthew 10:28. Cullmann's substitution, furthermore, of "inner man" for "soul" merits comment.[87] To imply that "inner man" and "outer man" have less connotations with Greek philosophy than the terms "soul" and "body" does not harmonize with Greek philosophical thought from the time of Plato to Plotinus.

St. Paul employs the appellation "inner man" on three occasions. In Romans 7:22-23 he writes: "For I delight in the law of God after the inward man: But I see another law in my members, warring against the law of my mind, and bringing me into captivity to the law of sin which is in my members." In 2 Corinthians 4:16 we read: "For which cause we faint not; but though our outward man perish, yet the inward man is renewed day by day." Ephesians 3:16 states: "That he would grant you, according to the riches of his glory, to be strengthened with might by his Spirit in the inner man." A detailed analysis of the psychological, anthropological, and theological implications of Paul's phrase "the inner man" (*ho eso anthropos*) is unnecessary for the present purpose,[88] which is merely to show that by substituting an immortality of the "inner man" for that of the "soul" Professor Cullmann is not accomplishing what he apparently intends — to avoid concepts of Greek philosophy.

The concept of "inner man" is as Platonic as the claim for an immortal soul. In the *Republic* (589a-d) Plato compares the tripartite soul to a mythical composite of man-lion-many headed beast surrounded by a human form, advising his readers to cultivate the "inner man" (*ho entos anthropos*), also referring to this element as that which is "human" or "divine" in contrast to that which is "beastly" or "wild." Similarly at the conclusion of the *Phaedrus* (279b) Socrates prays: "Give me beauty in the inward soul; and may the outward and inward man be at one."[89] In the words of a current scholar of Greek philosophy also Aristotle thought in terms of an "inner man": "At any rate, the 'inner man' occurs prominently in the tenth book of the *Nicomachean Ethics* (1178A) — and, it should be noticed, in a passage which is full of Platonic echoes and refers explicitly to the attaining of likeness to God."[90] Stoic philosophers speak of the "inner spirit,"[91] while the Epicureans refer to "inner life."[92] Plotinus in his *Enneads* (5.1.10) discusses "the inner man" (*ho eiso anthropos*); while Philo, one of the main links between Greek philosophy and Jewish thought, mentions the intellect or reason as "the truly inner man."[93] Thus the term "inner man" is as replete with connotations embedded in Greek philosophy as the concept of an immortal soul.

An Interim Sleep

It remains now to examine Professor Cullmann's second premise concerning the experience of the "soul": that there is an interim state of sleep between physical death and the time of Christ's return. Cullmann asserts: "They are 'with Christ' or 'in paradise' or 'in Abraham's bosom' or, according to Revelation 6:9, 'under the altar.' All these are simply various images of special nearness to God. But the most usual image for Paul is: 'They are asleep.' "[94] Cullmann refers respectively to the following passages:

> For I am in a strait betwixt two, having a desire to depart and to be with Christ; which is far better (Philippians 1:23).
>
> And Jesus said unto him, Verily I say unto thee, Today shalt thou be with me in paradise (Luke 23:43).
>
> And it came to pass, that the beggar died, and was carried by the angels into Abraham's bosom: the rich man also died, and was buried; And in hell he lifted up his eyes, being in torments, and seeth Abraham afar off, and Lazarus in his bosom (Luke 16:22-23).
>
> And when he had opened the fifth seal, I saw under the altar the souls of them that were slain for the word of God, and for the testimony which they held (Revelation 6:9).

Cullmann's premise presumes two assumptions: there is an interim, and the condition of this interim is a state of sleep.

The argument of Professor Cullmann for an interim between physical death and Christ's return is extremely brief. According to Luke 16:22-23 Lazarus went directly to "Abraham's bosom" and the rich man after burial was in hell. In Luke 23:24 the malefactor on the cross received the promise of being with Jesus at once in paradise. St. Paul preferred to die and to be with Christ, mentioning nothing about an interim period of waiting (Philippians 1:23). In the face of this evidence Cullmann briefly asserts that none of these passages "proves as is often maintained that the resurrection of the body takes place immediately after the individual death."[95] Cullmann's emphasis seems to be on the resurrection of the body not taking place immediately after death. He reiterates this emphasis in his footnote: "It is certain that Luke 16:23 does not refer to the resurrection of the body. . . . "[96] But no one, as far as we are aware, claims that these passages imply a resurrection of the body immediately upon physical death. The point at issue is whether these passages supply any evidence for, or against, an interim state. They appear to indicate that an element of a Christian person will be with Christ in paradise immediately after physical death (and the same element of a non-Christian person will proceed directly to a place of punishment). Such is the connotation also of Jesus' words in John 5:24: "Verily, verily, I say unto you, He that heareth my word, and believeth on him that sent me, hath everlasting life, and shall not come into condemnation; but is passed from death unto life." Our Savior clearly states that the Christian "is passed from death unto life," implying nothing of an interim state.

Cullmann's argument that "sleep" best describes the condition of such an interim period needs further comment. He presumes that of the New Testament expressions ("with Christ" and "in paradise" and "in Abraham's bosom" and "under the altar" and "are asleep") "are asleep" is the most accurate description, while the other phrases are merely figurative. The possibility that the description "are asleep" may be figurative, or a euphemism for death, while the phrases "with Christ" and "in paradise" may be more literal and accurate expressions for a deceased Christian he relegates to a footnote: "The interpretation which K. Barth (*Die Kirchliche Dogmatic,* III, 2, p. 778) gives of the 'sleeping', as if this term conveyed only the 'impression' of a peaceful going to sleep which those surviving have, finds no support in the New Testament."[97] To relegate the possibility that "sleep" may be merely a euphemism for death to a footnote and then to dismiss this possibility in such a dogmatic fashion, without any serious consideration of it in the main body of the text, is lacking in fairness. But even more negligent is Cullmann's failure to scrutinize the word employed in the New Testament for "are asleep."

To decide between Cullmann's assumption and the traditional view as expressed by K. Barth, a study of the connotations of *koimao* and its cognates is absolutely essential. The point at issue is specifically whether *koimao* in Greek literature and in the New Testament may be a euphemism, a figurative expression for physical death. Cullmann asserts categorically that there is "no support in the New Testament." He must make such a claim to bolster his entire thesis; but the correctness of his assertion depends on the evidence concerning the connotation of *koimao* in Greek literature. Let us look more closely at the meaning of this verb.

Homer recounts the slaying of Iphidamas by Agamemnon as follows:

> Then wide-ruling Agamemnon caught the spear with his hand and drew it toward him furiously, like a lion, and smote his neck with the

sword, and unstrung his limbs. So even there he fell, and slept (*koimesato*) a sleep of bronze most piteously, far from his wedded wife . . . (*Iliad* 11. 238-242).[98]

Thus already Homer employs *koimao* as a euphemism for death. Also in Sophocles *koimao* has the same figurative meaning:

> O chariot race of Pelops long ago, source of many a sorrow, what weary troubles hast thou brought upon this land! For since Myrtilus sank to rest (*ekoimathe*) beneath the waves, when a fatal and cruel hand hurled him to destruction out of the golden car, this house was never yet free from misery and violence (*Electra* 504-515).[99]

Other instances of *koimao* and its cognate *koimizo* from classical Greek where the connotation definitely is a euphemism for physical death are: Callimachus, *Epigrammata* 11.2; Sophocles, *Ajax* 832; Euripides, *Hecuba* 473-474, *Hippolytus* 1386-1387, and *Trojan Women* 594. No one could dare to deduce from these passages that the Greeks believed in an interim sleep.

The evidence from the New Testament is equally as convincing that *koimao* may and does denote figurative language for death. The verb, of course, literally means to experience physical sleep or bodily rest and in such a sense appears four times in the New Testament (Matthew 28:13; Luke 22:45; John 11:12; and Acts 12:6), with its cognate noun, *koimesis*, as the sleep of slumber occurring once in the New Testament (John 11:13). Figuratively, however, as a euphemism for physical death, *koimao* occurs much more frequently in the New Testament (Matthew 27:52; John 11:11; Acts 7:60 and 13:36; 1 Corinthians 7:39; 11:30; 15:6; 15:18; 15:20; and 15:51; 1 Thessalonians 4:13; 4:14; and 4:15; and 2 Peter 3:4) — fourteen times in all.[100] It will be necessary to examine merely several of these occurrences of *koimao* to show that the connotation is a euphemism for physical death rather than a description of any presumed interim state.

1 Corinthians 7:39 reads: "The wife is bound by the law as long as her husband liveth; but if her husband be dead, she is at liberty to be married to whom she will; only in the Lord." The Greek for "be dead" is *koimethei*, which the Revised Standard Version, Moffatt, and Goodspeed translate "dies" and the New English Bible renders "die." There is a parallel passage in Romans 7:2: "For the woman which hath a husband is bound by the law to her husband so long as he liveth; but if the husband be dead, she is loosed from the law of her husband." Here the Greek for "be dead" is *apothanei*, as is a variant reading in the Greek text of 1 Corinthians 7:39. In brief, St. Paul employs *koimao* as a synonym for *apothneisko*, or as a figurative expression for physical death, not as a description of any interim state.

The eleventh chapter of St. John speaks of the raising of Lazurus thus:

> These things said he: and after that he saith unto them, Our friend Lazarus sleepeth (*kekoimetai*); but I go, that I may awake him out of sleep (verse 11).
>
> Then said his disciples, Lord, if he sleep (*kekoimetai*), he shall do well (verse 12).
>
> Howbeit Jesus spake of his death (*thanatou*): but they thought that he had spoken of taking of rest in sleep (*tes koimeseos tou hupnou*) (verse 13).
>
> Then said Jesus unto them plainly, Lazarus is dead (*apethanen*) (verse 14).

Verse twelve is an example of the literal meaning of *koimao*, to experience physical sleep or bodily rest. But the eleventh verse reveals that the same verb has a figurative meaning, to undergo physical death, as the noun for death (*thanatos*) in verse thirteen and the verb for die (*apothneisko*) in verse fourteen amply substantiate. Again the entire passage agrees with 1 Corinthians 7:39 (and its parallel in Romans 7:2) as evidence that *koimao* is a euphemism for *apothneisko*, or a figurative term for physical death rather than a description of some interim state.

The story of the stoning of Stephen includes the following account:

> And they stoned Stephen, calling upon God, and saying, Lord Jesus, receive my spirit. And he kneeled down, and cried with a loud voice, Lord, lay not this sin to their charge. And when he had said this, he fell asleep. And Saul was consenting unto his death (Acts 7:59-8:1).

The Greek for "he fell asleep" is *ekoimethe*, translated "he died" in the New English Bible. Once more there can be no doubt that the verb *koimao* is synonymous to *apothneisko*, employed merely as a euphemism for physcial death. Also the succeeding sentence, that Saul consented to Stephen's *death*, substantiates such a deduction. The context, furthermore, indicates that *koimao* is a figurative term for death rather than a description of an interim state, for Stephen expects that one element will go to Jesus ("Lord Jesus, receive my spirit")—apparently at once, since his words imply nothing about any interim between his stoning and his reception by Jesus.[101]

"Soul" and "Spirit"

The account of the stoning of Stephen suggests that also pertinent are passages that teach the immortality of an element of human beings called the "spirit" (*pneuma*). In fact Arndt-Gingrich gives as one meaning of *pneuma* "breath, (life-) spirit, soul." 1 Corinthians 15:45, furthermore, seems to employ the two terms *psyche* and *pneuma* interchangeably, implying that at times they overlap. The first part of the verse retains the Septuagint *psyche,* as it quotes Genesis 2:7, while the latter clause uses *pneuma*. Luke 23:46 records: "And when Jesus had cried with a loud voice, he said, Father, into thy hands I commend my spirit (*pneuma*): and having said thus, he gave up the ghost."

In Luke 8:55, after Jesus commands the dead daughter of Jairus to arise, we read: "And her spirit (*pneuma*) came again, and she arose straightway." In the case of Jairus' daughter, then, an element of her being, termed "spirit," exists after death, and its return revives the corpse. 1 Peter 3:19 clearly affirms that Jesus "preached unto the spirits (*pneumasin*) in prison." Thus these passages (ranging from a Gospel through the Acts of the Apostles and an Epistle) definitely imply the survival of an element of a human being after physical death — an element at times called "soul" and at times termed "spirit." These passages plus the account of the stoning of Stephen agree with the previous evidence that the immortality of the soul or spirit is not an idea foreign to the New Testament.[102]

Nor is the concept of the immortality of the soul or spirit of a human being foreign to the early Christians, as Professor Wilken clearly demonstrates in his article in *Dialog*.[103] Instead of attempting to drive a wedge between the immortality of the soul and the resurrection of the body, as many modern critics attempt to do, they maintained both tenets and considered them as complementary.

Lest we appear to be excessively critical of Professor Cullmann, we must add that his distinction between Scriptural teaching on the soul and the Platonic soul is a major contribution to correct Biblical exegesis. According to Plato the soul is eternal, being immortal because of its nature, and it exists prior to any joining with a human body. Scriptures, however, teach that immortality and eternal life are gifts of God, not endowments of nature; they do not speak of any pre-existence of the soul.

The distinction between a Platonic and Scriptural soul, as Professor Cullmann emphasizes is a distinction which also the early Church Fathers held, as Professor Wilken clearly points out.[104] It is also a distinction properly drawn in the document of our Commission on Theology and Church Relations,' "Statement on Death, Resurrection, and Immortality," approved by the New Orleans Convention. The document rejects the teaching "that the soul is by nature and by virtue of an inherent quality immortal, as the pagans thought and as is taught in a number of fraternal orders today." The CTCR, moreover, affirms "the continued existence of all men with their personal identity intact between death and the resurrection, and thereafter," and rejects the claim "that the soul 'sleeps' between death and the resurrection in such a way that it is not conscious of bliss."[105]

Conclusion

The evidence corroborates the traditional view that *koimao* definitely may denote merely a euphemism for physical death, not a description of a presumed interim state, and that the phrases "with Christ" and "in paradise" describe the condition of a deceased Christian more literally than the figurative phrase "are asleep." Stephen clearly states that he saw "the glory of God, and Jesus standing on the right hand of God . . . and the heavens opened and the Son of man standing on the right hand of God" (Acts 7:55-56). Instead of mentioning an interim period, Stephen plainly expects to be united with Jesus at once; that is, to be "with Christ" according to St. Paul (Philippians 1:23) and "in paradise" as Christ promised the malefactor on the cross (Luke 23:43).

Where is Christ? Stephen asserts that He is "on the right hand of God"—an expression which does contain an anthropomorphic figure, but certainly implies close proximity to God rather than an unconscious period between the physical demise of the body and the return of Christ. Where are Christ and God? "In paradise," asserts our Savior. There also will be the deceased Christians —as they may with confidence hope and trust while they still enjoy the gift of human life — after their physical death. Those who die as Christians may expect to be "with Christ" "in paradise" at once, since the presumed evidence for an interim of sleep upon closer examination amounts to no more than a euphemism for physical death. In short, "sound, scientific exegesis" of the New Testament teaches both the immortality of the soul and a resurrection of the dead.

Notes

[1]*Dialog*, vol. 15, no. 2 (Spring, 1976), p. 111. Cf., for example, *Immortality and Resurrection*, edited by Pierre Benoit and Roland Murphy (New York: Herder and Herder, 1970); *The Intermediate State in the New Testament*, by Karel Hanhart (Franeker, 1960); and *Immortality and Resurrection*, edited by Krister Stendahl (New York: The Macmillan Company, 1965).

[2] Herbert T. Mayer, *"And He Shall Reign Forever and Ever"*: A study of the message, ministry and mission of the Christian Church for use in pastoral conference study programs. Based primarily on the Gospel according to St. Mark, this is an inductive study in Bibli-

cal theology. Produced by the Faith Forward Committee of The Lutheran Church—Missouri Synod (St. Louis: Concordia Publishing House, no date), p. 36.

[3] Cullmann originally delivered his paper as an Ingersoll Lecture at Harvard University on April 26, 1955. It was published in the *Harvard Divinity School Bulletin*, vol. 21 (1955-1956), pp. 7-36. Cullmann's study, published also in Switzerland and summarized in French periodicals, appeared in book form with a significant change in title: *Immortality of the Soul or Resurrection of the Dead? The Witness of the New Testament* (New York: The Macmillan Company, 1958; reprinted in 1959, 1960, 1962, 1964). For the convenience of the reader I shall refer to both English editions with the following abbreviations: to the former as "Harvard" and to the latter as "Macmillan."

[4] Macmillan, pp. 5-6; the Preface is not in the Harvard edition.

[5] Norman Wentworth DeWitt, *St. Paul and Epicurus* (Minneapolis: University of Minnesota Press, 1954); cf. *The Classical Journal*, vol. 51, no. 3 (December, 1955), pp. 134-136.

[6] Eric A. Havelock, *Preface to Plato* (Cambridge: Harvard University Press, 1963); cf. *Classical Philology*, vol. 59, no. 1 (January, 1964), pp. 70-74.

[7] Macmillan, pp. 19-27.

[8] Harvard, pp. 9-14.

[9] Macmillian, p. 25; Harvard, p. 12 ("resurrection" not capitalized).

[10] Macmillan, p. 22; Harvard, p. 10.

[11] Macmillan, p. 23; Harvard, p. 11 (with some changes: "but in sublime repose he discourses"; "trembles and quakes and begs"; "his" and "him" when referring to Jesus are not capitalized).

[12] Macmillan, p. 24; Harvard, p. 12.

[13] Macmillan, pp. 28-39.

[14] Harvard, pp. 14-21.

[15] Macmillan, p. 30; Harvard, p. 15.

[16] Macmillan, p. 31; Harvard, p. 16 (with the following differences: "corporeal phantasm" for "corporeal appearance"; "future creation of the resurrection" for "future creation brought into being by the resurrection"; "and the new creation" for "and new creation").

[17] Macmillan, pp. 32-33; Harvard, p. 17 ("also knows" for "certainly knows"; "This distinction, also present in the New Testament," for "This distinction").

[18] Macmillan, p. 33; Harvard, p. 18.

[19] Macmillan, p. 34; Harvard, p. 18.

[20] Macmillan, p. 36; Harvard, p. 19.

[21] Macmillan, p. 36; Harvard, p. 20.

[22] Macmillan, p. 37; Harvard, p. 20.

[23] Macmillan, pp. 37-38; Harvard, p. 20 ("but the concrete objects" for "but concrete objects").

[24] Macmillan, p. 38; Harvard, p. 21.

[25] Macmillan, p. 37; Harvard, p. 20.

[26] Macmillan, pp. 40-47.

[27] Harvard, pp. 21-26.

[28] Macmillan, p. 40; Harvard, pp. 21-22 ("Shall no more die" for "should no longer die"; "earliest time" for "earliest days"; "ascertained" for "discovered").

[29] Macmillan, p. 42; Harvard, p. 23.

[30] Macmillan, p. 45; Harvard, pp. 24-25 ("resurrection body" not capitalized).

[31] Macmillan, p. 45; Harvard, p. 25.

[32] Macmillan, p. 46; Harvard, p. 25 ("Biblical" capitalized).

[33] Macmillan, pp. 48-57.

[34] Harvard, pp. 26-31.

[35] Macmillan, p. 51; Harvard, p. 27 ("merely various images" for "simply various images"; "of the special nearness" for "of special nearness"; "they are asleep" not capitalized).

[36] Macmillan, p. 54; Harvard edition does not contain paragraph in which this statement appears.

[37] Macmillan, pp. 55-56; Harvard, p. 30 ("Greek teaching of immortality" for "Greek doctrine of immortality"; "must have already" for "must already have").

[38] Macmillan, p. 60; Harvard, p. 32.

[39] Macmillan, p. 31; Harvard, p. 16.

[40] *Ibid.*

[41] Macmillan, p. 37; Harvard, p. 20.

[42] Macmillan, p. 46; Harvard, p. 25.

[43] John Burnet and A. E. Taylor. Cf. A. E. Taylor, *Plato: The Man and His Work* (London: Methuen & Co., 1949) *passim*, especially pp. 348, 503-516.

[44] David Ross, *Plato's Theory of Ideas* (London: Oxford Clarendon Press, 1953), pp. 176-245; Konrad Gaiser, *Platons Ungeschriebene Lehre* (Stuttgart: Ernst Klett Verlag, 1963), pp. 15-331; cf. my review in *Classical Philology*, vol. 60, no. 2 (April, 1965), pp. 136-139.

[45] *The Riddle of the Early Academy* (Berkeley: University of California Press, 1945).

[46] *Ibid.*, pp. 31-59.

[47] Cf. Aristotle, *Metaphysica* 990a33-993a10, *Ethica Nicomachea* 1096a11-1097a14.

[48] 69e-70a. I have cited the translation of R. Hackforth, *Plato's Phaedo* (Cambridge: University Press, 1955) lest anyone fear my translation might be slanted.

[49] 107b: "I am compelled still to have doubt personally about what has been said."

[50] Werner Jaeger, *Aristotle: Fundamentals of the History of His Development*, translated by Richard Robinson (London: Oxford University Press, Second edition, 1948), p. 45; cf. p. 40. Cf. also D. Allan, *The Philosophy of Aristotle* (London: Oxford University Press, 1952), pp. 63-66. Cf. Aristotle, *De Anima* 412a1-413a10.

[51] Eduard Zeller, *Outlines of the History of Greek Philosophy* (New York: Meridian Books, 1955), p. 255. Cf. Diogenes Laertius 10.124-126, 139 for the views of Epicurus concerning his denial of the soul's immortality.

[52] Norman Wentworth DeWitt, *Epicurus and His Philosophy* (Cleveland and New York: The World Publishing Company, 1967), pp. 328-348. Cf. Lactantius, *Divinae Institutiones* 3:17; Lucretius 5.19-21; Cicero, *De Finibus* 1.7.25, 2.9.28, 2.14.44, 2.15.49, 2.25.81, 2.34.115, *Tusculanae Disputationes* 2.3.7, 3.21.50, 4.3.6, 5.10.28, *De Officiis* 3.33.116; Diogenes Laertius 10.9; Pliny, *Epistulae* 10.96; Lucian, *Alexander* 25; *Corpus Inscriptionum Graecarum* 4149.

[53] Cf. Cicero's statement: "Sunt qui discessum animi a corpore putent esse mortem; sunt qui nullum censeant fieri discessum, sed una animum et corpus occidere animumque in corpore exstingui" (*Tusculanae Disputationes* 1.9.18): "Some think that death is the separation of the soul from the body; others believe that no separation occurs, but that the soul and body perish together and that the soul is extinguished with the body." For the view of Panaetius, a famous Stoic philosopher of the second century B.C. who taught that souls perish at death, cf. Cicero, *Tusculanae Disputationes* 1.32.79. For the views of two other Stoics (of the third century B.C.), Cleanthes and Chrysippus, cf. Diogenes Laertius, 7.157 to observe their failure to agree with Plato's *Phaedo*.

[54] *Phaedo* 60a.

[55] *Phaedo* 117c-e.

[56] *Apology* 34b-d.

[57] Diogenes Laertius 10.125.

[58] *Symposium* 223b-d; Jowett translates: "Agathon arose in order that he might take his place on the couch by Socrates, when suddenly a band of revellers entered, and spoiled the order of the banquet. Some one who was going out having left the door open, they had found their way in, and made themselves at home; great confusion ensued, and every one was compelled to drink large quantities of wine. Aristodemus said that Eryximachus, Phaedrus, and others went away—he himself fell asleep, and as the nights were long took a good rest: he was awakened towards daybreak by a crowing of cocks, and when he awoke,

the others were either asleep, or had gone away; there remained awake only Socrates, Aristophanes, and Agathon, who were drinking out of a large goblet which they passed round, and Socrates was discoursing to them. Aristodemus did not hear the beginning of the discourse, and he was only half awake, but the chief-thing which he remembered, was Socrates insisting to the other two that the genius of comedy was the same as that of tragedy, and that the writer of tragedy ought to be a writer of comedy also. To this they were compelled to assent, being sleepy, and not quite understanding his meaning. And first of all Aristophanes dropped, and then, when the day was already dawning, Agathon. Socrates, when he had put them to sleep, rose to depart, Aristodemus, as his manner was, following him. At the Lyceum he took a bath and passed the day as usual; and when evening came he retired to rest at his own home."

59 Macmillan, pp. 33-34; Harvard, pp. 17-18.

60 Psalm 142:2 in Rahlfs' edition of the Septuagint.

61 The variant reading *humon* has no bearing on the question at hand.

62 In my *Saint Paul's Shorter Letters* I render these verses thus: "O you foolish Galatians! Who has cast a spell over you? The crucifixion of Jesus Christ has been vividly described in your presence. I wish to ask you merely one question. Did you receive the Spirit as a result of your performance of the law, or by faith as a result of hearing the gospel? Are you so foolish? Are you trying to complete by human means what you have begun by spiritual means? Have you experienced so many things for nothing?—that is, if they are for nothing. Now does God furnish you with his Spirit and perform miracles among you as a result of your performance of the law, or by faith as a result of hearing the gospel?"

63 That is, in addition to Galatians 6:12 and 6:13 cited above: Galatians 5:13, 5:16, 5:17 (twice), 5:19, 5:24, 6:8 (twice).

64 I have italicized the words which are a translation of *sarx*. In *Saint Paul's Shorter Letters* I render *sarx* as "human nature" in these passages: "Yes, fellow Christians, you have been called to freedom; only do not interpret your freedom as an excuse for your human nature. On the contrary, with love you should render service to one another" (5:13). "This is the point I am trying to make—follow the Spirit; then you will not submit to the passion of human nature. For human nature has passions opposed to the Spirit, and the Spirit opposes human nature. In fact they are directly opposite to each other" (5:16-17). "Now the expressions of human nature are well known; namely, prostitution, impurity, lewdness . . ." (5:19). "Those who belong to Christ Jesus have nailed to the cross the evil desires and passions of their human nature" (5:24). "Do not be misled; you cannot outwit God. In fact a person will harvest whatever he plants. I mean that whoever plants for the benefit of his human nature will harvest destruction from his human nature; but whoever plants for the benefit of the Spirit will harvest eternal life from the Spirit" (6:7-8).

65 An English translation and adaptation of the fourth revised and augmented edition, 1952, appeared in 1957; *A Greek-English Lexicon of the New Testament and Other Early Christian Literature*, by William F. Arndt and F. Wilbur Gingrich (University of Chicago Press and Cambridge University Press).

66 Oxford: Clarendon Press, 1940. This edition of the two-volume lexicon is usually referred to as "Liddell-Scott-Jones."

67 For the entire New Testament and other early Christian literature Bauer adds only one more meaning of *sarx* in only one New Testament passage: "The *sarx* is the source of the sexual urge without any suggestion of sinfulness connected with it" (John 1:13); but also in this passage the meaning of *ek thelematos sarkos* is "physical or bodily impulse." Bauer lists *sarx* in Galatians 6:12 under the general meaning of "*the external* or *outward side of life*" while I have construed it with Galatians 6:13 as referring to circumcision.

68 Diogenes Laertius, *Lives of Eminent Philosophers* 10:145.

69 Macmillan, p. 46; Harvard, p. 25 ("Biblical" capitalized each time, and "in a time" for "at a time").

70 7.3: "I desire the 'bread of God,' which is the flesh (*sarx*) of Jesus Christ, who was 'of the seed of David', and for drink I desire his blood, which is incorruptible love" (Kirsopp Lake, Loeb Edition).

71 4: "Be careful therefore to use one Eucharist (for there is one flesh [*sarx*] of our Lord Jesus Christ, and one cup for union with his blood . . . .)" (Kirsopp Lake, Loeb Edition). 5.1: " . . . making the Gospel my refuge as the flesh (*sarki*) of Jesus, and the Apostles as the presbytery of the church" (Kirsopp Lake, Loeb Edition).

72 7.1: "They abstain from Eucharist and prayer, because they do not confess that the Eucharist is the flesh (*sarka*) of our Saviour Jesus Christ who suffered for our sins, which the Father raised up by his goodness" (Kirsopp Lake, Loeb Edition).

73 8.1: "Therefore adopt meekness and be renewed in faith, which is the flesh (*sarx*) of the Lord, and in love, which is the blood of Jesus Christ" (Kirsopp Lake, Loeb Edition).

74 *To the Smyrnaeans* 3.1 (Kirsopp Lake, Loeb Edition; also cited by Eusebius, *Historia Ecclesiastica* 3.36.11).

75 Two additional passages are pertinent. St. Paul writes in 1 Corinthians 6:16: "What! know ye not that he which is joined to an harlot is one body (*soma*)? for two, saith he, shall be one flesh (*sarka*)." In the following chapter Paul continues (7:28): "But and if thou marry, thou hast not sinned; and if a virgin marry, she hath not sinned. Nevertheless such shall have trouble in the flesh (*sarki*): but I spare you." The New English Bible renders the last sentence: "But those who marry will have pain and grief in this bodily life, and my aim is to spare you." In each of these passages St. Paul employs *sarx* as synonymous to "body."

76 Macmillan, p. 36; Harvard, p. 20.

77 Macmillan, pp. 32-33; Harvard, p. 17 (cf. variations listed in note 17 above).

78 Macmillan, pp. 51 and 54; Harvard, p. 27 (cf. variations listed in notes 35 and 36 above).

79 Macmillan, p. 36; Harvard, p. 20.

80 Macmillan, p. 33, n. 5; Harvard, p. 34, n. 16.

81 Macmillan, p. 36; Harvard, p. 19.

82 Macmillan, p. 36; Harvard, pp. 19-20.

83 Cf. note 65 above.

84 Cf. note 66 above.

85 *Breviarium Ab Urbe Condita* 3.11.4.

86 Below we shall discuss some passages that teach the immortality of an element of man called the "spirit."

87 Macmillan, pp. 32-33 and 54-56; Harvard, pp. 17 and 30 (cf. variations listed in notes 17, 36, and 37 above).

88 Such a study would consider also the contrast between the "old man" and the "new man" in Romans 6:6, Ephesians 4:22-24, Colossians 3:9-10 as well as the "hidden man of the heart" in 1 Peter 3:4. We suspect that it would be difficult to disprove the judgment of Arndt-Gingrich (under *anthropos* 2ca) that "the outer man" and "the inner man" distinguish "between the two sides of human nature . . . man in his material, transitory, and sinful aspects" and "man in his spiritual, immortal aspects, striving toward God."

89 Translation of Benjamin Jowett. R. Hackforth translates: "Grant that I may become fair within, and that such outward things as I have may not war against the spirit within me." For additional comments on Plato's "inner man" cf. Paul Friedländer, *Plato: The Dialogues, Second and Third Periods* (Princeton: Princeton University Press, 1969), pp. 125, 128, 136, 149, 402, and John M. Rist, *Eros and Psyche: Studies in Plato, Plotinus, and Origen* (Toronto: University of Toronto Press, 1964), pp. 175-181.

90 John M. Rist (cf. note 89), p. 177. In a footnote he refers also to *Nicomachean Ethics* 1166A and 1169A.

91 Or "inner god" or "inner selves" or "inner part" or "divine part within." Cf. William L. Davidson, *The Stoic Creed* (Edinburgh: T. & T. Clark, 1907), pp. 141-142; R. M. Wenley, *Stoicism and Its Influence* (New York: Longmans, Green and Co., 1927), pp. 97-98, 103, and 106; and Marcus Antonius, *Ad se Ipsum* 2.13, 2.17, 3.3, 3.4, 3.5, 3.6, 3.7, 3.12, 3.16, 4.1, 5.10, 12.1, 12.3, 12.19.

Election and Analogy of Faith

The doctrine of election to salvation from eternity frequently fails to receive its proper emphasis, perhaps because pastors and teachers concentrate more on the difficulty of its presentation than on its importance in the analogy of faith. That election is a difficult doctrine is clear from the way it has been misunderstood and misapplied in the history of Christianity. Disagreement concerning this Scriptural teaching has separated various denominations of Protestantism and has been a doctrine disputed also among branches of the Lutheran church bodies. That election to salvation is an important auxiliary tenet of the Christian faith often may be bypassed through fear of the inability to explain adequately this "mystery" and hence the danger of confusing Christians. Article XI of the Formula of Concord deals with eternal election in order "by God's grace to prevent . . . disunity and schism in this article among our posterity." For its fuller treatment the reader ought to consult paragraphs 14-24 of the Solid Declaration, which emphasize eight points that should never be excluded in a discussion of God's election.

This brief article will attempt to allay some of the fear which all serious students of Scripture experience in approaching the doctrine of election, by offering a diagram which we found helpful in presenting the doctrine of election particularly to Bible classes, followed by some comments on the important relationship of this Scriptural teaching to other articles of the Christian faith (analogy of faith). Analogy of faith, according to J. Gerhard, "means that the interpretation of Scripture should be undertaken and properly done in such a way that it harmonizes with the whole thought set forth in Scripture concerning each article of the heavenly doctrine" (Locus I, chap. XXV [*De interpretatione scripturae sacrae*], par. 531).

	Source of Salvation	Source of Damnation	
1.	man	man	(synergistic)
2.	God	God	(Calvinistic)
3.	God	man	(Scriptural)
	(Ephesians 2:8-9)	(Matthew 23:37)	

This diagram wishes to illustrate that throughout the history of the church basically three sets of answers have been given to the question, "What are the causes, respectively, of salvation and damnation?" The first two sets of replies are logical, comprehensible to our natural reason, because the same cause appears in both columns (as indicated by the broken vertical line). If some human beings are able to attain salvation by their own actions or decisions, the failure of other individuals to do likewise must be the cause of their damnation. This synergistic answer (that man is responsible for, or cooperates in, his salvation) covers a wide spectrum, from the gross work-righteousness of the heathen to the fine synergism of "decision" or "lack of rejection" as the ultimate factor in separating the "saved" from the "lost." The Calvinistic approach, making God responsible for damnation as well as for salvation, is also logical, since the election of some persons implies to our natural reason that the lack of election is the reason for the damnation of others. Also this answer covers a wide spectrum, from the teachings of certain Reformed theologians to the fatalism of Islam.

Only the third set of answers — God as the source of salvation and man as the source of his own damnation — is Scriptural, on the basis of Ephesians 2:8-9 and Matthew 23:37. "For by grace are ye saved through faith; and that not of yourselves; it is the gift of

---

Dr. Hoerber is Associate Professor of Exegetical Theology at Concordia Seminary.

God: not of works, lest any man should boast" makes it clear that our faith is not our work, but the gift of God the Holy Spirit; therefore God's grace is the only cause of salvation. Mourning over the Jerusalem of His day, Jesus laments, ". . . how often would I have gathered thy children together, even as a hen gathereth her chickens under her wings, and ye would not!" God our Redeemer desired the salvation of the inhabitants of Jerusalem, but the cause of damnation was their own negative response—"ye would not!" Although not logical according to the canons of human reason, which argues for similar causation in both columns of the diagram, the third reply is the only one based on Scripture.

This very fact—that the answer to any theological question must be based on Scripture alone, regardless of the canons of human reason—is the basic tenet of sound exegesis. When Scripture speaks, reason yields—whether the teaching concerns the Triune God, the two natures of Christ, His virgin birth, the empty tomb, the presence of Christ's body and blood in the Lord's Supper, or the doctrine of election. So, according to the analogy of faith, the divine truth that God is the source of our salvation (but not of anyone's damnation) is intricately entwined with the principle of *sola Scriptura*—Scripture alone decides doctrine.

Two other basic principles of Lutheran theology are also intimately connected in the doctrine of election: *sola gratia* and *sola fide*. In fact, the Scriptural teaching of salvation by grace alone through faith alone retains its essential purity only if taught together with election. Without our election to salvation by God from eternity, grace may be thought of as an infused quality in us, instead of as a favorable disposition of God for Christ's sake, and faith may be viewed as a positive contribution on our part, instead of the "receiving" means created by the Holy Spirit through the "giving" means of grace. Only through a proper understanding of God's gracious election to salvation do we begin to appreciate the fullness of God's grace and our complete dependence on the work of the Holy Spirit, initiating and sustaining faith in the hearts of the believers. Again, according to the analogy of faith, the divine truth that God is the sole source of our salvation by His eternal election is basic to the Biblical principles of *sola gratia* and *sola fide*.

Another essential principle of Scriptural and Lutheran theology concerns the means of grace, the Word and Sacraments, the written Word and the visible Word. Today, as well as in the time of Luther, people frequently raise the question of "signs" or "marks" of a person's spiritual state, particularly in regard to their feelings. How does one know that one has "saving faith," especially if one experiences little or no emotional indications, ranging from daily delight to the ecstasy of speaking in tongues and healing? To overcome such doubts and to assure Christians of their salvation, Scripture clearly teaches that in the kingdom of grace the Holy Spirit works only through the Word and Sacraments and not apart from them. "So then faith cometh by hearing, and hearing by the word of God" (Rom. 10:17). "For this is my blood of the new testament which is shed for many for the remission of sins" (Matt. 26:28). It is through Word and Sacrament that the Holy Spirit calls us and keeps us in faith. The Word, Baptism, and the Lord's Supper are the means of grace. They are the instruments by which God "signs, seals, and delivers" salvation to believers, whose faith is the result of the Spirit's work, assured by God's promise, and not by a human work (such as prayer) or human feelings or emotional ecstasy. Also here, according to the analogy of faith, the divine truth that God is the sole source of our salvation by His eternal election is basic to the essential assurance that our spiritual state is the work of the Triune God through Word and Sacrament—preventing us from relying on prayer, on sacrificial acts on our part, or on personal feelings.

The doctrine of election involves another essential principle of Scriptural and Lutheran theology—the distinction between Law and Gospel, Scripture alone, grace alone, faith alone, Word and Sacrament as the only means of grace by which the Holy Spirit engenders faith—all these teachings are intricately entwined with the Gospel. Gospel must not be confused with Law. The above diagram attempts to illustrate this point by the solid vertical line separating the source of salvation from the source of damnation in the third set of answers. Damnation is the result of violating the Law and cannot be confounded with salvation, which is Gospel. The confusion of Law with Gospel occurs, according to the diagram, when one ignores the distinction made in the third set of answers (emphasized by the solid vertical line), thus yielding to human reason, which would impose the same source in both columns. Law shows us our sin. Gospel shows us our Savior. Our natural depravity is so great that sin alone has doomed us to damnation. God's mercy abounds even more, so that only God's election, ratified and sealed through Christ's atonement and applied to believers through the work of the Holy Spirit, saves us from our deserved doom. God's grace and our human depravity must be retained in two separate columns—otherwise Law and Gospel are being confused. While both Law and Gospel are to be applied to each Christian each day, they must be kept distinct and separate. And so, according to the analogy of faith, the divine truth that God is the sole source of our salvation by His eternal election is *consistent* with the Scriptural principle that Law cannot be confounded with Gospel—although human reason would hold that it is *logical* to credit the same source in each column.

Consistent! Logical! Do these terms not imply similar meanings? Can one be consistent without being logical? Although the two terms are somewhat synonymous, it is vital to note that we distinguish between "consistent with Scripture" and "logical according to human reason." But, for the moment, let us look at the doctrine of election on the basis of human reason and logic. St. Paul reminds us that "the foolishness of God is wiser than men" (1 Cor. 1:25), which is a compressed way of saying "the foolishness of God is wiser than the wisdom of men." Is it really logical to insist—or even to expect—that the truths of our gracious God be reduced to tenets comprehensible to human reason? Is it logical to impose the canons of human reason on the doctrine of election? Is it not more logical to expect that God's wisdom is far superior to our limited human reason?

Permit an illustration from human experience. When a new library was constructed on our campus a few years ago, no doubt some ant hills were disturbed by a bulldozer. The operator of the machine was following the orders of the contractor, who was being guided by the blueprints of the architect, who in turn was pursuing the plan of the Board of Control to furnish a building for more adequate storing and studying of books and periodicals. The complicated process was guided by logical human planning and comprehensible to the workmen and the officials of the seminary. But what about the ants that were dislocated? Could the plan and the process be explained to them? What a foolish question! But no more foolish than insisting that God's plan of election to salvation be explained on a logical basis to human reason, for "the foolishness of God is wiser than the wisdom of men." Is it not logical to suppose that God's wisdom is to a greater degree superior to human wisdom than man's wisdom is to that of ants?

Finally, the doctrine of election to salvation from eternity is an important truth of Scripture because it is most comforting. When a Christian, particularly in later years of life, ponders his or her spiritual situation and possibly even wonders whether he or she will remain in faith at the hour of death, the doctrine of election offers assurance. If faith were the accomplishment of the Christian, fear that faith might fail before death would present some cause for alarm. The devil, the world, and our flesh might overcome human endeavors, including a faith resulting from human choice. But, thanks to our election to salvation from eternity by our gracious God, our faith is the result of God's choice and is engendered and sustained by the endeavor of the Holy Spirit through Word and Sacrament. Only a hardened shutting ourselves off from the Holy Spirit by continuously resisting or refraining from the means of grace would result in the loss of faith. A Christian, however, who shows concern for his or her spiritual condition and who relies on God's Word, on God's Sacraments, on the work of the Holy Spirit, and on Christ's atonement can and should be assured that faith will not fail, as God promises:

> Who shall separate us from the love of Christ? . . . For I am persuaded that neither death, nor life, nor angels, nor principalities, nor powers, nor things present, nor things to come, nor height, nor depth, nor any other creature shall be able to separate us from the love of God, which is in Christ Jesus our Lord (Rom. 8:35, 38f.).

What a comfort to know that our salvation is the result of the divine choice of our almighty and gracious God from eternity! This assuring doctrine of election must be taught to mature Christians, if we follow Paul in his address to the elders from Ephesus: "For I have not shunned to declare unto you all the counsel of God" (Acts 20:27). For, according to the analogy of faith, it is essential to teach the doctrine of election to salvation, since with it are inextricably involved such basic tenets as Scripture alone, grace alone, faith alone, Word and Sacrament as the only means by which the Holy Spirit engenders and sustains faith, and the clear-cut distinction between Law and Gospel—all essentially hallmarks of Scriptural Lutheran theology.

Several Classics Reprinted

On the Language of the New Testament and the Reliability of Acts

Seldom does a publisher merit commendation as does Baker Book House for reprinting in inexpensive paperbacks in the "Twin Brooks Series" several extremely important contributions to the language of the New Testament and the reliability of the Acts of the Apostles. Since some of these volumes have been out of print and not readily available to students of the New Testament, we take this opportunity to comment briefly on their value, in the hope of stimulating their serious study also by the younger generation.

Adolf Deissmann

Adolf Deissmann, a professor of New Testament at the universities of Heidelberg and Berlin, first published in 1908 *Light From the Ancient East: The New Testament Illustrated by Recently Discovered Texts of the Graeco-Roman World.* In May 1978, Baker Book House reissued the fourth edition of 1922 (557 pages — $8.95), retaining the eighty-five illustrations of ostraca, stelae, tombstones, numerous letters from the papyri, a Quirinius inscription from Antioch in Pisidia as well as a Roman milestone, both of which confirm the first Syrian governorship of Quirinius at 11-8 B.C., a contract of sale for a part of a vineyard, a hereditary lease of a vineyard, etc.

Previous to Deissmann scholars of the New Testament were wont to compare in morphology, syntax, vocabulary, and literary style the authors of the New Testament with the writers of the classical period in fifth-century and fourth-century Athens. Attempts to explain the differences, whether by regarding the New Testament as peculiar Greek of the Holy Ghost or as replete with Semitisms, usually left the Biblical documents wanting. It was Deissmann's classic which showed that the Greek of the New Testament was the Greek of everyday life and business in that period. Although it is our considered judgment that Deissmann emphasized too strongly the non-literary aspects of Biblical Greek — not appreciating, for example, the numerous figures of speech in the New Testament — his utilization of the papyri, ostraca, and monuments served as a landmark in New Testament studies.

Mention may be made also of the appendices and indices (pp. 413-535). Eleven appendices include such topics as "On the Text of the Second Logia Fragment from Oxyrhynchus," "Lucius — Luke," and "Unrecognized Biblical Quotations in Syrian and Mesopotamian Inscriptions" — reprints of articles by Deissmann that appeared previously in professional journals. The various indices make the volume extremely useful for background material in private study, homiletical preparation, and Bible class illustration: places, ancient persons, words and phrases in Greek, subjects, modern persons, and passages cited — which are divided into the following categories: Greek Bible (Septuagint, Aquila, Symmachus, and New Testament), Latin Bible, inscriptions, papyri and parchments, ostraca, wooden tablets, glass goblets, coins, and ancient authors (other than Biblical). Still recalling vividly our titillating experience as a student at the seminary in seeing and studying the photographs of the actual ancient documents, we trust that current students also will experience the same pleasurable excitement with Deissmann's volume. It should arouse new insights in the parish pastors who are searching for solid aids to their mental rejuvenation.

Dr. Hoerber serves as Associate Professor of Exegetical Theology.

Richard B. Rackham

The second classic, also reissued by Baker in May 1978 (640 pages — $8.95), is *The Acts of the Apostles: An Exposition* by Richard Belward Rackham. This is the 1908 fourth edition of a commentary that first appeared in 1901. The forte of Rackham's commentary is its emphasis on the theological aspect of the Acts of the Apostles, stressing such features as Luke's interest in women, the brotherly unity of the early church, the resurrected Lord at work in the church, prayer, joy in the Spirit, and the work of the Holy Spirit. Some critics feel that Rackham wrote too much from the point of view of the subsequent theology of the church and from his own high-church position — he was a member of the Community of the Resurrection, an Anglican community in Mirfield, Yorks, England — yet, many scholars would agree that his *opus* is among the half-dozen most important commentaries on Acts which have appeared in English.

Rackham seems to be the first English author to suggest a twofold parallelism between Luke's Gospel and the Acts of the Apostles (p. xlvii). The following table will illustrate the parallel structure:

	Luke	*Acts*
Introductory period of waiting and preparation	1-2	1
Baptism of the Spirit	3	2
Active ministry	4ff.	3ff.
Early anticipations	9:51	19:21
Journey to Jerusalem	17:11-19:48	20:1-21:17
Last words of the sufferer	20-21	20:17-38
Passion proper	22-23	21:17-29:31

Rackham, furthermore, points out similar parallelisms between the two parts of Acts (1-12 and 13-28). Each opens with a special manifestation of the Holy Spirit (2:1-4; 13:1-3). A period of work and preaching, persecution and opposition follows (2:14-11; 13:4-19). Each ends with a passion or a passing of the chief actor, who passes through suffering to a deliverance (12; 20-28). There is also a parallelism, extending even to verbal details, between the activities and experiences of the two main characters, Peter and Paul. Dissenting from the negative conclusion of the Tuebingen critics concerning the historicity of these parallels, Rackham argues that "the parallelism arises out of the facts" (p. xlix).

James Smith

A third classic, a 1978 reprint of the 1880 fourth edition of a work originally appearing in 1848, issued by Baker (391 pages — $5.95), is a most careful study of Acts 27. We refer to James Smith's *The Voyage and Shipwreck of St. Paul: With Dissertations on the Life and Writings of St. Luke and the Ships and Navigation of the Ancients,* which F. F. Bruce calls "an indispensable handbook to the study of this chapter." James Smith was not a theologian but a layman, the son of a wealthy merchant of Scotland, devoting his life to yachting and the study of geography, nautical matters, and Luke's account of Paul's voyage to Rome.

As a yachtsman of thirty years experience, Smith travelled to Malta and combined a firsthand investigation of that region and sailing conditions in the Eastern Mediterranean with a careful study of Acts 27-28:16, following with research in the important libraries and museums of Europe. The results were published in the volume that remains the classic study of the subject to the present day.

Smith's book contains a detailed analysis of Acts 27-28:16 in the light of geography, archaeology, and his personal knowledge of seamanship, both ancient and modern (pp. 61-158). It includes also several valuable essays of the narrative in Acts, the most important being "On the Ships of the Ancients," that ranks among the best of the early studies of this subject (pp. 181-244). The results of Smith's scholarship render forever implausible the suggestion that Luke's account of the sea journey and shipwreck of Paul is merely a literary device based on the examples of such Greek authors as Homer, Josephus, or Lucian. Smith argues, furthermore, that the narrative implies considerable experience in traveling on the part of the author, though not as a sailor. James Smith typifies the approach of British scholars to the Book of Acts, with emphasis always on the solid facts of historical research.

After the publication of *The Voyage and Shipwreck of St. Paul,* Dean Henry Alford wrote to Smith as follows:

> I may venture to congratulate you on the fact that your name will now, in all ages and countries, be handed down as having done substantial service in settling once and for all a point in dispute deeply interesting for its own sake, and for the authenticity and credibility of the sacred narrative. When we commentators are deservedly forgotten, you will be known in enviable connection with the great Apostle's course of Perils (back cover).

The other major work on this topic agrees with Smith's judgments, although differing concerning various technical details, namely, A. Breusing's *Die Nautik der Alten* (Bremen, 1886).

A. N. Sherwin-White

The fourth classic to which we wish to call attention is likewise by a layman in theology, a British scholar and Roman historian, A. N. Sherwin-White. His volume, *Roman Society and Roman Law in the New Testament*

(Oxford, 1963), is perhaps the most important of all the recent studies on the historicity of the Acts of the Apostles. Although of later vintage than the classics described above, it soon was out of print. Since November 1978 it is available again in Baker's "Twin Brooks Series" (204 pages — $3.95).

This monograph is the published version of The Sarum Lectures for 1960-61. It looks specifically at the trial of Jesus in the context of Roman law, at the legal, administrative, and municipal background of Paul's activities as portrayed in Acts, and at the social and economic conditions in the synoptic narrative on Jesus in Galilee. This book is extremely important since it presents a trained historian's careful appraisal of some of the most difficult problems of New Testament historical criticism. It is not the work of an apologist, but of an experienced Roman historian who comes to grips with the historical elements of the New Testament. In addition, it contains many valuable exegetical insights concerning the interpretation of specific passages in Acts.

In his study of the Pauline section of Acts, Sherwin-White shows that in detail after detail the account fits to a tee the historical conditions prevailing at the middle of the first century A.D. He concludes that the essential historicity of the narrative in Acts which pertains to Paul's adventures, when tested by the canons of historical criticism, is demonstrated beyond any serious doubt. A few examples will suffice.

Concerning St. Paul's appeal to Caesar, for example, the type of the appeal process reflected in Acts *(provocatio)* is an example of the procedure prevailing up to about the beginning of the last decade of the first century rather than the modified practice of a slightly later date or the *appellatio* procedure of still later. Another illustration is Felix's decision to hear Paul's case when he heard that Paul came from Cilicia (Acts 23:34-35). Ordinarily Paul would have been sent back to his home province for trial. But, as Sherwin-White notes, Cilicia at that particular time and *only* at that time was merely a part of the larger province of Syria, and the legate of Syria would not wish to be bothered with a relatively minor case from an outlying section of his territory. The situation was different during the Flavian period (69-96 A.D.), when Cilicia was a province in its own right (pp. 55-56).

Another example of Luke's remarkable accuracy is Claudius Lysias' statement (Acts 22:28) that he obtained his Roman citizenship by the payment of a large sum of money — that is, by a bribe — a practice that was common under Emperor Claudius (41-54 A.D.) but was exposed and effectively ended in the time of Nero (54-68 A.D.). Both the incidental statement of Claudius Lysias and his name fit the historical facts perfectly (pp. 154-156). There is also the accurate designation of the two Roman centurions mentioned in Acts — Cornelius (10:1) and Julius (21:1) — only by their gentile *nomina* (the name of the clan or gens). This type of name represents an old-fashioned practice found only in the Roman army by the middle of the first century A.D. (pp. 160-161). That the Acts of the Apostles gives this type of Latin name to only two people, both soldiers, at the precise time in history when only soldiers were likely to be using it, is surely no mere coincidence.

We could go on and on about the accuracy of Luke concerning the titles of both the municipal officials and the Roman provincial officials appearing in the narrative of Acts — a feat of no mean accomplishment, which points to an author who either was personally acquainted with the events or derived his information from sources that were reliable — but these few examples should whet the appetite of current students and parish pastors to peruse these reissued classics for themselves as mines of valuable information for their professional ministry.

Implications of the Imperative in the Sermon on the Mount

Some students of Greek regard the literature from the blind bard of Smyrna through Plato and Paul to contemporary Athens as basically one language. Be that as it may, one element of syntax is consistent throughout Greek epic, lyric, and dramatic poetry as well as historical, philosophical, and oratorical prose—in classical, koine, and modern Greek authors—namely, the distinction between the present and aorist tenses of the imperative mood. The aorist imperative implies punctiliar ("snap-shot") or ingressive ("beginning") or categorical ("once for all") action, while the present imperative denotes durative ("continuous") or iterative ("repeating") action.

Two pertinent examples should suffice. One is the statement of Jesus during the cleansing of the temple: "Take these things away! Do not make My Father's house a house of merchandise!" (John 2:16; NKJB). Both verbs are in the imperative mood, but the tenses in the Greek text are different. "Take" is in the aorist tense, while "make" is in the present tense. A change in tense for the imperative is proper and expected, completely in line with the distinction throughout Greek literature. The merchants had not begun to remove their paraphernalia (animals, tables, etc.). "Take these things away" (in the aorist imperative), therefore, implies a new pattern of behavior viewed as a single act once and for all. But the merchants were using the temple to transact business. So Jesus changes to the present imperative, which should be rendered: "Stop making My Father's house a house of merchandise!"—indicating the discontinuation of their present behavior.

Dr. Hoerber, Professor of Exegetical Theology, delivered this study to a meeting of Studiorum Novi Testamenti Societas *at Toronto on August 25-29, 1980.*

Another example, pertinent to the present point, is the apparent prohibition to Mary from touching the risen Master (John 20:17) in contrast to the invitation to Thomas a week later to thrust his hand into Jesus' side (John 20:27). The key lies in the tenses of the verbs. The present imperative to Mary, connoting continuous action, cautions her not to continue to touch, or to stop clinging to, Jesus—for there was work to be done. The aorist imperative to Thomas, denoting "snap-shot" action, instructs him to make physical contact with the risen Christ—a new action which Thomas as yet had not dared to do.

The present paper attempts to make a careful study of the imperatives in the Sermon on the Mount—particularly in respect to the tenses in the Greek text—noting the implications concerning the behavior patterns of Jesus' disciples—insights which are lost in most translations and usually overlooked by commentators. In fact, the only comments along this line, so far as I am aware, appear in a few pages of *Grammatical Insights Into the New Testament* by Nigel Turner (Edinburgh: T. & T. Clark, 1965, pp. 29-32).

We shall observe the nuances of Jesus' address as reflected in Matthew's version. Even on the assumption that Jesus spoke originally in Aramaic, as Professor Turner states, ". . . there is no denying that the written record in Greek aims at preserving his [Jesus'] meaning very carefully" (p. 30). A case in point is the consistent use in Matthew and other synoptic accounts of the name "Jesus," employing the appellation "Christ" only to make a theological point, although the latter term is normal in Paul's letters.

The first imperatives occur at Matthew 5:12. The present tense means "continue to rejoice and be glad." The disciples had not been sullen and gloomy, or the aorist imperative would be appropriate. Jesus is urging them to continue in their joyful attitude. Then, after telling His followers that they are the salt of the earth and the light of the world, our Lord advises them: "Let your light shine before men" (5:16). His advice shifts to the aorist tense. Up to this time apparently the disciples had tended to keep their joy to themselves. Now Jesus encourages them to begin a new pattern of behavior, to start displaying their joyful peace and hope to others.

The rest of chapter 5 concerns the Jewish law, specifying five examples: murder, marriage, oaths, retaliation, and love. The introduction to this section (5:17) employs the aorist subjunctive of prohibition, which replaces the aorist imperative in negative commands. The choice of tense says emphatically: "Don't begin to think [or "Don't entertain the idea" or "Do not for one moment suppose"] that I have come to destroy the law and the prophets." The disciples apparently had not drawn such a conclusion. They were not regarding the Master as an opponent of the Law and the Prophets or as any instigator of revolt. Jesus is warning them against beginning to entertain such an idea for one moment.

Concerning the commandment against murder, interpreted as covering angry thoughts and words, Jesus advises a spirit of forgiveness toward fellow human beings before offering sacrifice (5:24). The change in tense at the end of the sentence is instructive. "Leave your gift" and "be reconciled to your brother" are in the aorist tense, signifying a new pattern of behavior and a completed action once and for all. ". . . then come and offer your gifts" is in the present imperative, indicating a continuation of the originally intended act as well as a possible continued activity. That is, Jesus seems to be implying: "Leave your gift and be reconciled once and for all, thus adopting a new attitude of forgiveness to your brother (aorist); then continue in your original intention and offer as many gifts as you wish (present)."

The next few imperatives, in the section on marriage, need only brief comment. They are in the aorist tense, referring to the removal of an offending eye and hand (5:29-30). The aorist implies a new action rather than the continuation of present behavior. Also, the citation from the Old Testament, ". . . let him give her a certificate of divorce," employs the aorist tense since it refers to the beginning of a new action to be performed once and for all (5:31).

Were the followers of our Lord a docile or a forceful group? The use of the aorist tense in the discussion on oaths (5:33-37) and on retaliation (5:38-42) describes rather a docile group. They had not been given to the taking of oaths, and Jesus urges them not to begin the practice (5:34, 36). Nor had they previously engaged in forceful resistance, and Jesus encourages them not to start such action (5:39). That is the implication of the aorist tense—the same distinction in tense is applicable, although two of the verbs are aorist infinitives used for commands. Yet, while docile rather than forceful, the Master's followers apparently had not yet reached the point of turning the other cheek (5:39) and surrendering the second garment (5:40) and giving or loaning to those wishing to borrow (5:42). Such charitable conduct they had not yet attained, so Jesus encourages them to commence these practices, as the aorist imperatives suggest.

It is noteworthy that in this passage there is inserted one present imperative, referring to the going of the second mile (5:41). Either the verb does not appear as an aorist imperative (as is probably the case, which is true also of the verb "to be") or the present imperative indicates the continuation of a journey already in progress, advocating the extension to one more mile. Also noteworthy is the apparent previous renouncing of oaths by Jesus' disciples as implied in the aorist tense (5:34, 36). Such behavior would agree with the information at John 1:35-40, that some of our Lord's disciples previously had followed John the Baptist. They may have adopted their practice concerning oaths prior to the transferring of allegiance to Jesus. Professor Turner notes that according to Josephus (*De Bello Judaico* II, viii, 6) "the people called Essenes, whom John resembled in many ways, denied themselves the use of oaths" (p. 31).

That the followers of our Lord spurned violence and exhibited docile behavior is indicated further in the last two imperatives in Matthew 5, the section on the law of love (5:43-48). Jesus' commands, ". . .love your enemies" and "pray for those who persecute you" (5:44) are in the present imperative, thus encouraging His disciples to continue in their present peaceful manner of conduct. Note that the two additional imperatives in the *apparatus criticus* ("bless" and "do good") are also in the present tense, suggesting a continuation of the current docile behavior.

The first half of Matthew 6 contains remarks on three examples of Jewish piety: almsgiving, prayer, and fasting. The brief section on charity (6:1-4) begins with a present imperative, by which Jesus tells the disciples to continue to take heed that they not make an open display of their righteous conduct (6:1). The same thought continues in the following two verses (6:2-3), which shift to the aorist tense (a subjunctive of prohibition and a third person imperative): Do not for a moment consider (or commence) the practice of hypocrites who call attention to their almsgiving by sounding a trumpet; do not let your left hand begin to know what your right hand is doing. The disciples apparently had not been accustomed to "wearing their piety on their sleeves," and Jesus encourages them to continue their current behavior in this respect.

Concerning prayer (6:5-15) our Lord may be suggesting a new practice by the use of two aorist imperatives: ". . .go into your room, and when you have shut the door, pray" (6:6). In the next two verses (6:7-8) the Master continues with the aorist tense (the subjunctive of prohibition for the imperative), advising His followers not to begin the practice of "vain repetitions" in prayer and thus not to start imitating the *ethnikoi* (heathen). That is, their prayer habits were commendable, but more privacy might be advisable in order to continue avoiding ostentatious display.

Jesus then presents a model prayer, introducing it by a present imperative "pray" (6:9), which suggests that the model should continue to be prayed and should be prayed frequently. The model prayer itself in Matthew (6:9-13) employs only the aorist tense (six imperatives and one subjunctive of prohibition). Prayers to God usually use the aorist tense, emphasizing a categorical request (e.g., "forgive us our debts *once and for all*") or a peremptory demand ("forgive us *now*") or a punctiliar petition, which would connote that God hears our single request—although He invites continuous prayer.

It is pertinent to note that at Luke 11:3 we have a change in tense from Matthew 6:11. In the fourth petition Luke's use of the present imperative is to be expected in view of the phrase "day by day" (*to kath' hemeran*) for "this day" (*semeron*) in Matthew 6:11. In other words, the continuous action expressed in the phrase "day by day" necessitates the shift to the present imperative.

The third example of Jewish piety, fasting (6:16-18), begins with a present imperative: ". . .do not continue to be [i.e., stop being] like the hypocrites, with a sad countenance." Then follow two aorist imperatives: ". . .anoint your head and wash your face" (6:17). The disciples seemingly were tending to assume sad expressions while fasting. The Master wishes them to discontinue that behavior and to begin the practice of anointing and washing—advice parallel to that concerning almsgiving: not to "wear their piety on their sleeves." The fasting by Jesus' followers probably occurred in the early period of their discipleship, and it may indicate (as in the case of oaths) a prior association of some with John the Baptist, whose disciples were strict about fasts. Jesus' disciples, however, soon followed His advice and even discontinued the practice of fasting (Matt. 9:14; Mark 2:18; Luke 5:33).

The last half of Matthew 6 employs imperatives in the remarks on material resources (6:19-24) and on anxiety about physical needs (6:25-34). Each of these sections begins with the present imperative, implying a current weakness of our Lord's followers. Concerning financial matters Jesus states: "Stop laying up for yourselves treasures on earth" (6:19). While they were manifesting some concern for mundane assets, they were not rank materialists, for the Master adds: ". . .continue to lay up for yourselves treasures in heaven" (6:20). Apparently the disciples had some concern for earthly resources, while at the same time realizing the importance of spiritual treasures. Jesus is telling them to stop the former and to continue the latter.

Some anxiety about physical needs seems to have been another weakness of Jesus' followers, as the present imperative indicates: ". . .stop worrying about your life" (6:25)—that is, about food and clothing. They apparently had not considered the birds in the air and the lilies in the field—two examples of their heavenly Father's care for His creation. The Master suggests that they initiate reflection on God's nurture in nature to assuage their anxiety, so he shifts to aorist imperatives (6:26, 28). Yet, the concern for physical needs apparently was not excessive. They were seeking first the kingdom of God, as Jesus' use of the present imperative advises a continuation of that current practice (6:33). Also the aorist tense in two of the concluding verses of this section implies that our Lord's followers were inflicted with only slight anxiety about their physical needs. The aorist (subjunctive of prohibition for imperative) may indicate that the Master's discourse on worry, with its several illuminating illustrations, probably did calm their needless concerns, and that He is cautioning them against beginning anew such foolish anxiety: "Do not, therefore, begin to be anxious again" (6:31); and "Do not, therefore, begin to worry again about tomorrow" (6:34). Or the aorist tense in these two verses may connote merely encouragement for future behavior. In either interpretation the conjunction *oun* is pertinent.

The few imperatives (or equivalents) in Matthew 7 follow the same pattern in respect to tenses that is apparent in the previous two chapters of the Sermon on the Mount. A brief reference to each imperative should suffice. As is too normal in human behavior, our Lord's disciples showed a tendency to be judgmental. With the present imperative Jesus sharply warns: "Stop judging, that you be not judged" (7:1). The removing of a speck or a plank from an eye would initiate a new practice; hence we have the aorist imperatives (7:4, 5). His followers were not in the habit of giving holy things to dogs or pearls to swine; so the aorist tense (subjunctive of prohibition) advises against commencing such behavior (7:6).

The disciples apparently were accustomed to make requests from their heavenly Father, referred to by the terms "asking," "seeking," and "knocking"; for the present imperatives imply the continuation of current practice (7:7). They also were accustomed to treat others as they wished to be treated; such is the connotation of the present imperative, denoting the continuation of present behavior (7:12). Entrance "at the narrow gate" would be a new venture, as indicated by the aorist tense (7:13). One might suppose that many of Jesus' contemporaries were wary of being misled by false prophets, in view of the circumstances of the day. Jesus' caution, therefore, is not surprising in the present imperative: "Continue to beware of false prophets" (7:15); it reveals that His disciples were in the habit of being on the alert for false prophets. Finally, on the day of judgment our Lord will say to some: "I never knew you; depart from me" (7:23). The present imperative denotes the continuation of a present condition—the separation from the Savior—a condition already present in their earthly life. A better rendering might be: "I never knew you; continue to stay away from Me, you who practice lawlessness."

The present paper should be helpful at least in three areas: 1) It should delineate the attitudes, practices, and behavior of Jesus' followers at the time of the Sermon on the Mount; 2) It should apprise us of the foibles and weaknesses of our Lord's disciples as a group—as an addition to the general knowledge of the failures of a few, such as Peter and Judas; and 3) It may shed some light on the relation between Matthew's Sermon on the Mount and Luke's Sermon on the Plain—a topic which would involve a separate study reserved for the future.

Paul Our Paragon

Students of Shakespeare have written volumes analyzing the unique qualities of his dramas. John A. Scott of Northwestern University made a similar study on the Greek epic in his book, *The Genius of Homer.* It may prove helpful as various phases of Christian education begin anew in September — from parish elementary schools through church-related colleges, from confirmation classes through specialized training in seminaries — to mention briefly some of the essentials in the successful career of St. Paul which we should emulate on every level of Christian education.

The key to Paul's success is his divine call on the road to Damascus and the subsequent working of the Holy Spirit through the Word proclaimed in his Scriptural preaching. He is convinced that he is called by God (Romans 1:1-6), that he has a revelation from Jesus Christ (Galatians 1:12), and that he would be utterly miserable if he did not serve his Savior (1 Corinthians 9:16).

St. Paul shows his sense of divine mission in his tenacious convictions and in the authority he assumes in addressing Christian congregations — even those churches where he is unknown personally. When dealing with the major Jewish-Gentile controversy, when settling local disturbances over the Lord's Supper, or when urging contributions for the poor in Judea, he is clear as to the spiritual basis of his work. His authority is based on his sense of divine vocation, realizing that an appointment from God carries its own stamp of authenticity. It is with deep conviction that he expounds the great truths of justification, salvation by grace, the redemptive work of Christ, the ministry of the Holy Spirit, and the cosmic significance of the Christian Church.

Such a relation vertically with the Triune God results in sincere concern horizontally for his converts. Paul commands, encourages, corrects, and rebukes only because of a real affection for God's people. When expressing gratitude to the Philippian Christians for their generosity, when admonishing those at Corinth whose actions cause him pain, or when instructing believers in Rome with a fully developed doctrinal document, his basic longing is for the welfare of fellow Christians. To the congregation that apparently causes the most concern, Paul pens his chapter on charity. The Paul of authority is also the Paul of love — expressing love for his readers and capable of drawing out their love.

St. Paul's love for people, the result of God's love for him, enables him to be versatile. He sets for himself the goal of being all things to all people — basically a desire to see the other person's point of view. Paul reveals a dexterity of mind and an ability for adaptation which is astonishing. Yet, he never adapts his principles, his theological convictions, to suit a situation. He is adamant in doctrine, but tolerant in adiaphora.

Paul our paragon! Are we able to emulate him? "If to do were as easy as to know what were good to do, chapels had been churches and poor men's cottages princes' palaces" (*The Merchant of Venice,* Act 1, Scene 2). Thanks be to God, we may draw on the power of the Holy Spirit, as Paul did, for guidance and, if it is His will, for some small success in our ministry of the Word.

Lent: Law and Liberty

"For me to live is Christ" (Philippians 1:21) is the central focus for St. Paul. His confrontation with the risen Lord on the road to Damascus and his identification of the crucified Jesus with the Messiah of the Old Testament change his attitude during the remainder of his life. Persecutor becomes preacher. Realizing that Judaic legalism is invalid before God, in Christ he sees true liberty from the curse of the Law, but does not allow liberty to become license.

The crucified Savior is the basis of Paul's preaching throughout his journeys (1 Corinthians 2:2), enabling him both to withstand staunchly those who would minimize the significance of Jesus' person and work by demanding a fulfillment of the Law (Galatians) and at the same time to tolerate weak and immature followers of Christ who fail to comprehend fully Christian liberty (1 Corinthians 8-11). St. Paul allows nothing to obscure the centrality of Jesus Christ — whether it is a form of legalism or the unwise exercises of Christian liberty.

The teaching and practice of the apostle are based on the lesson of Lent — on Jesus' fulfillment of the Law and His death on the cross in our stead, that we may live as redeemed servants in His Kingdom. The lesson of Lent is authoritative for Christians today. Liberty from the letter of the Law does not imply freedom from the Scriptures through private interpretation. Freedom through Christ carries corporate implications for Christians as members of the Body of Christ, His Church, in the use of their liberty. In Paul's practice we have an example worthy of emulation.

The New and the Old: Truth in Tension

With the new calendar year replacing the old, following after a brief span the juncture of the new and the old church years, one is reminded of change also in areas other than time. St. Paul speaks of the "new man" and the "old man," the "new lump" and the "old leaven," the "present aeon" and the "aeon to come," also no doubt frequently reflecting on his past conduct in contrast to his converted career.

Change or conversion or sanctification in the Christian entails tension. There may be tension in his actions: "For I do not do the good I want, but the evil I do not want I do" (Romans 7:19). There may be tension in his emotions — a rage of anger versus a spirit of forgiving. Tension is emphasized both in Scripture and in Luther by the contrasting of certain pairs: flesh-spirit, Law-Gospel, kingdom of God-Kingdom of the world, faith-works.

All these tensions, characteristic of a Christian and resulting from change implied in sanctification, point up the truth expressed in the phrase: *simul iustus — simul peccator*. The Biblical truth that Christians are both "saints" and "sinners" is a fundamental fact in Lutheran theology, true throughout all change in calendar time, and basic to the Gospel of God's grace through Jesus' death and resurrection. The tensions in the life of a Christian will continue during his time on earth. But these tensions, by-products of his being *peccator,* may be resolved by God's gift of his being *simul iustus* through Christ.

The true tenet, *simul iustus — simul peccator,* is the key that unlocks the apparent enigma of St. Paul's attitude to the Law when he writes to the Romans that Christ is the "end" (goal) of the Law (10:4) and also that his preaching "establishes" the Law (3:31). This truth of *simul iustus — simul peccator* must be proclaimed during the new calendar and church years to the world, following its application first to each one of us in our own lives every day of the new year.

Commencement: Christian Growth

May is the month in which most academic programs reach a conclusion. At Concordia Seminary, as well as on numerous other campuses, the exercise observing the completion of a program of studies is called "Commencement" rather than "Graduation." The choice of the term "Commencement" is appropriate because it indicates the proper forward focus. "Graduation" (from the Latin *gradus,* "step" or "degree") connotes a successful fulfilment of past studies. "Commencement," however, emphasizes the utilization of an academic attainment in the future, implying that the person is beginning or commencing a new period in life.

Underlying the concept of commencing or beginning a career is the implication of growth or advancement. The graduate should look to the future with fond expectation of developing, improving, and maturing in a chosen endeavor -- in brief, the neophyte should expect to grow. Such a positive attitude toward growth is necessary in order to avoid deterioration. It is also equally imperative that growth and development be directed properly.

Our Lord, we are told, "increased in wisdom and stature, and in favor with God and man" (Luke 2:52). His fourfold growth -- physically, mentally, spiritually, and socially -- all Christians should emulate, from the neophyte graduate to the more mature professional. The growth of Christians should not neglect any of the four aspects of Jesus' development. The goal of Christian growth, furthermore, must be service in God's Kingdom. As our Savior served us, so we are constrained to grow in service to Him -- with humility, gratitude, and joy.

The Concordia Seminary community congratulates the class of 1977, prayerfully wishing the members successful Christian growth in their various areas of "planting" and "watering." We pledge our continued efforts toward improvement in our mutual goal of serving in God's vineyard -- humbly, gratefully, and joyfully. As His workmen we give glory to Him who will continue to "give the increase."

Treasure in Clay Jars

In describing his task as the apostle to the Gentiles, St. Paul writes: "But we have this treasure in jars of clay to show that this all-surpassing power is from God and not from us" (2 Cor. 4:7 NIV). The "treasure," as Paul has clarified in a preceding verse, is the Gospel concerning Jesus Christ as Lord (v. 5). In contrast to the pricelessness of the Gospel message Paul underlines the worthlessness of human messengers — Paul, the apostles, pastors, and teachers of today — by calling them jars of clay, a relatively cheap and omnipresent material in the society of his day. The priceless treasure of the "light of the knowledge of the glory of God" (v. 6) is entrusted to sinful people created from dirt — to emphasize that the power of the Gospel is from God, not from human beings.

As jars of clay we are not only of insignificant value but we are also weak when relying on our own abilities. The triune God, however, comes to our aid and supplies the necessary strength. The four metaphors used by St. Paul may reflect gladiatorial or military combat (vv. 8-9): 1) hard pressed on every side, but not completely cornered or without room for movement, never driven to surrender; 2) bewildered, but never at his wits' end — or, to retain the word play of the Greek, at a loss but never totally at a loss; 3) hounded by the foe, but not left to his mercy; 4) knocked to the ground, but not permanently grounded.

Although we may not suffer the extreme hardships of Paul, we do experience obstacles and reverses in our various tasks as messengers of the Gospel. At such times of stress and distress we must recall St. Paul's metaphor of "treasure in clay jars." The pricelessness of our message is worth any inconvenience the messengers may undergo. Not only is the Gospel message the power of God, it is the power of God the Father, Son, and Holy Spirit that supports us, jars of clay, and protects us from being completely overwhelmed. Confident that we are proclaiming God's message with the aid of His power through Word and Sacrament, we continue the fight of faith, giving glory and praise to God for entrusting His treasure to clay jars of mortal men.

New Creation

The new calendar year, following closely upon a new church year, reminds us of St. Paul's description of a Christian as a "new creation" (2 Cor. 5:17; cf. Gal. 6:15). But this reminder, at first seemingly pointing to a comparison, on closer reflection develops into a decided contrast, for "new" has two different implications.

A new calendar means newness in time—a manmade artificial device for dividing a continuum into years, months, etc. A Christian as a "new creation" denotes newness in quality—a divine change, a difference from what has preceded. As the apostle Paul states, "...the old has passed away (aorist), behold, the new has come (perfect)" (2 Cor. 5:17).

The two connotations of "new" frequently are distinguished by two Greek adjectives: *neos* and *kainos*. *Neos* refers primarily to something new in time, recent, young. It is the word for the new wine in Mark 2:22 and its parallel passages. The wine is not necessarily different in quality from that produced in previous years; it has been recently freshly made. The comparative of *neos* is used for a younger person (e.g., the younger son in Luke 15:12).

Kainos, in general, implies a newness in quality. It is employed to modify the wineskins in Mark 2:22. They are not merely freshly made but different in quality from the old ones, supple and elastic instead of hard and brittle. In Mark 1:27, this adjective implies that there is a newness of quality in Jesus' teaching, different from anything the audience had heard previously. Also Paul's preaching at Athens was new in quality (Acts 17:19). In Revelation we read of a Jerusalem new in quality (3:12; 21:2).

Although the distinction between *neos* and *kainos* is not always observed in the New Testament (e.g., forms of both are used for the new covenant in Hebrews 8:8 and 12:24), the frequent distinction between the two Greek adjectives should stress the vital difference between a new year *(neos)* and a Christian as a "new creation" *(kainos)* . We are not to be content with merely beginning a new calendar in 1978, essentially no different from the one recently discarded. The new year should remind us that as "new creations" we are on a new level of life—through God's creative power in Baptism and His Word. "All this is from God, who through Christ reconciled us to himself and gave us the ministry of reconciliation" (2 Cor. 5:18).

Gratitude: Three Phases

November commemorates an annual national holiday — Thanksgiving — originating among the early colonists in gratitude for material blessings of a successful harvest. As Christians we share in the civic observance of the day — frequently with excessive gusto — and we also attempt to instill a religious significance through special worship services.

In this respect we are patterning ourselves after the precedent of St. Paul, who so frequently in his Letters took a secular word (*eucharisteo,* still employed in modern Greek) and its cognates (*eucharistia, eucharistos*), but infused them with spiritual overtones, employing them no less than thirty-eight times. Specific examples occur at 1 Thessalonians 1:2; 2 Thessalonians 1:3; Philippians 1:3; Colossians 1:3; Ephesians 1:15.

In most cases Paul expresses his gratitude to God for the blessings of faith and love found in the believers. In Philippians 1:1 Paul, who terms himself a "servant" of Jesus Christ, is grateful for those whom he calls "saints" or "sanctified" by God's grace. At first glance it may appear that the members of the local congregation ("saints") have a higher rank than the great missionary to the Gentiles, who refers to himself merely as a "servant."

To appreciate the significance of these terms and their interrelationship, we may note three phases of gratitude as exemplified in Latin idioms. Latin distinguishes as follows:

1) *gratiam habere* is "to have a *feeling* of gratitude" or "to be grateful or thankful";
2) *gratias agere* means "to *express* a feeling of gratitude" or "to thank" (in words);
3) *gratiam referre* implies "to *return* gratitude" (through deeds).

St. Paul's use of the terms "saints" for his readers and "servant" for himself should show that Christian thanksgiving embraces all three phases of gratitude. A Christian, contemplating through the Holy Spirit the spiritual blessing of the person and work of Jesus our crucified Savior, cannot but *feel* grateful. But the gratitude of Christians does not stop with an attitude. It *expresses* gratitude in words — by sincere praise, prayer, and thanksgiving — as the Spirit gives utterance. The example of the Lord's Prayer and Paul's frequent expression of gratitude should make it clear that our thanksgiving and prayer also ought to concentrate on our spiritual blessings rather than be an attempt at bargaining for mundane benefits.

Nor should genuine Spirit-filled gratitude stop at the second phase — expression in words. Here lies one essential thrust of Paul's reference to himself as "servant" (besides putting himself in succession to the prophets of the Old Testament). His thankful feeling and expression blossom forth in *deeds,* in *activity,* in *working* and *laboring* for his Savior; in spite of all opposition from within and without the congregations — again through the guidance of God's Holy Spirit. St. Paul, if we look more carefully, does not call himself a "servant," but "a servant of Jesus Christ." The motivation and inspiration of Christ Jesus impel him to put his *feeling* and his *verbal expression* into *active* gratitude for the cause of the Gospel. As a "servant of Jesus Christ" St. Paul exemplifies for us the third phase of gratitude — *gratiam referre* — in a genuine spirit of thanksgiving.

Sovereign Servants

Although rulers rode on horses in the time of Solomon and servants walked beside them, Ecclesiastes describes the reverse situation: "I have seen servants upon horses and princes walking as servants upon the earth" (10:7). The contrast between princes and servants and between riding and walking raises an interesting question. Where do Christians fit into such a dichotomy—as sovereigns or as servants?

That God created human beings in His own image indicates that man is to be a sovereign, as does the enjoinder to Adam to have dominion over the earth. Man was meant to ride as kings, not walk as servants. But the disobedience of our first parents changed the scene. Human beings lost their royal jewels, becoming slaves to sin instead of rulers of their destiny—completely helpless to alter their situation.

But God the Father, who created us to be kings, came to our rescue by sending His Son to fulfil the Law for us. Christ's death, burial, and resurrection undid everything that Adam's sin had accomplished. "For if by one man's offense death reigned by one; much more they which receive abundance of grace and of the gift of righteousness shall reign in life by one, Jesus Christ" (Rom. 5:17). The redemption by Jesus put believers back into the saddle. Christians once again may live like kings—through the power of the Spirit of God, "who worketh in you both to will and to do his good pleasure" (Phil. 2:13). Left to ourselves we are doomed to failure, but by the power of the Holy Spirit once again we are sovereign.

Yet, though sovereign through Christ, who conquered and subdued the forces of evil in our behalf, we show our gratitude by serving our Lord. The object of our service has changed. We serve Christ, not sin. Since we have been crucified with Christ, Christ lives in us; the life which we live, we live by faith in the Son of God who gave Himself for us (Gal. 2:20); our sanctified life serves the cause of Christ.

Are Christians sovereigns or servants? As redeemed through the cross we are sovereigns. As grateful sovereigns we are servants. We are both sovereigns through Christ and servants to Christ—we are sovereign servants.

Grace and Gratitude

Lutheran theology distinguishes between justification and sanctification—between what God has done for us and what our response should be. This distinction is Scriptural, in line with the division St. Paul makes in his Epistles, generally presenting the message of the Gospel in the first part of each Letter and following with ethical principles in the latter portion. In Greek the key words that summarize these two aspects of Biblical theology are the cognates *charis* (grace) and *eucharistia* (gratitude).

That salvation depends on the good news of free grace is a tenet which permeates Paul's Epistles. It is also a tenet that is explicit in Jesus' teaching and embodied in His passion and resurrection. The synoptic Gospels and John may not employ the term *charis* as does the apostle Paul, but the lesson of several parables is that God freely forgives the sinner, while Jesus clearly declares "your sins are forgiven," and the prodigal son is welcomed home by a forgiving father.

The triune God performs great wonders—creating the universe from nothing and calling the dead to life. But an even greater wonder is the justification of the ungodly. Creation and revival of corpses are deeds consistent with an almighty God who controls a kingdom of power. Also other religions accept such divine persons. The forgiveness of sinners through undeserving love, however, is a gift limited to the triune God of Christianity in His kingdom of grace.

Not only is God's grace *(charis)* the source of our salvation; it is also the power which transforms the life of the Christian into the response of gratitude *(eucharistia)*. The two usual sections of Paul's Letter are intertwined. Justification and sanctification cannot be separated. "Good works are necessary," but not "for salvation." According to Thomas Erskine, "in the New Testament, religion is grace, and ethics is gratitude" (*Letters* [Edinburgh, 1877], p. 16). We readily cite Ephesians 2:8-9; we should not neglect the tenth verse.

Grace and gratitude are two key words that contain the kernel of Christianity. The divine grace of God's free love calls forth a life of gratitude, which is a response generated and maintained by the Holy Spirit. Both grace and gratitude are imparted and cultivated through Word and Sacrament. It is more than accidental that St. Paul chooses two cognates (*charis* and *eucharistia*) to teach the true relationship between God's grace and a Christian's response. As he states in Romans 3:31, grace through faith does not annul the Law, but establishes it.

Not *By* Faith

Proverbs frequently are misunderstood. People then cite these maxims with incorrect application. How often, for example, do we hear the advice, "Feed a cold and starve a fever," when our respiratory system is not up to par? The adage usually is misunderstood. It really means: "Do not eat too much when experiencing respiratory trouble; for, if you feed a cold, you may develop a fever and then refraining from solid foods will be a necessity." The axiom, when misunderstood, leads to an application directly opposite to the one originally intended.

Another instance of a proverb often misunderstood and wrongly applied is: "The exception proves the rule." The true meaning is: "The exception *tests* the rule." The verb is derived from the Latin *probo,* whose basic meaning is *test,* as in the derivative *probation,* or period of testing. So the maxim, cited correctly, indicates that any exception should merely test a premise, not prove its correctness.

Besides proverbs, translations of axiomatic sentences and phrases can be extremely misleading, causing deductions completely at variance to the author's intention. One such sentence, commonly misconstrued, comes from Aristotle: "Man is a political animal." Such a rendering of the Greek *politikon zoon* may conjure up visions of Aristotle as cataloging (which was one of his major endeavors) human beings as a step above animals, whose primary distinctiveness is an interest in politics and political science. How different from Aristotle's original intention! He actually is characterizing human beings as people who are to live in society with other persons in a city-state *(polis)*—not as hermits. A more correct rendering of Aristotle would be: "Man is a social creature"—a far cry from the rendition frequently found in discussions and translations of the Greek philosopher from the fourth century B.C.

Likewise a possible misunderstanding could result when Christians glibly cite the English text of Romans 1:17, Galatians 3:11, and Hebrews 10:38: "The just shall live by faith"—references to Habakkuk 4:2. The possible misunderstanding could involve a false deduction that *by faith* implies a work, act, attitude—or, at least, a contributing factor—on our part in attaining salvation. We realize, of course, from other passages of Scripture that it is only God's grace which is the source of salvation. "All our righteousness is as filthy rags" (Is. 64:6).

An examination of the Greek text of these and similar passages makes it abundantly clear that faith is not our contribution. The verses referred to above read: *ho de dikaios ek pisteos zesetai* and should be translated: "He who is justified as a result of faith shall live." The Greek *ek pisteos* means *"as a result of faith."* In other passages we read that we receive justification or salvation *dia pisteos, through faith. Pistis* is never used in connection with justification in the dative case with the preposition *en,* which would imply means or instrument and be rendered correctly *by faith.* The New Testament consistently avoids constructions which could be construed as if *our faith* is a *means* or *instrument* contributing to our salvation. Instead, the usual prepositional phrases are: *as a result of faith (ek pisteos)* and *through faith (dia pisteos).*

Romans 3:28, however, does employ *pistei*—a dative case without a preposition—which construction at times could indicate means, as well as manner plus several other usages. This is not the usual construction occurring in the New Testament, but rather the two mentioned previously. The context of Romans 3:25-31 indeed makes it crystal clear that *pistei* is to be construed as parallel to *dia pisteos* and *ek pisteos,* each of which occurs several times in this context. (The *pistei* in Romans 3:28, an exception, *tests* the rule. It neither proves nor overthrows the rule.)

Technically, then, we are not saved or justified *by faith*—*en pistei* never occurs in the New Testament in connection with justification.* It is the Holy Spirit who works faith in our hearts. Faith is not our contribution. Ephesians 2:8-9 is so eminently specific: "For by grace you have been saved through faith, and that not of yourselves; it is the gift of God, not of works, lest anyone should boast" (NKJB). Note that we are saved *by grace* (*tei chariti*—dative)—the source of our salvation—*through faith (dia pisteos).* Faith is God's *gift (doron),* not our accomplishment.

Through the work of the Holy Spirit—or, as a parallel phrase in other passages—*as a result of* the work of the Holy Spirit, who engenders faith in us, we are saved. To say glibly "We are saved *by* faith" could be misunderstood and could be misleading, as some proverbs often are misunderstood and misapplied. Faith is the *avenue* through which the Holy Spirit accomplishes in us the fulfillment of God's grace, the source of our salvation. Or faith is the *result* of the Holy Spirit's operation in our hearts. We are not saved *by* faith in the sense of our faith contributing to our salvation. *Soli Deo Gloria!*

* There are sixteen occurrences of *en pistei* in the entire New Testament: 1 Cor. 16:13; 2 Cor. 13:5; Gal. 2:20; 2 Thess. 2:13; 1 Tim. 1:1, 4; 2:7, 15; 3:13; 4:12; 2 Tim. 1:13; Titus 1:13; 3:15; James 1:6; 2:5; 2 Pet. 1:5. In fifteen instances sanctification is discussed—e.g., "stand firm in the faith," "live in the faith," "my true son in the faith," "teacher of the true faith," "continue in the faith," "sound in the faith," "rich in faith," etc. In the sixteenth instance, 2 Thess. 2:13, the subject is *election* by God, which rules out faith as our own contribution.

Love and Esteem

To love and be loved, to have self-esteem as well as esteem for others are among the basic needs of human beings. But love and esteem on the human level may appear difficult to some individuals in the face of the facts of life. It is a humbling experience, for example, to read that the chemical elements in the human body are worth less than a dollar — before inflation. A poor self-image may result from physical handicaps, a failure to achieve one's goals, or an inability to make friends. To become more lovable and of greater esteem to themselves and others, Americans spend, we are told, over five million dollars annually on diet pills, hair tonics, devices to remove wrinkles, etc. All this for human love and esteem!

Divine love and esteem as detailed in Scripture, however, present a much more encouraging picture. Our human frailties, our original sinfulness, our numerous errors of commission and omission against God's holy Law portend a dark fate for humanity. But the Gospel of Jesus Christ can change our sorrow and remorse to repentance and salvation. God's love and esteem for us in the supreme sacrifice of His Son bring us peace, joy, and hope. We are assured that Easter follows Good Friday and that eternal life follows our natural death.

The promises of Scripture should help fulfill our basic needs for love and esteem, when we read what Christ has planned for us. "I go to prepare a place for you" is His guarantee to every Christian (John 14:2). "I will come again, and receive you unto myself," He continues. "The Lord himself shall descend from heaven with a shout . . . we shall be . . . in the clouds to meet the Lord in the air; and so we shall always be with the Lord," St. Paul assures us as well as the Thessalonian believers (1 Thess. 4:16-17).

David's treatment of Mephibosheth is an Old Testament shadow of our future (2 Sam. 9). This son of Jonathan, whose name means "breathing shame," was lame from a bad accident and lived "on the wrong side of the tracks" in an out-of-the-way place called Lodebar. He was hiding out from David, supposing that David wished to kill him in order that he could not claim the throne as King Saul's grandson. But that was before David changed the picture.

Sending for Mephibosheth, who termed himself a "dead dog," David gave him land, servants, and a free meal ticket to eat at the king's table as one of the king's sons. David said in effect, "Mephibosheth, you are moving in with me. My home — the palace — is your home."

In a similar way Jesus says to us, "Someday you are going to move in with Me. My home — heaven — will be your home." Jesus will escort us personally to His eternal home — David merely sent for Mephibosheth. Such high value placed on us more than meets our basic needs for love and esteem.

Son and Servant

In two successive homiletical helps of this issue the terms "son" and "servant" are placed in juxtaposition: the healing of a centurion's servant and the raising of the son of the widow at Nain (pp. 114 ff.). Twice in the Letter to the Galatians St. Paul contrasts son and servant—the son who becomes the heir in contrast to the offspring born of a servant (4:1-3), and the specific reference to Isaac, the son of a free-woman, versus Ishmael, the child from a servant (4:21-31).

The juxtaposition of servant and son evokes scenes and situations of struggle, of opposition, of tension in social, political, and economic areas. The New Testament, however, employs these two terms primarily to illustrate the sharp distinction between the holy or righteous and sin or wickedness—between man's natural condition and the sanctified situation of Christians through Christ—between Law and Gospel.

Through Christ the situation is solved, sin is forgiven, servants become sons, the wicked are declared righteous. For "when the fullness of time had come, God sent forth His Son . . . to redeem [i.e., to serve] those who were under the law, that we might receive the adoption as sons" (Gal. 4:4-5). Through the life and death of Jesus, the divine Son-Servant, we are no longer servants of sin but sons of God.

Already at Jesus' Baptism our heavenly Father indicates the role of Christ as Son-Servant when the voice exclaims: "You are My beloved Son, in whom I am well-pleased" (Mark 1:11). While the voice calls Jesus specifically God's *Son,* the phrase "in whom I am well-pleased" implies His role as *Servant,* for it is a quotation from Isaiah 42:1, one of the "Servant Songs" of Isaiah. The voice, furthermore, infers the conquest of the Son-Servant over evil, since the brief sentence "You are My beloved Son" reflects Psalm 2:7, the Psalm that celebrates the coronation of King David and foreshadows the "King of kings and Lord of lords."

Jesus, the Son-Servant, is also the King who is victorious over all opposition, struggle, and tension. Such situations, while still present in our earthly lives even as Christians, we can overcome in part through Christ on this side of the grave as we serve His church as sons of God. And—all glory be to God!—we have the promise of ultimate and complete conquest over all ills as we shall reign with our Son-Servant-King in eternity.

Oikodomeo

The Great Commission Convocation, scheduled for three to four thousand people in St. Louis in November, undoubtedly will explore such passages as Matthew 16:18, as well as the closing verses of this Gospel. One basic requisite for proper exegesis, of course, is the correct comprehension of vocables, particularly the key words in a sentence. At Matthew 16:18, following Peter's confession, the nouns *Petros, petra,* and *ecclesia* commentators usually consider quite carefully—to such an extent, in fact, that they at times neglect the verb *oikodomeo.* It is the purpose of these few paragraphs to call attention to the basic connotation of this verb.

Oikodomeo appears in Classical Greek as "build," "erect," "build up," both literally and figuratively. Its occurrences in the Septuagint, approximately three hundred and fifty times for the Hebrew *banah,* denote in most cases the erection of a building. In Jeremiah, in particular, we find the figurative meaning: God Himself, for example, will rebuild Israel (31:4; 33:7); God builds up Israel by putting His words in the mouth of the prophet (1:9-10); God builds up neighboring peoples by bringing them into fellowship with the people of Israel (12:14-16).

The New Testament also employs *oikodomeo* both literally and figuratively—literally, for instance, as "building a house" (Luke 6:48) and "built a tower" (Matt. 21:33); figuratively, as "being built up a spiritual house" (1 Pet. 2:5); "build on another man's foundation" (Rom. 15:20); and "build again those things which I destroyed" (Gal. 2:18).

In Matthew 16:18 *oikodomeo* definitely is used figuratively: ". . . you are Peter, and on this rock I will build My church. . . ." The reference is to the resurrection and the power of Pentecost to erect the new Temple, the Christian church or community—as our Lord foretold also when He declared that He would destroy the temple made with hands and within three days build another made without hands (Mark 14:58; Matt. 26:61; cf. John 2:19-22).

There are numerous other non-literal occurrences of *oikodomeo* in the New Testament. They concern the *spiritual progress* and *inner growth* of the members of the Christian community:

> . . . all things are lawful for me, but all things do not edify (*oikodomei,* 1 Cor. 10:23). Knowledge puffs up, but love edifies (*oikodomei,* 1 Cor. 8:1). . . . the word of His grace, which is able to build you up . . . (*oikodomesai,* Acts 20:32). He who speaks in a tongue edifies *(oikodomei)* himself, but he who prophesies edifies (*oikodomei*) the church (1 Cor. 14:4). Therefore comfort each other and edify *(oikodomeite)* one another . . . (1 Thess. 5:11). . . . will not the conscience of him who is weak be emboldened *(oikodomethesetai)* to eat those things offered to idols (1 Cor. 8:10)?

The verb *oikodomeo* does not connote numerical growth or statistical increase. For this idea the New Testament employs *plethuno* and *auxano:* ". . . the number of the disciples was multiplying . . ." (*plethunonton,* Acts 6:1; cf. 6:7); ". . . the people grew *(euxesen)* and multiplied *(eplethunthe)* in Egypt . . ." (Acts 7:17). That the two ideas of numerical increase and inner growth are separate concepts, implied by separate vocables, is illustrated in Acts 9:31:

> Then the churches throughout all Judea, Galilee, and Samaria had peace and were edified *(oikodomoumene).* And walking in the fear of the Lord and in the comfort of the Holy Spirit, they were multiplied *(eplethuneto).*

The one rule which applies to everything that happens in the Christian community is that it must serve to *build up* the community *spiritually* in the *inner growth* of its members. The verb *oikodomeo* with its cognates and compounds (*synoikodomeo* and *epoikodomeo*) connote that inner spiritual growth. At times the New Testament adds the metaphors of planting and of the human body to the figure of building. Such metaphors teach that Christians are rooted *(errizomenoi)* and built up *(epoikodomoumenoi)* in Christ (Col. 2:7), who has given apostles, prophets, evangelists, and pastors and teachers for the edifying *(eis oikodomen)* of the Christian community as Christ's body (*tou somatos tou Christou,* Eph. 4:11-12), "built *(epoikodomethentes)* on the foundation of the apostles and prophets with Jesus Christ Himself as the chief cornerstone . . . in whom you also are being built together *(synoikodomeisthe)* for a habitation of God in the Spirit" (Eph. 2:20, 22).

In brief, *oikodomeo* in Matthew 16:18, as well as in the entire New Testament, denotes the spiritual foundation on which Christ builds His church and the spiritual growth of the members of the Christian community, the new Temple, through their nourishment from Word and Sacrament.

Mathetes

The initial editorial in the previous issue of our periodical attempts to clarify what our Lord implies by the verb *oikodomeo* in the sentence, "I will build My church" (Matt. 16:18) — that is, inner spiritual growth rather than numerical increase. The present paragraphs will try to delineate the connotation of the imperative *matheteusate* in Christ's great commission, "make disciples of all nations" (Matt. 28:19).

The verb *matheteuo* appears only twice in the New Testament (Acts 14:21 and Matt. 28:19). The noun *mathetes,* however, occurs over two hundred and sixty times, exclusively in the Gospels and Acts. To investigate the basic connotation of the verb, therefore, an examination of the uses of the noun should prove enlightening.

A *mathetes* is much more than a follower; he is one who hears the call of Jesus and joins Him. When crowds of people—including the curious—merely follow Jesus, the New Testament frequently employs the verb *akoloutheo* (Matt. 4:25; 8:1; 21:9). *Mathetes,* however, is cognate to *manthano* (aorist stem: *math*), which involves a process of learning—not merely the acquisition of knowledge, but the surrender of one's person to Christ in faith and service.

A comparison of the Old Testament with Rabbinic Judaism on the use or lack of use of *mathetes* should give some clues concerning its meaning in the New Testament. Most surprising at first is the fact that *mathetes* appears in the Septuagint only in alternative readings at Jeremiah 13:21; 20:11; 26:9, being weakly attested. Also the Hebrew noun for pupil *(talmid)* occurs only at 1 Chronicles 25:8; at Isaiah 8:16 some translators render *limmud* as disciples. This dearth of vocabulary for a learner in a teacher-pupil relationship stems from Israel's consciousness of being an elect people. The individual Israelite always remains a part of the whole chosen race. This concept excludes any possibility of a disciple-master relationship between men, in which the priest and prophet teach on their own authority. The attendants of Moses and of the prophets, therefore, are called servants and sons (Ex. 24:13; Num. 11:28; 1 Kings 19:19-21; 20:35; 2 Kings 2:3; 4:12). In the words of Professor Rengstorf, "In the sphere of revelation there is no place for the establishment of a master-disciple relation, nor is there the possibility of setting up a human word alongside the word of God which is proclaimed, nor of trying to ensure the force of the divine address by basing it on the authority of a great personality (*TDNT,* 4:431).

The situation in Rabbinic Judaism, however, is quite different. The pupil is concerned with the entire Jewish tradition—the written Torah (the writing of the Old Testament) and the oral Torah (the traditions of the fathers). The pupil *(talmid* or *mathetes)* subordinates himself to his teacher in almost servile fashion, attributing a value to human authority that was unknown in previous Judaism. The Rabbi becomes a sort of mediator between the Torah and his pupils. The verbs for learn *(lamad* and *manthano)* still connote the discovering of God's will in the Torah, but learning now is determined by the authority of the teacher and his interpretation of the Torah. The pupil-teacher relationship of Rabbinic Judaism becomes an important institution for the study of the Torah, in contrast to the previous practice as indicated in the Old Testament. Some scholars see the origin of the Rabbinic innovation through Judaism's contact with Greek philosophy.

The New Testament evangelists probably take over the term *mathetes* from Hellenistic Judaism, but they give it a completely new character through its association with Jesus. They employ *mathetes* to indicate total attachment to someone in discipleship. A frame of reference wider than the followers of Christ also appears, when the New Testament refers to the disciples of John the Baptist (Matt. 11:2; Mark 2:18; 6:29; Luke 5:33; 11:1; John 1:35, 37), the disciples of Moses (John 9:28), and the disciples of the Pharisees (Matt. 22:16; Luke 5:33).

It is indisputable that our Lord called people to be His *mathetai*—a relationship that entails several distinctive characteristics, in contrast to the custom prevailing in Rabbinic Judaism. While the disciples refer to the Master as Rabbi (Mark 9:5; 11:21; John 1:38; 4:31), one basic distinction is that Christ's call is decisive: Jesus takes the initiative in calling people into discipleship, whereas in Rabbinic circles a person makes a voluntary decision to join a master (Luke 5:1-11; 9:59-62; Mark 1:17; 2:14; John 1:43). The Rabbinic pupil aims at becoming a master himself, furthermore, while a *mathetes* of Christ is to submit to the unconditional surrender of his whole life for his entire life (Matt. 10:24-25, 37; Luke 14:26-27; John 11:16). Unlike the Rabbis, Jesus breaks through the barriers of social distinction by calling the fisherman and the tax-collector, although the latter is outside the contemporary worshipping community—that is, God's grace is basic in Christ's call.

Also basic is that the Lord's call entails service, as when He sends out the "twelve" and the "seventy" (Mark 6:7-13; Luke 10:1-12). Such service may include also suffering (Matt. 10:24-25, 38; 16:24-25). The promised reward, which exceeds any kind of merit, is fellowship with God through Jesus, culminating in a new and future life (Matt. 16:25; John 14:6).

In brief, faithfulness to Christ is crucial in being a *mathetes.* The Master summarizes the promise and the dangers involved thus: "Whoever confesses Me before men, him the Son of Man will also confess before the angels of God. But he who denies Me before men will be denied before the angels of God" (Luke 12:8-9). The essence of a *mathetes* lies in saving faith, which motivates the fulfilment of his duty as a witness to his Lord in his entire life.

It is pertinent to note that, as Luke implies at Acts 11:26 and later in his volume (26:28), in the early church the terms "disciple" and "Christian" are interchangeable (cf. 1 Pet. 4:16). Any attempt to distinguish between a disciple and a Christian is unwarranted and has no basis in Scripture.

Comments on Christ's Commission

Our two previous editorials—*Oikodomeo* in July and *Mathetes* in September—clearly indicate that our Lord is stressing primarily the inner spiritual growth of His church in Matthew 16:18 and the total commitment of His followers to the cause of the Gospel in Matthew 28:19-20. The present comments on Christ's commission will attempt to elaborate briefly on some pertinent points in the commission and its context.

The context is important because of the contrast between human endeavor and divine power. As the eleven arrive at the designated mountain in Galilee and worship the resurrected Savior, we read, "some hesitated" (Matt. 28:17). In spite of the various "proofs" of the true identity of Jesus of Nazareth, both during His ministry through numerous miracles and after His resurrection through frequent encounters with the risen Christ, some of His closer associates still *hesitate*—or, as some render the verb, some of His intimate disciples still *have doubts*. It is these fickle followers who are to begin carrying out the great commission with all of their frailties and foibles.

Our Lord realizes the limitations and weaknesses of human endeavor by itself. So He frames the great commission with the promise of divine power. He prefaces His instruction with the basic premise which should have been obvious to the eleven during the previous years: "There has been given to me all authority in heaven and on earth" (Matt. 28:18). Immediately after His instruction Jesus again assures His disciples: "And lo, I am with you all the days until the close of the aeon" (Matt. 28:20). Not only does Christ here emphasize by contrast the need for divine power to give impetus and success to human endeavor; the concluding sentence of Matthew's Gospel is an artistic and pointed reminder of the citation from Isaiah at the beginning of the Gospel: "They shall call His name Emmanuel, which is translated 'God with us'" (Matt. 1:23). The primary Person of the Gospel, called "God with us" in the initial chapter, promises to be "with you," His followers, as disciples are added among all nations.

How are peccable people—then and now—to carry out the commission Christ commanded to His church? Again, the means of making disciples stress divine power. The two participles, *baptizontes* and *didaskontes,* are without the definite article, thus denoting circumstantial and adverbial use. That is, disciples are to be added to the church *by baptizing* in the name of the triune God and *by teaching* all things which Jesus commanded. The means of making disciples, in brief, are *by Sacrament* and *by Word,* the only means by which the Holy Spirit works in the hearts of humans. People are saved by God's grace through faith *propter Christum.* Jesus has accomplished everything for us; the Holy Spirit works faith in us (Eph. 2:8-9). The power of persuasion and the success of evangelistic endeavors come from above—to overcome the hesitation and doubts of natural man. The conversion of sinners is God's work entirely. Our faith (Eph. 2:8-9) and our faithful stewardship (Eph. 2:10) in carrying out Christ's commission are both gifts from God.

It is pertinent to note the use of *didaskontes,* rather than *kerussontes* in the great commission. To carry out Christ's command through proclamation in public preaching is not enough. Constant and consistent toil of teaching is imperative. The verb *didasko* has a wide connotation in Greek literature, denoting the imparting not only of knowledge, opinions, and facts, but also of artistic and technical skills—all of which are to be acquired systematically and thoroughly as a result of the repeated activity of both teacher and pupil. Herodotus, for example, employs *didasko* to describe the work of a chorus-master, who took on the task of training the chorus of a Greek drama in intricate lyrical poetry and dancing (1.23; 6.21). In the New Testament *didasko* occurs ninety-five times basically in two senses: 1) in the Gospels and Acts, primarily to address people in teaching them those things which God requires of the whole person; 2) in the Pastoral Epistles and in 2 Thessalonians, mainly to hand down a form of doctrine to be mastered and preserved intact.

That the toil of teaching is imperative in following Christ's commission is clear, furthermore, from the phrase: " . . . teaching them to observe all things, as many as I have commanded you" (Matt. 28:20). What did Jesus teach during His earthly ministry?—the nature of God, God's will for humans, God's activity in history, His plan of salvation, His kingdom, His judgment for eternity.

Christians, then, are to bear in mind the pertinent points of Christ's commission. Word and Sacrament are the only means of building the church. Discipleship implies total commitment to the cause of Christ. Constant and consistent toil is required. The message must be all inclusive of what our Lord teaches. Final evaluation will be based on the content of evangelistic endeavors—"gold, silver, precious stones" rather than "wood, hay, straw" (1 Cor. 3:12-15). The success of serious human endeavor is measured by inner spiritual growth and is the result of the divine power of our Emmanuel, our "God with us."

Apropos of the New Year

The beginning of the new year 1981 — and, in spite of frequent claims to the contrary during the past twelve months, the beginning of a new decade — provides the occasion for several observations. In fact, every dating of a document in any year — a will, a contract, a letter, a newspaper — is an eloquent testimony to our Savior, for since the sixth century the division of dates into *"Anno Domini"* and "Before Christ" testifies to the great significance of the ministry of Jesus on earth.

But this division, introduced by Dionysius Exiguus around 525, also reminds us of the shortcomings of human reason; for, as Ripley's column occasionally points out, Dionysius Exiguus miscalculated, possibly misconstruing in Luke 3:1 the "fifteenth year of the reign of Tiberius Caesar," who became co-ruler with Augustus several years before occupying the throne alone. Hence, while we shall date our documents this year as A.D. 1981, we must acknowledge that in actuality the date is incorrect, for our Lord was born more than nineteen hundred and eighty-one years ago. Human reason errs frequently and should not be a touchstone for judging divine truth — particularly when a relatively simple human mathematical calculation on the yearly calendar turns out to be in error.

The distinction between human reason, frequently fallible, and divine wisdom, always infallible, furthermore, is reflected in the difference between our secular calendar and the church calendar, which has a separate beginning and reflects a different purpose. While the secular calendar indirectly testifies to Jesus' ministry, the church calendar has as its prime purpose the celebration of events in the life of our Lord and His church. It is, therefore, proper that the two calendars be distinct — suggesting to us Christians that we live in two separate kingdoms and challenging us to give evidence in our lives as to which kingdom is more important.

The measurement of time is a convenient and conventional method of reckoning human events. But to God a thousand years are as one day. As its Creator He is above time. Attempts to entangle God with mundane temporal calculations lead to confusion — to wit, the frequent predictions of dating the end of the world and some current calculations of millennialists. God's covenants and promises have a far greater implication than any interpretation of contemporary events in the Middle East. His Word sheds light on our justification and sanctification; it does not pretend to predict the chronology of the future. Scripture attests to the *kairos* of the *parousia,* not its *chronos.* In the words of our Lord, "It is not for you to know times or seasons which the Father has fixed by his own authority" (Acts 1:7).

The arrival of a new year, with economic and social conditions similar to those of the old year, should also remind us of the close connection between the Old and New Testaments. As our lives in the new year will be closely parallel to what we experienced in the old year, so God's Word is the same in both Testaments. The one is not of the Law and the other of the Gospel. Both show God's grace. They form one book, a careful reading of which reveals that Yahweh is concerned with sin, judgment, *and grace* in the Old Testament as well as in the New. The early church in Acts and the apostle Paul did not reject the Old Testament, but cited it frequently, finding God's promises of the Old Testament fulfilled in the New. Our human heritage of previous years is helpful in understanding the present; so our spiritual heritage from the Old Testament is a necessary requisite for fully appreciating God's grace today.

The new and the old, finally, are terms pertinent to the Christian's response to God's grace. In the words of St. Paul, " . . . put off, concerning your former conduct, the old man which is corrupt according to the deceitful lusts, and be renewed in the spirit of your mind, and . . . put on the new man which was created according to God, in righteousness and true holiness" (Eph. 4:22-24; NKJB). Then in eternity, when the tension between the old man and the new man has been resolved, the goal *(telos)* of God's grace will arrive: a new heaven, a new earth, a new Jerusalem (Rev. 21:1-2). *Soli Deo Gloria!*

A Significant Shift

One of the focal points in the church year is the period of Lent climaxed by our observance of Easter. The suffering, death, and resurrection of our Lord entail a significant shift, with ramifications not always readily comprehended. That is, the resurrection is the point at which Jesus becomes the interpreted rather than the interpreter—the One who is proclaimed rather than the One who proclaims.

One ramification of this significant shift is that the historical Jesus leaves His earthly ministry to be exalted on the right hand of the Father as both the Lord of the universe and the Head of the church, becoming the Christ of faith. There is no denying that Jesus seen through the eyes of resurrection faith looks very different from Jesus according to the flesh. His visible presence, except on the occasions of several post-resurrection appearances, disappears, and the presence of His Holy Spirit working with special signs becomes dominant. The One Son, the embodiment of the new Israel, extends His kingdom through the expanding church, the body of Christ which is also the new Israel. It is only natural, then, that the continuity between the events recorded in the Gospel accounts and the inspired writings of the Pauline Epistles on Christ and the church suffers a significant shift—a shift that seems to bother many current scholars unduly. There is a definite continuity and identity, but a change in emphasis—a change resulting from the significant shift involved in the resurrection.

The death and resurrection of Jesus also cause a significant shift in the thought of Paul. As a Jew St. Paul has to rethink all his ideas about his own relationship with God. What sort of a God would permit the Messiah's death? Could Deity shed human blood? Scrupulous obedience to the Law has to make room for a crucified Messiah raised from the dead. The Gospel message is a "scandal" or "stumbling block" to Paul the Jew, as it is foolishness to the non-Jew. People

In reality it is the significant shift of Lent and Easter which is basic to the continuity from the evangelists to Paul. The Gospel of Paul is identical with that of the Gospels. While the Gospels *culminate* in Jesus' death and resurrection, with the ministry of Jesus leading up to this significant shift, St. Paul bases his writings largely on the *foundation* of Christ's death and resurrection. The initial sentence in Romans, for example, makes clear that Paul's Gospel is based on God's "Son Jesus Christ our Lord, who was born of the seed of David according to the flesh, and declared to be the Son of God, according to the Spirit of holiness, by the *resurrection* from the dead" (1:3-4).

The significant shift entailed in Jesus' death and resurrection is evident, furthermore, in Paul's Letters. References to Jesus' earthly ministry are noticeably scanty in the Pauline corpus. It is Jesus' death, not His life, which is significant in Paul's Epistles. The dearth of references to the earthly life of Jesus does not mean that Paul has no interest in the historical Jesus. There is a significant shift in perspective caused by Jesus' death and resurrection. While the evangelists record the miracles, sayings, parables, and three-year ministry of *Jesus,* Paul centers his writing on what God has done through *Christ.* Paul writes about the *risen* Jesus Christ, not so much about the *ministry* of Jesus of Galilee. Although the purpose and aim of the evangelists and Paul are the same—the response which the readers are to make to Jesus—the emphasis changes. The Gospels write about Jesus; Paul writes about what God's actions through Jesus imply—a change in emphasis brought about by the significant shift involved in Jesus' death and resurrection.

Evangelism in Acts

In light of the current emphasis on evangelism and church growth, it may be well to point out some salient items in the Acts of the Apostles, which covers approximately the first thirty years of the Christian church—a period in which Christianity grew proportionately more than in any other time in her history.

Numerically we read of one hundred and twenty persons present at the choosing of Matthias (1:15)—not counting, of course, at least five hundred people who saw the resurrected Jesus, probably in Galilee (1 Cor. 15:6). To this number of followers about three thousand souls were added at Pentecost (2:41), and the total number of converts soon reached five thousand (4:4). But this movement was only in its embryonic stage, limited to Jews and proselytes in Palestine. The theme of Acts is much more comprehensive, as Jesus promised before His ascension: "But you will receive power when the Holy Spirit has come upon you; and you will be witnesses to me in Jerusalem, and in all Judea and Samaria, and to the end of the earth" (1:8; NKJB).

The theme of Acts describes two prime aspects of early evangelism: geographically, the spread of Christianity from Jerusalem throughout the eastern Mediterranean as far as Rome; theologically, the growth of the church from a group consisting primarily of Jews to a movement which included numerous Gentiles of various national backgrounds throughout the Graeco-Roman world, possibly even predominantly Gentiles. The importance of the latter aspect of early evangelism, which involves some basic theological and social problems for the church as well as soul-searching rethinking of native axioms and principles by such leaders as Peter and Paul, the Acts of the Apostles underlines and emphasizes in various ways. Acts reports the incident of Peter and Cornelius, the first Gentile convert, in two successive chapters (10 and 11); it retells the conversion of Paul, the apostle to the Gentiles (9), on two later occasions (22 and 26); and it places in the center of the document the Jerusalem Council (15), which deals with two basic issues present in a Jewish-Gentile church: How may Gentiles become members? How can unity be maintained in a Jewish-Gentile church?

How did the church achieve such growth in the first thirty years in spite of the tremendous problems within and opposition from without, particularly from Judaism? The answer, of course, is simple and singular, as stated in Acts. Jesus promised the growth and specified its source: "But you will receive power when the Holy Spirit has come upon you" (1:8). The source of evangelism in the early church was the work of the Holy Spirit, poured out at Pentecost (2:1-13) and continually active (e.g., 4:31), particularly in Word and Sacrament, and evidenced in prayer and fellowship (1:14; 2:42, 46). Acts emphasizes throughout the work of the Holy Spirit in Baptism, beginning with Peter's appeal at Pentecost (1:38). The six summary statements (6:7; 9:31; 12:24; 16:5; 19:20; 28:31) underline the work of the Holy Spirit in the growth of the church through the Word, by alternating between "word" and "church" in the first five summaries and by citing the content of the message in the sixth summary, the final verse in Acts: "preaching the kingdom of God and teaching the things which concern the Lord Jesus Christ with all confidence" (28:31; NKJB).

Equally noteworthy with the Holy Spirit being the source of evangelism in the early church are the foibles and shortcomings of the witnesses. At first they did not comprehend the implications of the movement and its Leader, querying, "Lord, will You at this time restore the kingdom to Israel?" (1:6; NKJB)—after three years of daily association with the One who assured them that His kingdom is not of this world! Then, after experiencing the outpouring of the Holy Spirit at Pentecost, they refused (adamantly, it seems) to carry out Jesus' commission that they should be witnesses in Jerusalem, in Judea and Samaria, and to the end of the earth; they continued to observe the hours of prayer at the temple (2:46; 3:1; 5:21; 5:42) and did not budge from Jerusalem. Apparently the apostles planned to spread the Word through their contacts at the temple, where they hoped to make converts among the dwellers in Jerusalem and those adherents to Judaism who visited from various regions of the dispersion. In fact, it took a persecution to begin the preaching of the Gospel beyond Jerusalem (8:1-4)—even then the apostles themselves preferred to remain in Jerusalem.

The weaknesses of the two prominent leaders, Peter and Paul, are also pertinent in evaluating the witnesses of the early church. In each case divine intervention was necessary—Peter's vision on the housetop before his willingness to enter the home of a Gentile; and Paul's vision on the road to Damascus before he changed from a persecutor to a promoter of Christianity. Without the work of the Holy Spirit in their hearts, effecting a radical change in their understanding and attitude, Peter and Paul would not have been successful instruments in the evangelism of the early church.

That the Holy Spirit used witnesses who in themselves were prone to human weaknesses is apparent also in the incident of the quarrel between Paul and Barnabas over John Mark (15:36-41). We read: "Then the contention became so sharp between them that they departed from one another" (15:39; NKJB). It is true that God used this dissension to develop two missionary trips instead of only one, with Barnabas and Mark sailing to Cyprus while Paul and Silas journeyed to Cilicia. But the time of the disagreement is extremely pertinent—immediately after the Apostolic Council! Think of it for a moment! The leading witnesses had thrashed out a basic doctrinal dispute with implications for the essence of the Gospel and the unity of the church, when two of the witnesses clashed over personal preferences of a personality. Agreement in doctrine did not shield them from showing human foibles and shortcomings.

Today the task of the church is the same as in the Acts of the Apostles—to engage in evangelism in carrying out Christ's commission. The source is the same—the working of the Holy Spirit through Word and Sacrament. The witnesses today, sad to say, frequently exhibit weaknesses and shortcomings similar to the early leaders in Acts. At times personalities may loom as more important than unity in teaching. But, evangelism will continue and the church will overcome opposition—not by gimmicks and new techniques, but by the blessing of the Lord of the church, who has promised to be with His people "always, even to the end of the age" (Matt. 28:20).

Paul's Gospel

Paul summarizes the Gospel which he preached to the Corinthians in four verbs: Christ died, was buried, rose, was seen (1 Cor. 15:1-8). Since burial implies death and being seen confirms resurrection, Paul's Gospel may be reduced to two verbs: Christ died and rose. These two facts of the Gospel Paul emphasizes in other passages of his First Epistle to the Corinthians: "For I determined not to know anything among you except Jesus Christ and Him *crucified*" (2:2; NKJB); "And if Christ is not *risen*, then our preaching is vain and your faith is also vain" (15:14; NKJB).

But since the Corinthian congregation had some questions about the resurrection of the dead (1 Cor. 15:12), the apostle may be summarizing the Gospel message to them in this way for that reason. How, then, does Paul summarize the Gospel to the Romans? In the same way: " . . . the gospel of God . . . concerning His Son Jesus Christ our Lord, who was born of the seed of David according to the flesh, and declared to be the Son of God with power, according to the Spirit of holiness by the *resurrection from the dead*" (1:1, 4-5; NKJB); "that if you confess with your mouth the Lord Jesus and believe in your heart that God has *raised* Him from the *dead*, you will be saved" (10:9; NKJB). Paul sums up the Gospel also to the Roman Christians in two facts: God *raised* Christ, who had *died*; furthermore, it is through the resurrection that Jesus is acknowledged as Lord and Son of God.

If Paul's Gospel can be reduced to two verbs or two facts, why are his Letters so theological? Because the "simple" Gospel of death and resurrection is really not so simple after all. Paul describes this "simple" Gospel as a "stumbling block" to the Jews and "foolishness" to the Greeks (1 Cor. 1:23). To Paul, a Jew, it was no simple message to preach that the Jewish Messiah had died—even the death of crucifixion. He had to rethink all his ideas about God and about his relationship with God. What sort of God would permit the Messiah's death? Previously the apostle had considered his relationship with God as a matter of his own obedience to the Law. Now he has to make room for a crucified Messiah whom God raised from the dead. People in general, Jews and Gentiles, associate deity with glory and power. What is this talk of the Son of God dying in shame and weakness? The "simple" message of Christ crucified and risen has far-reaching implications.

The implications of the "simple" Gospel, for example, are evident in Paul's correspondence with Galatia and with Corinth—although in each case the conditions are quite different. In Galatia the context is the Jewish understanding of God's Law and the character of righteousness; in Corinth the situation involves a taste for philosophy and human wisdom. In either case the problem is parallel—an attempt to add something to the "simple" Gospel of Christ's death and resurrection.

Why should Paul become so "hot under the collar" when some people in Galatia urged that after Baptism into Christ's death and resurrection the next step was acceptance of the Jewish rite of circumcision and obedience to the regulations of Judaism? Although Paul's reaction may have seemed absurdly violent to some early Christians, his teaching is controlled by a deeper logic grounded on the basic facts of the "simple" Gospel that Christ died and rose. The Law, which Paul had obeyed for so long, had condemned the Messiah as a criminal. The attempt to keep the Law had caused people to seek their own righteousness instead of accepting God's, to try to earn salvation by their own merit rather than trusting in God, to return to self-reliance, and thus to deny the grace of God, which offers salvation as a free gift through the "simple" Gospel that Jesus died and was raised.

Also in Corinth some people were attempting to add something to the Gospel and as a result were destroying it. They wished to add, not the rules of Judaism, but human wisdom. Although expressed in different terms, the danger at Corinth was basically the same as in Galatia—a temptation to rely upon oneself—upon one's own cleverness, ability, intellect. Paul contrasts the Gospel of Christ crucified and risen with the search for wisdom, which can empty the cross of all meaning. He declares that the apparent folly and weakness of God, as seen in the cross, are wiser and stronger than the wisdom and strength of human beings, whose efforts can never earn them salvation: " . . . so that no man may boast before him. It is because of him that you are in Christ Jesus, who has become for us wisdom from God—that is, our righteousness, holiness, and redemption" (1 Cor. 1:29-30; NIV). If Christ is our wisdom and righteousness, it is folly to look any further.

Although to Galatia the apostle writes in terms of Law and grace and to Corinth in terms of wisdom and folly, the fundamental antithesis in both Epistles is the same—between self-reliance and reliance upon God, between pride in one's own achievements and trust in the achievements of God. At first Galatians and 1 Corinthians—two Letters of unquestionable authenticity—seem to talk about the Gospel in totally different ways. Yet, as we examine the meaning of the different passages, we see that Paul's basic theological position is the same in both. It is the same "simple" Gospel of Christ's death and resurrection, which causes him to react as he does in addressing these two different groups of people. The differences in expression are the result of the different situations with which he is dealing. In each case the apostle is defending salvation by grace, the Gospel of Christ's death and resurrection.

Justification unto Life

The basis of our justification is the grace of God, not our merit, as St. Paul emphasizes in Romans 4:4-5: "Now to one who works, his wages are not reckoned as a gift but as his due. And to one who does not work but trusts him who justifies the ungodly, his faith is reckoned as righteousness." A person who has worked at a job receives earnings or wages in proportion to his labors — if his employer is fair and square. But since mankind is ungodly and has even rebelled against God and therefore is incapable of acquiring merit, we must depend solely on the grace of God.

In the Parable of the Laborers in the Vineyard (Matt. 20:1-16) those who worked shorter hours received far more than they had reason to expect. While the householder had specified wages for the first group and had promised the next group a fair wage, there is no mention of such an agreement with the men hired around 5:00 P.M. That the last received the same remuneration as those who had worked all day, must be attributed to the grace of the householder. None can say he was unfair. The first men had agreed to work for a denarius, and that is what each received. In the case of the "eleventh-hour" laborers, the employer simply went beyond what they had earned and expected.

The "blessed" man of Psalm 32 is not the sinless man, but the one whose sins God does not count against him, whose sins are forgiven. It is not a matter of being and doing good; it is being in a new relationship with God through the imputed righteousness of Christ.

The receiving hand is faith, not the works required under the Law. What did faith mean to Abraham? 1) Total dependence on God, even when it meant leaving home without knowing where he would be taken. 2) A reliance upon God to perform the impossible and the unreasonable. 3) An unswerving allegiance to God, even if it meant obeying the command to sacrifice his only son Isaac.

The beneficiaries of justification are Abraham and all who believe — from among the circumcised and uncircumcised (Rom. 4:11-12). We must, with St. Paul, distinguish between Israel *after the flesh* (which produced Judaism and all the restrictive legalism of post-exilic law) and the Israel *of God* (which springs from the true heart of Old Testament faith and carries us back from Christ through the insights of the prophets to the Covenant with God at Sinai and beyond that to the faith of Abraham). To the "Israel of God" (Gal. 6:16) belong Jews *and* Gentiles. As Paul says in Galatians 3:7, "So you see that it is men of faith who are the sons of Abraham."

God's grace not only forgives sin, it also gives life — to Abraham, to his offspring, and to every believer. God gives life to the dead. As Paul states in Romans 4:17, God calls into existence the things that do not exist. In the working of the divine plan there are two creations. The first is that of Genesis 1 and 2. The second is described in 2 Corinthians 5:17: "Therefore, if any one is in Christ, he is a new creation."

Both creations are accomplished by the concurrent operation of the Spirit and the Word of God. According to Genesis 1:2b, 3a, "the Spirit *(ruach)* of God was moving over the face of the waters. And God *said*. . . . " The Psalmist declares: "By the word of the Lord the heavens were made, and all their host by the breath (*ruach*) of his mouth" (33:6).

Jesus Christ, the eternal *Logos* (Word), is the mediator of both creations. "All things were made through him" (John 1:3). When the time had fully come, "the Word became flesh and dwelt among us" bringing grace and truth (John 1:14, 17). Jesus' death provided the basis for the new creation (Col. 1:20). Paul affirms: "For it is the God who said, 'Let light shine out of darkness,' who has shone in our hearts to give the light of the knowledge of the glory of God in the face of Christ" (2 Cor. 4:6).

An element of mystery is present in both creations. No one can fully understand how the Almighty created and shaped matter in the beginning nor how one is "born of water and the Spirit" (John 3:5; cf. v. 8). How the physical universe shall figure in the reconciliation of all things by Jesus Christ, only God knows. Abraham believed that God would restore life to his and Sarah's well-nigh "dead" bodies (cf. Gen. 18:11-14). He believed there would be a son called into existence in keeping with the divine promise.

The object of our faith is the same as that of Abraham: God Himself. Yet the sphere is different, for we live in the presence of an accomplished redemption. "Upon us the fulfillment of ages has come" (1 Cor. 10:11; NEB). Through Jesus Christ's once-for-all saving work, God gives life to the spirtually dead (Eph. 2:1-7). By virtue of Christ's resurrection, He will one day grant spiritual bodies to the physically dead (1 Cor. 15:44). With this firm faith in God's grace, which grants justification unto life, we are strengthened in our service as a response to His grace.

Christian Hope

Christian hope frequently expresses itself in reference to the future—a future glory which surpasses the present, a future situation which is far superior to present hardships, a future recompense which makes up for present inequities. There is a break between present and future with no real continuity. The negatives of the present existence cease, and the blessings of the future commence. Such a view of Christian hope is Scriptural, with Christ's *parousia* and the final judgment separating the present world from eternal glory for Christians.

But also Scriptural is a more profound view of Christian hope—that it is not limited to the future but belongs also to the present. Christians already are glorified, although their glory may not be evident to the world. Christians already are conforming to the pattern of Christ by sharing in His life and in His death. God's power, which raised Christ from death, already is transforming death to life in the lives of those who are in Christ.

Christians are not limited to experiencing present sorrow and suffering and death with the hope of future joy and glory and life. They already experience a joy which comes from sorrow, a glory found in suffering, and a life emerging from death. The paradox of Christian hope is explained in the cross of Christ, where life and death, glory and suffering, joy and sorrow coalesce. Through the cross restoration is no longer just a future hope but a present experience—and in many ways experience is more real than hope.

There are two means by which the present hope of Christians is proclaimed: Baptism and the Lord's Supper. Baptism is dying with Christ, an incorporation into Christ's death; it also assures the believer of resurrection to life through Jesus' resurrection. Baptism coalesces death and resurrection at a point in present time. Baptism commences a new life at the very moment the believer dies to what is past. Also the Lord's Supper looks back to the death of Christ; it also is a foretaste of the Messianic banquet of the future. But at the same time it is a present experience of the living presence of Christ.

Through these two means of grace—Baptism and the Lord's Supper—Christians experience present hope by being united with the death and resurrection of Christ. In Christ opposite experiences—life and death, joy and sorrow, glory and suffering—are fused together. That is the paradox of the cross. Paul sums it up when he describes himself as "always carrying in the body the death of Jesus, so that the life of Jesus may also be manifested in our bodies. For while we live we are always being given up to death for Jesus' sake, so that the life of Jesus may be manifested in our mortal flesh. So death is at work in us, but life in you" (2 Cor. 4:10-12).

To Equip the Saints

May and June are the months for most graduation or commencement programs. We take this opportunity, therefore, to congratulate the members of the class of 1982 at Concordia Seminary, whose basic goal in their calling will be to equip the saints.

The function of the pastoral office, we trust, has been defined for our students during their instruction at the seminary—to proclaim God's grace through Word and Sacrament, properly applying both Law and Gospel in a multitude of varying situations. Also the motivation, we hope, has been clearly delineated—God's glory and love as manifested in Jesus' life and death for the redemption of sinful mankind.

St. Paul refers to those who perform the pastoral ministry as Christ's gifts to the church; he then specifies the purpose of these gifts as *pros ton katartismon ton hagion* (Eph. 4:11-12). This phrase briefly presents the prime purpose of the pastoral office. Christ's gifts to the church are to be instrumental in the lives and growth of each and every Christian. The task of carrying out the Great Commission is far too large to be accomplished by a select few leaders. Every follower of Christ must be equipped to contribute his or her share of the task.

Note that it is not sufficient to encourage each believer to carry out Jesus' commission. Incentive and motivation must be present, to be sure. The prime purpose of the pastor is to equip the members of his flock. The noun *(katartismos)* is used in the setting of a broken bone (BAG, p. 419); Matthew employs the cognate verb in the mending of nets (4:21). That is, the physician sets a broken bone in order for it to perform its proper function, and the fisherman mends the net for it to do its task—the physician will not do the work of the bone, nor will the fisherman perform the task of the net. The specialists see to it that the bone and net are equipped to do their respective work.

Jesus Himself set the example. He equipped the apostles to spread the Gospel throughout the Mediterranean world after His ascension. Under the guidance of the Holy Spirit God's Good News spread from Jerusalem to Rome and from Jews to Gentiles within one generation. Also our generation of Christ's body, the church, faces internal problems and external opposition to the Gospel. Under the guidance of the same Holy Spirit such challenges may be met when God's gifts to the church follow the example of Jesus. They are "to equip the saints for the work of ministry, for building up the body of Christ."

That is the assignment to all in the pastoral office, including the class of 1982.

Twenty-Five Years in Retrospect

25 Years Ago

Twenty-five years ago, as a recent graduate of Concordia Seminary in St. Louis and as a professor of Greek and Latin in a college of the Synodical Conference, I read with interest "A Statement" of the "forty-four" and the explanatory pamphlet **Speaking the Truth in Love.** After examining all the voluminous literature written on both sides of the question and upon a most careful and prayerful study of the Greek text of the New Testament, I became aware that each "camp" was mustering its missiles from an inadequate and erroneous use of Greek grammar. In spite of my youth and relative inexperience in theology (some of the "warriors" on each side had been my instructors a few years previous), my training and relatively wide reading in Greek gave me the courage to call attention to the fact that both factions were misunderstanding and misapplying basic rules of Greek in the exegesis of a passage considered to be of key importance. My findings were published in a monograph, **A Grammatical Study of Romans 16, 17,** mailed **gratis** to all the clergymen in the Synodical Conference in 1947, with a second printing (1963) currently available from the Lutheran Synodical Book Company in Mankato, Minnesota.

Soon the Statement of the forty-four and its accompanying pamphlet were withdrawn and, so far as I am aware, no one ever attempted a rebuttal of my monograph. But currently "A Statement" is being resurrected through a recent issue of **Concordia Historical Institute Quarterly** (November, 1970) and a "Newsletter" (No. 15, February 17, 1971) as a historic landmark in the conflict between a "legalistic and an evangelical direction" for the Missouri Synod. This attempt to memorialize a position of twenty-five years ago, that ignorantly (I assume) ran afoul of many basic rules of Greek syntax, as an important step in freeing Missouri from "legalism" to an "evangelical" approach to Scripture (supposedly based on all the latest scholarly methods of research) invites us to take stock of the situation at present in regard to where the battle-line is being drawn currently.

Situation Today

Today the situation has changed tremendously—in fact, almost inconceivably. Twenty-five years ago proponents of each party, judging from their published statements, agreed to the traditional Lutheran theology as expressed in the Brief Statement—particularly on the inerrant Word of Scripture, or the historicity of the entire Bible. The battle-line was drawn primarily over the question of fellowship with Lutherans in other denominations who seemed to some to be close enough in doctrine and practice so that altar and pulpit fellowship was possible in the near future on the basis of Scriptural unity. Today the situation is quite different. Only after personal conversation and correspondence with some of my Christian friends and brothers in Christ could I believe that the current battle-line had changed so considerably. Some no longer feel it necessary to accept, for example, as historical fact the appearance of the Holy Spirit in the form of a dove and the voice of God at the baptism of Jesus—these embellishments, they say, may have been later additions by the evangelists as mere literary figures. Others find no objection in taking the account of the Virgin birth as merely figurative language—adding that such an interpretation "would make the miracle more wondrous."

If the current situation is the result of the "evangelical direction" begun by the Chicago forty-four, let us not memorialize an interpretation of Scripture that then was found so wanting in scientific exegesis and now has progressed so far along rationalistic lines. On the basis of literary figure instead of historical accuracy, we would not know how to interpret Scripture, nor could we begin to draw the line between fact and myth in the Bible, either for ourselves or for any Christian souls under our care (although we have had thirty years experience in similar attempts with the dialogues of Plato). From our observation, spanning almost twenty-five years, at a church-related college of a Protestant denomination, we realize all too well that a rationalistic approach to the Bible (currently erroneously equated with an "evangelical direction") soon—rather, very rapidly—leads to accepting as historical fact in the second article only the phrase: "suffered under Pontius Pilate, was crucified, and was buried"—the rest becomes "myth" or "literary figure." Since the battle-line currently is no longer a skirmish with the rear-guard, but currently is a frontal attack on the central position of Biblical Christianity, we must take inventory of the situation today and also look ahead to the immediate future.

Prospects for the Future

Assuming that we all are humble Christians who are willing to submit our pet human theories (even though derived and copied from some of the "leading" theological seminaries) to the guidance and direction of the Holy Spirit through a scholarly and scientific study of the original texts, the prospects for the immediate future should be clearly and candidly appraised. We must stop at once all engaging in personalities and emotional attacks. (I suspect that difference in personalities played no small part in the conflict already twenty-five years ago.) Instead of bombasting on another either with emotional frenzy or with sweeping generalities that lack scholarly support, let us begin to discuss some key moot questions calmly, scholarly, and—most important—prayerfully, with supreme confidence that the Holy Spirit will lead us to see divine truth as revealed in the Holy Scriptures.

The battle concerning Isaiah 7:14, for example, currently is being waged on the basis of generalities. One side claims that **almah** occurs here and elsewhere in the Bible to describe young women who are clearly not virgins. Others retort that no one ever has cited a passage in which **almah** does not specifically refer to a virgin. Let us cease such generalities. There are only approximately seven or eight occurrences of **almah** in the Hebrew Old Testament. It should not be difficult, therefore, to present a scholarly study that will examine carefully and prayerfully each of these instances of **almah** and will come to a conclusion acceptable to open-minded readers.

Another key question is the immortality of the soul. Several contemporary writers in our circles have proposed the thesis that "the traditional division of man into body and soul is not possible Biblically any more than it is medically." This generalization claimed to be based on "recent studies." After all our attempts to procure these "studies" (with full "exegesis" of Scriptural passages) failed, we became aware that the root study from which "progressives" in our circles were deriving their theories was a paper, later published in book form, by Professor Oscar Cullmann. Since in his Preface he invited a scholarly exegetical refutation on his thesis, we have prayerfully obliged. The results, according to present plans, will appear in the October issue of **Concordia Theological Monthly** under the title: "Immortality and Resurrection–A Reply to Oscar Cullmann." It contains no name-calling or sweeping generalizations that lack scholarly support. We trust it will serve as a pattern for future studies by others on similar current moot points. We hope it at least will help to clear up some of the present doubt on a traditionally basic tenet of Christian belief. (A few years ago one of the vice-presidents of our synod in preaching a funeral sermon glaringly omitted any reference to the soul of the departed being with Christ in heaven; he merely referred to "jewels in his/her crown" at some time in the distant future.)

Twenty-five years ago our attempt to correct the misuse and misunderstanding of basic principles of Greek grammar apparently fell on many deaf ears. Both factions had preconceived notions, which they attempted merely to bolster by exegesis or, if necessary, by "eisegesis." Many were not willing to correct their "eisegesis" and thus to alter their preconceptions. We pray that our present study on the immorality of the soul as taught in Scripture may find a more open reception. Point out any mistakes and erroneous deductions–we make no claim to divine inspiration–but do so on the basis of scholarly exegesis. Try not to approach this basic question or others with preconceived notions. Be willing to let the Holy Spirit guide both groups in all matters mooted today. Let us not repeat the mistake of twenty-five years ago. Christ, the personal Savior of each of us has promised to lead us "into all truth" (John 16:13). Take Him at His Word. Prayerfully and humbly "fight the good fight of faith" (I Timothy 6:12).

After this item appeared in **CN,** the article, "Immortality and Resurrection," was returned to the author, although it had been accepted previously by **CTM** and was scheduled for publication in a forthcoming issue of **CTM**. It later appeared in **Concordia Journal**.

Why I Accepted a Call to Concordia Seminary

Recently under the guidance of the Holy Spirit I made what was virtually one of the easiest decisions of my life. The choice was between a Distinguished Service Professorship with tenure at a sizable salary and an Associate Professorship with a two-year term at a marked reduction in remuneration.

(Incidentally, the implications of *Missouri In Perspective*—that I was "bribed" to accept, or "rewarded" for accepting, by an advance in salary and rank, and that I was "screened" previously concerning my opinion on Resolution 3-09 so that any function on an important committee appears to be "rigged"—are not only directly contrary to the facts, but also scurrilous and libelous, casting such aspersions on my integrity that the impression erroneously and stupidly given is tantamount to professional suicide in scholarly circles. The facts are: Neither in my interview nor at any other time was I asked any question regarding my attitude on Resolution 3-09. My rank was not and has not been changed, nor has my remuneration been altered. I received only one letter concerning pecuniary recompense, and that letter arrived more than two weeks after I accepted the Call.)

But, to return to the theme, "Why I Accepted a Call to Concordia Seminary," the basis for my decision may be summarized in one word—OPPORTUNITY. Over against any material advantages of professional standing, security of tenure and pecuniary remuneration, stood the OPPORTUNITY to work daily with the Word of God and assist more directly in the training at Concordia Seminary of future missionaries, pastors, teachers, and other servants of the Word and Sacrament. The Call to such service so clearly illuminated the ramifications involved in the choice that my decision was virtually one of the easiest of my life. It was no doubt an easier decision than that of many of my colleagues who must decide whether their service is needed more at Concordia Seminary or in their present position either as a pastor of a congregation or as a teacher in one of our sister institutions.

The OPPORTUNITY to serve at Concordia Seminary, furthermore, is particularly challenging at the present time in view of the current crisis in the Missouri Synod. It is now that our church needs servants to assist in the rebuilding process at Concordia Seminary. It is now that our Lord is calling on the resources within our synod—both, resources being used currently in other "arms" of the church as well as latent resources previously prepared for more direct service in His kindgom—to come forth and assist the seminary which God has blessed so bountifully for one hundred and thirty-five years. Not only is Concordia Seminary "likely to survive" (as acknowledged by a news reporter not known for any sympathy to our cause), Concordia Seminary *has* survived and *will* survive what historians probably will term the crisis in her history—in spite of unfriendly press reports and attempts by "fellow" Lutherans at "discrediting" the institution—simply because God both is calling servants with certain God-given talents out of the "woodwork" of the church to assist in the rebuilding process at Concordia Seminary, and He is blessing their endeavors, as it has become very evident and clear to one who has witnessed and participated in the activities at Concordia Seminary during the spring quarter and the June session of the summer school.

There is an additional OPPORTUNITY in my positive decision regarding the Call to teach at Concordia Seminary. I refer to my thirty-five years of experience as a graduate student and as an instructor in the Greek and Latin classics and the OPPORTUNITY of applying this experience to the current basic problem confronting our synod, other Lutheran church-bodies and in reality confronting all branches of Christianity—the problem of the reliability of Scripture. I have studied in detail the skeptical approach in classical philology during the eighteenth and nineteenth centuries to the "Homeric Question" and to the genuiness of the Platonic dialogues. Avoiding the details, I may summarize the history of classical scholarship by noting that the extremely skeptical attitude of the two previous centuries has proved to be subjective, exaggerated and in many cases not even scholarly or scientific. The pendulum in classical research has swung back—that is, away from source-hypothesis in Homer and away from the rejection of the genuineness of the majority of Plato's dialogues. So the current skeptical attitude toward much of the New Testament (and of the Old Testament) is not a new discovery or a new problem—although it seems to be new and the "in-thing" to some of the past professors from Concordia Seminary. I see, in brief, my Call to Concordia Seminary as an OPPORTUNITY to demonstrate in a small way that the traditional position (that is, the position generally held before the onslaught of modern "scholarship") is based on genuine scholarship rather than on any emotional premise of "Wir bleiben beim Alten."

Allow me to mention what I consider another OPPORTUNITY in accepting the Call to Concordia Seminary. I refer to the possibility—and I pray it will become a reality—of discussing the issues (avoiding the political procedures and the personality clashes) with my fellow Christians at Seminex and in ELIM, many of whom were personal friends of mine during our days at the seminary, and with whom I currently remain on sincerely friendly terms. I am bold enough to pray and hope (to convert a popular phrase to the order of importance) that we will have and will take the OPPORTUNITY of discussing the issues calmly, candidly and humbly with a view to delineate between apparent disagreements and actual divergence in theology, and between acceptable variance and divisive difference in doctrine, if such exists, always under the tutelage of God's Holy inspired inerrant Word.

I have mentioned the great OPPORTUNITIES in serving at Concordia Seminary. I do so in all humility, for the other side of the same coin involves equally large RESPONSIBILITIES on the shoulders of the faculty and administration of Concordia Seminary in the current process of rebuilding. My contemplation of the huge RESPONSIBILITIES coupled with the awareness of my own deficiencies caused me to pause, to hesitate, and to consider in all honesty the declining of the Call—in spite of the tremendous OPPORTUNITIES. I found the antidote to my fear and trepidation in the Scriptural comfort and assurance that we at Concordia Seminary will be mere agents of our Heavenly Father. God, Who so loved the world that He sent His only begotten Son as our Redeemer (John 3:16), also has promised through Jesus to send us His Holy Spirit, Who will guide us into all truth (John 16:13). My fears of the tremendous RESPONSIBILITIES were soon allayed by the promises of God's Word. Since God bestows on us the guidance of the Spirit, my fear and trepidation soon changed to courage and confidence. I readily accepted, thanking Him for the OPPORTUNITIES, confidently accepting His guidance in meeting the RESPONSIBILITIES, humbly giving all credit and glory to Him in the rebuilding of Concordia Seminary.

I request and urge, in conclusion, the prayers of the pastors, teachers and lay members of our church, and I repeat the concluding paragraphs from my letter of acceptance, dated Pentecost Sunday, June 2, 1974:

> Throughout my career as teacher and scholar I have prefaced my work each day with the prayer

***Call . . .* Continued**

that the Holy Spirit somehow may bless my endeavors to the glory of our Savior and the benefit of His Church. I am most grateful, therefore, for the opportunity to labor more directly in the preparation of ministers of the Gospel during the remaining years of my career.

May Christ bestow upon me and all of our colleagues a generous portion of His Holy Spirit, as on the original Pentecost, to guide us as teachers and scholars, and may our Lord grant us health to continue for many years in service to His Kingdom.

Soli Deo Gloria!

Christian Courage (Acts 7:54–8:3)

Introduction

Certain questions concerning human character have been, and will continue to be, debated. Is environment or heredity more important in determining character? Can virtue be taught? Do individual leaders guide the course of history, or do trends in history influence the leaders? Challenging as such questions may be, the text suggested for our homily this morning presents a study in one aspect of character—*Christian Courage*—and clearly indicates the source of this virtue.

The Setting

The setting occurs within a few years after Jesus' ascension—probably around A.D. 32, certainly not later than A.D. 35. Stephen, chosen as one of the seven to care for the widows of the Jerusalem church, also began debating in a synagogue, possibly the same one attended by Paul, since it was frequented by men of Cilicia.

Stephen's courage is clear from the contents of his speech, in which he boldly reprimands Judaism for its excessive emphasis on Jerusalem and the temple—the pride of Jewish civic and spiritual life. Stephen's speech, as pointed out by Dr. Martin Scharlemann in his monograph *Stephen: A Singular Saint,* should be read against the backdrop of the running argument between Judea and Samaria. It took courage for Stephen to treat a topic not too popular with the populace in Jerusalem. But Stephen's courage is most evident in his charges against his opponents immediately preceding our text:

> How stubborn you are and pagan at heart and deaf to the truth! You're always opposing the Holy Spirit. Your fathers did it, and so do you! Was there ever a prophet your fathers didn't persecute? They killed those who announced, "The Righteous One will come!" and now you betrayed and murdered Him. Angels were ordered to give you the Law, but you didn't keep it!

Reaction

Stephen's courage is evident also when his hearers react to his speech. His bold accusations were too much for them. They were not able to restrain themselves without immediate reaction. According to the King James Version and the Revised Standard Version, it may not appear certain whether Stephen had the opportunity to finish his address. Both versions read "When they heard these things," as if the reaction of the opponents took place after the conclusion of the speech, which does not seem to arrive at a natural finish. The present participle in the Greek text (*akouontes*), however, indicates that Stephen was not finished, since the present participle, as a rule, implies the same tense as the main verb, or verbs, which in our text are imperfect indicative. The implication is that the opponents "got furious" and "began to grind their teeth at him" "while they were still listening" to his accusations. They did not, apparently, allow Stephen to finish before reacting.

Commentators debate whether the incident recorded in our text was a legal trial or a mob-murder. One conclusion, that the text seems to bear out, is that what began as a legal trial ended as a furious attack by an enraged mob. Stephen's vision of "the heavens opened and the Son of Man standing at God's right hand"—note Jesus is standing in our text, as if ready to welcome Stephen to his heavenly home—this vision infuriated the opponents and kindled the mob spirit.

We read:

> They yelled at the top of their voices, held their ears shut, and all together rushed at him. They threw him out of the city and started to stone him (vv. 57-58; another imperfect tense overlooked by the King James translators and others).

This is hardly the scene of an orderly legal trial, but rather one of an infuriated mob. Confronted by the reaction of the mob, Stephen manifests *Christian Courage*, rather than fear. He prays—first for himself and then for others. It is natural for a person in time of danger to pray for himself—to utter a phrase such as, "God, help me," or "Lord, save me." But it is unnatural for human nature to pray as Stephen does: "Lord Jesus, receive my spirit." His prayer does not stem from fear, but from courage. His prayer is an affirmation of his trust. Because of his trust he is able to maintain his courage while, as the text says, "they kept throwing stones at him" (another imperfect tense missed by some translators). Stephen is courageous because of his confidence that, whatever happens, Christ is adequate for any emergency.

The second part of Stephen's prayer—his prayer for others—is also unusual for human nature. It is natural in the face of imminent death—for by this time many stones had crushed his body violently, but had not crushed his spirit—it is natural under such circumstances for a person to pray for others—for his loved ones, his spouse, his children, his friends. But Stephen prayed for his attackers—a nonnatural act, similar to the prayer of his supernatural Savior.

Source of Stephen's Courage

Prayer throws light on a person's nature and character. When "the chips are down," it is difficult to maintain a pretense. In the face of danger or death, a person's true character tends to become apparent. Stephen's prayer, while the stones were dashing upon him, reveals his *Christian Courage* and lack of fear. His final words, requesting forgiveness for his attackers, show the confidence, trust, and courage in his heart.

Stephen's courage is not a temporary attempt to put on a good front. His courage is the result of an attribute deeply engrained in his character. The source of Stephen's courage is that he was "full of the Holy Spirit" (v. 55). That the influence of the Holy Spirit was not a passing fancy, but a condition of long-standing with Stephen, is clear from the same reference to Stephen when he was chosen as one of the seven in Acts 6:5. Stephen is mentioned first, and to his name alone is added the phrase "a man full of faith and of the Holy Spirit." Furthermore, our text indicates that the influence of the Holy Spirit in Stephen's life was of long-standing by the use of *hyparchon*—a verb usually implying a more permanent condition than the simpler participle of the verb "to be" (*on*). That is, "being full of the Holy Spirit" was a quality not merely suddenly come upon him, but one which he had possessed for some time—as Scripture teaches, a gift, a divine gift which Christians receive through Word and Sacraments. It was this divine gift which was the source of Stephen's *Christian Courage*.

Saul

Novels and dramas present antagonists in contrast to their protagonists. At times it may be a villain versus a hero. In western movies the "good guys" ride white horses and wear white hats, while the "bad guys" have black horses and black hats. In our text Saul, who would be wearing a black hat and riding on a black horse, makes his first appearance in Acts. His appearance illustrates the three steps to evil: 1) as a silent witness (7:58); 2) as a consenting spectator (8:1); and 3) as an active participant (8:3). Saul, the persecutor of the church, is as sincere as Stephen, the promoter of the church. What later caused Saul, the persecutor, to become Paul, a promoter of Christ? Paul's "change-over" (technically, his "conversion") had the same source as Stephen's courage—the influence of the Holy Spirit. It took the supernatural, the divine gift of the Holy Spirit, to change Paul's attitude and understanding from what he had learned from Gamaliel—particularly in two points: 1) that Deity actually died on the cross; and 2) that the Law, given to a select people, was not a cause for boasting and pride, but explicitly resulted in a curse to all people, for no one could fulfill its demands—"no one is righteous . . . all have turned away and one and all have become worthless" (Rom. 3:10-12). What else can account for the one hundred eighty degree reversal in Paul, except divine revelation (Gal. 1:12)—not necessarily all at once, but as his heart and mind were enlightened by the Holy Spirit!

Conclusion

The lesson or application is almost too obvious to dwell on. We are "good guys"—thanks to God's grace, to Christ's suffering, death, and resurrection, and to the gift of the Holy Spirit through Word and Sacraments. Our "conversion" in the sense of justification is complete (Greek perfect tense). Our "change-over" in the sense of being promoters of God's kingdom through a sanctified life is one of progress (Greek imperfect tense). The source of our progress in service is the same as that of Stephen and Paul. We are here for serious study of God's Word, exegetically, systematically, historically, and practically. Through serious, humble, and diligent contact with His Word and Sacraments, God will use us as His agents, as promoters of His kingdom, and will endow us also with *Christian Courage*. God grant it in Jesus' name. Amen.

Martin H. Scharlemann, Septuagenarian

December 28, 1980 marked the seventieth anniversary of the birth of Concordia Seminary's Graduate Professor of Exegetical Theology. To fail to commemorate this anniversary would be remiss of the Biblical injunction: "Remember your leaders, those who spoke to you the word of God" (Heb. 13:7).

Scholar and theologian are only two of the attributes descriptive of the productive career of Professor Scharlemann. Indicative of his scholarship are his two earned doctorates — one at Washington University (Ph.D., 1938) shortly after his graduation from the seminary; the other at Union Theological Seminary (Th.D., 1964). The former degree entailed a doctor's dissertation on the Greek drama, which the advisor on more than one occasion in the presence of the undersigned rated as the best ever presented to the department of Classics at the university. Also pertinent to the quality of his scholarship is his election to the honorary society of Phi Beta Kappa as a doctoral graduate — a rare distinction indeed.

Enumerating only some of the other highlights of Professor Scharlemann's illustrious career, we should mention his being: ecumenical guest at the Pontifical Biblical Institute in Rome (1966); guest or visiting professor at Waldensian Seminary in Rome (1966), Nairobi University in Kenya, Africa (1972-73), Martin Luther Seminary in Adelaide, Australia (1973), Concordia Seminary in Nagercoil, India (1973); the author of numerous volumes and articles, particularly of *Stephen: A Singular Saint,* published by the Pontifical Biblical Institute in Rome (1968); member of various professional societies, including the prestigious international *Studiorum Novi Testamenti Societas,* in which membership is by election only on the basis of scholarly production.

The theologian, of course, is intertwined with the scholar in almost all of the accomplishments listed above. The theologian and pastor, however, come to the foreground especially in Professor Scharlemann's career as chaplain in the United States Air Force (1941-52, active duty; 1952-70, reserve duty) — in which post he rose to the rank of Brigadier General — and as interim pastor of the Waldensian Church in Cerignola, Italy (1944-45), preaching in Italian after using an interpreter for only a few weeks.

Theologian and scholar have been the hallmarks of Professor Scharlemann's career at Concordia (since 1952; acting president, 1974), where he is readily available to students in his office and at coffee breaks, directs most of the doctoral dissertations in New Testament, and still teaches a complete load of classes as a septuagenarian.

It is proper that the CONCORDIA JOURNAL observe Martin Scharlemann's seventieth birthday anniversary, for he was instrumental in organizing and formulating the present periodical, has written numerous theological and scholarly articles and editorials for our publication, and has served on the editorial committee continuously until a few months ago.

For the past, present, and future service of Professor Martin H. Scharlemann, scholar and theologian, we are grateful to our gracious and merciful God, and we wish him many happy returns of his birthday anniversary.

Roy Arthur Suelflow

1918-1981

Our gracious heavenly Father, the Creator and Giver of life, granted to Professor Roy A. Suelflow sixty-two years of earthly life in the Church Militant before calling him suddenly to the Church Triumphant on February 2, 1981. As missionary, historian, and professor, Dr. Suelflow faithfully served his Lord particularly in the Far East and in the United States, as well as throughout the globe as a member of the Board for Missions.

Born in Germantown, Wisconsin to A. Henry and Selma Kressin Suelflow on March 24, 1918, Professor Suelflow graduated from Concordia College in Milwaukee (1939) and Concordia Seminary in St. Louis (1944). His intellectual gifts and attainments are evident in the unusual accomplishment of two earned doctorates—the Th.D. degree at Concordia Seminary, St. Louis (1946; the first person to earn this degree at his alma mater) and the Ph.D. in Chinese History and Culture at the University of Wisconsin-Madison (1971).

As a classmate of the undersigned Roy exhibited an intense interest in taking to heart the Great Commission. Putting this desire into practice he spent the first fifteen years of his ministry as a missionary in the Orient—China (1946-1949), Japan (1949-1952), Taiwan (1952-1960). Dr. Suelflow was Instructor at the Tokyo Bible School, Director of the Institute of Japanese Language in Tokyo, and President of Concordia Seminary, Chia Yi, Taiwan, where he also taught exegetical theology in the Chinese language. As a linguist Professor Suelflow proclaimed the Gospel of Christ in four languages: Japanese, Chinese, German, and English.

As a result of international problems in the Far East, Dr. Suelflow returned to the States in 1960 and continued his career as professor, continuously retaining his interest in and service to foreign missions. He served on the faculties of his two alma maters—at Concordia College in Milwaukee as Chairman of the Department of Theology and Social Studies (1960-1974), and at Concordia Seminary in St. Louis as Professor of Historical Theology (1974-1981), Director of the World Mission Institute (1974-1978), and Mission Education Consultant (1978-1981).

Throughout his career Roy's pen produced numerous articles and books concerning missions and historical theology. These works include: *A Plan for Survival, Walking with Wise Men, The Chronicle of Rev. L. F. E. Krause, Christian Churches in Recent Times, Correspondence of C. F. W. Walther*. Scheduled for publication this summer is another volume by Roy, *Selected Letters of C. F. W. Walther*. As associate editor of the *Concordia Historical Institute Quarterly*, Roy's historical knowledge and sincere commitment to the church were of invaluable aid.

Colleagues at Concordia and associates in foreign missions are grateful to God for the contributions to the growth of the church accomplished by the Holy Spirit through the service of Roy Arthur Suelflow as missionary, historian, and professor. *Soli Deo Gloria!*

Notes on the Greek Article

Students of the Greek New Testament frequently find the definite article—its presence and absence—confusing. John 1:1, for example, reads in a number of translations (the New King James and the New International Version, for instance) as follows: "In the beginning was the Word, and the Word was with God, and the Word was God." A comparison with the Greek text, however, reveals three distinct differences: 1) there is no article before "beginning"; 2) Greek has "with the God"; 3) the concluding clause seems to say "and God was the Word." Since reliable exegesis depends on a correct understanding of the definite article in Greek (which has no separate indefinite article), a summary of its use should prove helpful, and even necessary, to the serious student of the original language.

Seven Simple Principles

We begin with seven simple principles—some of which will clarify the apparent discrepancies between the English and Greek text of John 1:1.

1. *Common prepositional phrases* tend to omit the article in Greek, which should be supplied in the English translation. Thus in John 1:1 the absent article in the opening phrase must be supplied in English: "In the beginning...."

2. The Greek article tends to be present with *proper nouns* and *names of well-known people*, and is usually omitted in English. So in the second part of John 1:1 we read: "and the Word was with God" (not "with the God"). To illustrate this rule facetiously, I always told my students that any person in class by the name of "John" would be called in Greek "the John."

3. To denote *collective groups* the Greek article is present but is not translated in English; *hoi anthropoi*, for example, may mean "men," "people," "human beings," or "mankind."

4. *Abstract nouns* usually have the article in Greek, but the article is omitted in English. Note *he agape* for "love" in 1 Corinthians 13:4–14:1.

5. *Possessive pronouns and adjectives* ordinarily take an untranslated article. "In our hearts" in Greek is *en tais hemeterais kardiais* (possessive adjective), and "his book" translates *to biblion autou* (possessive pronoun). The presence or absence of a definite article determines a difference in meaning. If a person owns one house, he would refer to it with the article in Greek as *ho oikos mou* ("my house"). A wealthy individual who possesses several homes, however, would speak of one of them as *oikos mou* ("a house of mine") without the article.

The Samaritan woman at the well, for instance, had five husbands; so Jesus refers to her present mate (without the article) as *sou aner* ("a husband of yours" and not, as it is usually rendered, "your husband") in John 4:18. But in the institution of the Lord's Supper our Savior says (Matthew 26:26): "...my body" (*to soma mou*) with the article because Jesus had only one body.

6. The Greek *demonstrative pronouns* for "this" or "that" (plural, "these" or "those") *always demand the presence of the article*. In Greek "this disciple" is *houtos ho mathetes* and "that village" becomes *ekeine he kome*. The absence of an article with a demonstrative pronoun indicates a slightly different sentence structure. At the conclusion of the pericope about the wedding at Cana (John 2:11) we read: *Tauten epoiesen archen ton semeion ho Iesous*. The

frequent rendering, "This beginning of signs Jesus did," technically is incorrect because of the absence of the article with the demonstrative pronoun. A more correct translation, although with little change in meaning, would be: "This Jesus did as a beginning of signs."

Another example of a lack of the article with a demonstrative pronoun, however, does involve a definite change in meaning with ramifications concerning the historical accuracy of Luke (2:2). The usual rendering, "This census first took place while Quirinius was governing Syria," cannot be correct since there is no article with "this." Also it exposes Luke to a historical error, as Quirinius ruled Syria in A.D. 6-9. Some attempt to defend Luke by assuming that Quirinius had a previous term in office in 6-4 B.C.—for which there is no definite historical evidence.

A more viable explanation and solution to the problem is to note the absence of the article with the demonstrative pronoun and to translate accordingly: "This took place as a census prior to Quirinius being governor of Syria"—taking *prote* ("first") as having comparative force ("prior") as it does in John 20:4,8, and the phrase "Quirinius being governor" as genitive of comparison instead of genitive absolute. The NET (New Evangelical Translation) is the only version which suggests this rendering, albeit in a footnote, which has also been proposed by Professor F. F. Bruce.

7. There are *two basic uses of the nominative case*: *subject and predicate nominative* (besides an occasional vocative use). In a sentence as John 1:1: *kai theos en ho logos*, cited above in the initial paragraph, the proper translation is "and the Word was God," not "and God was the Word," as the Greek word order would seem to indicate, since *the article determines the subject of the sentence* and the vocable without the article becomes the predicate nominative. Also according to "Colwell's Rule," because the predicate nominative precedes the verb (instead of following it) *theos* is to be rendered "God" and not "a god" (in spite of the claim of Jehovah's Witnesses)—see John 1:49: "you are the King [not a King] of Israel"; John 9:5: "I am the light [not a light] of the world"; John 19:21: "I am the King [not a King] of the Jews."

If both the subject and the predicate nominate, however, have the article, the two terms are to be considered as interchangeable or reciprocal. Thus if John 1:1 were: *kai ho theos en ho logos*, the implication would be that "the Word" and "God" identify the same person and that they are not two separate persons—together with the Holy Spirit comprising the Trinity. That is, such a sentence would signify personal identity of the Word with God the Father, while the New Testament text in John 1:1 attributes to the Word the divine nature of the Father.

Additional Principles

8. The article is used *with adjectives to form a noun* of the corresponding gender. Thus *hoi hagioi* means "the holy men," namely, "the saints." A similar usage of the article with an adjective to denote a substantive occurs also in English: "The good die young" indicates "The good men [or people] die young."

9. The article is used also *with prepositional phrases to form a noun* of the corresponding gender: *hoi en Joudaia* refers to "those [people] in Judaea." Some hold that also an *article with an adverb* forms a noun, as in *apo tou nun*, which denotes "from the present time" or "henceforth." But this construction rather seems to be an abbreviation for *apo tou nun chronou*, which is translated "from the present time"—the article indicting an original, but absent, noun for "time." Similarly in John 1:29 and 35 *te epaurion* is an abbreviation for *te epaurion hemera*, "the following day"—the noun for "day" being absent.

10. An *article between a noun and its modifying adjective shows emphasis*. Jesus declares in John 10:11,14: *Ego eimi ho poimen ho kalos*—which is not the same as: *Ego eimi ho kalos poimen*, the normal construction of article, adjective, noun. The latter word order should be rendered: "I am the good shepherd," as translated in NKJ and NIV and by others. But this translation misses the emphatic position of the adjective "good" in the Greek text. Any order of words in a Greek sentence which varies from the normal construction implies some emphasis—in spite of the view of Professor James Voelz in his *Fundamental Greek Grammar* (p. 43). A more correct rendition of Jesus' declaration would be: "I am the shepherd, the good one" or "I am the shepherd who is good." We agree with Maximilian Zerwick, S. J., who states that "an adjective in predicate use is sometimes equivalent to a relative clause of the type which in English is preceded by a comma" (*Biblical Greek*, p. 60, par. 187). The translation in NET comes the closest to showing the emphasis implied in the Greek text: "I am the Good Shepherd."

11. Participles occur either adjectivally (with the article) or adverbially (without the article). The adverbial use may be rendered in English as a participle (ending in "-ing"), although the fuller implication may be expanded into: 1) a temporal clause ("when"); 2) a causal clause ("since" or "because"); 3) a concessive clause ("although"); or 4) a conditional clause ("if"). It is the adjectival use which concerns the present paper—the participle with an article. Such a participle at times may be translated as a noun—for example, *ho speiron* is "the sower." Usually, however, a *participle with an article is best rendered by a relative clause*. Thus *makarioi hoi zetountes ton theon* means "blessed are those [or the ones] who seek God." Also, *ho speiron* (above) could just as well be rendered: "the one who sows." The use of the article with participles is similar to the article in the previous paragraph (no. 10)—which also could be translated in English by a relative clause: "the shepherd who is good."

12. The use of *one article before two or more nouns indicates a certain unity*, while the repetition of the article distinguishes two or more coordinated terms. In 1 Thessalonians 1:7 Paul praises the readers that they have become a model for all who believe *en te Makedonia kai en te Achaia* ("in Macedonia and in Achaia"), distinguishing the two Roman provinces. In the following verse, however, Paul gives the reason—for the word of the Lord has been spread by them not only *en te Makedonia kai Achaia* ("in Macedonia and Achaia"), but in every place their faithfulness to God has become known—grouping here the two provinces together as opposed to everywhere else.

The joining under one article the three regions (Antioch, Syria, Cilicia) to which the letter from the council of Jerusalem was addressed perhaps was meant to discourage a wider dissemination of its contents (Acts 15:23). The single article in Philippians 1:19 indicates that in Paul's mind the prayers of the believers and the help of the Spirit of Jesus Christ were intimately connected—possibly even regarding the entreaties of the faithful as being the help of the Holy Spirit.

According to the principle of one article with two or more nouns indicating unity, it is not farfetched to see an expression of the deity of Christ in a number of passages—"the kingdom *tou Christou kai theou*" (Ephesians 5:5); "*awaiting the coming of the glory tou megalou theou kai soteros Jesou Christou*" (Titus 2:13); see also 2 Peter 1:1,11; 2:20; 3:18. Although such passages are not final proofs, since the single articles could be explained as a conjunction in the author's mind of the ideas expressed, we may safely claim that these examples of a single article seem to corroborate the deity of Christ.

Two more passages merit some comments. On the basis of Acts 1:8 the single article with Judea and Samaria indicates a threefold division of the book, although four places are mentioned: Jerusalem, Judea, Samaria, the end(s) of the earth (an expression probably referring to

Rome). An acceptable outline of Acts, then, could be: I. Gospel in Jerusalem (chapters 1-7); II. Gospel in Judea and Samaria (chapters 8-12); III. Gospel to the end of the earth (chapters 13-28). In the English translation the prepositions likewise indicate a threefold division: "*in* Jerusalem, and *in* all Judea and Samaria, and *to* the end(s) of the earth" (NKJ and NIV, see also NET). A sixfold outline of Acts is also defensible on the basis of six summarizing statements: 6:7; 9:31; 12:24; 16:5; 19:20; 28:31. A twofold outline is also possible: I. Petrine section (chapters 1-12); II. Pauline section (chapters 13-28). All three outlines are legitimate and are based on internal evidence, and together they show the orderly arrangement of the document and the careful planning of the author.

The principle that one article before two or more nouns indicates a certain unity is extremely important in Ephesians 4:11. We refer particularly to the last phrase: *tous de poimenas kai didaskalous*—one article with two nouns. Four offices are mentioned in the verse, not five. As described in the note in the *Concordia Self-Study Bible*, each of the four offices (not five) had a separate function and purpose in the early church—the apostles, the prophets, the evangelists, and those who served as pastors and teachers. *CSSB* states correctly concerning the fourth office:

> Because of the Greek grammatical construction (one article with two nouns; also, the word "some" introduces both words together), it is clear that these two nouns describe one office. Those who have pastoral care for God's people (the image is that of shepherding) will naturally provide "food" from the Scriptures (teaching). They will be especially gifted as teachers (cf. 1 Ti 3:2).

All—yes all—the translations are true to the Greek text in listing *four* offices. Until a few years ago the nomenclature in *The Lutheran Annual* did not list parochial school *teachers*, as well as *pastors*, as "Ministers of Religion" (with a distinction between "ordained" and "commissioned"). Should we rethink our terminology, which to some appears unclear and misleading?

13. In English the article with an adjective may be used as a noun ("The good die young"; see item 9 above) and an infinitive may be employed as a noun ("To err is human"). In Greek *an article may be used with an infinitive, called an articular infinitive.* Such a construction is employed in Greek *as a neuter verbal noun, equal to the English gerund.* Only the neuter singular article appears, in all of its cases (nominative, genitive, dative, accusative), which really serves to decline the infinitive. Note that the Greek articular infinitive, as the English gerund, is a *verbal noun* ending in "ing," to be distinguished from a participle, which is a *verbal adjective* ending in "ing," and as an adjective agrees in gender, number, and case with a noun, expressed or implied. As a verbal noun the Greek articular infinitive does not demand agreement with a noun in gender, number, and case, but is similar to other nouns in functioning as subject, direct object, indirect object, after prepositions, etc. The subject of an articular infinitive, if it appears at all, is in the accusative case (as is the subject of a simple infinitive in Greek).

Many students at first have problems in translating an articular infinitive. But a method of approaching this construction which I employed in the classroom has proved helpful. Ease in dealing with the articular infinitive is necessary, because this construction appears frequently in the New Testament. So let me try my hand at instructing through the printed page, beginning with some simple examples.

agathon to eu graphein. First, translate the infinitive literally; *graphein* means "to write." Second, combine the article with the infinitive; *to graphein* is "writing" (a gerund or verbal noun in English). Adding *eu* ("well"), we have "writing well." Since there is no verb, we must supply the verb "to be" and we have "writing well is." Then adding *agathon* (a neuter form), we translate "writing well is a good thing."

to manthanein ginometha sophoi. First, the infinitive literally is "to learn." Second, add the article *to* (dative of means) to the infinitive; *to manthanein* is "by learning." The last two words mean "we become wise" and we render the entire sentence: "by learning we become wise."

The third example adds two more elements (or two more steps): 1) a preposition before the articular infinitive; 2) an accusative as the subject of the articular infinitive. *meta to grapsai hemas tauten ten epistolen.* First, the infinitive (*grapsai*) literally means "to write." Second, adding the article (*to*), we have "writing" (a gerund or verbal noun). Third, with the preposition (*meta* or "after") we may translate "after writing." Fourth, the accusative *hemas* is the subject of the articular infinitive or gerund; in English the subject of a gerund is in the possessive case ("our"). So now we have "after our writing." Finally, add the direct object "this letter" and the full phrase is "after our writing this letter."

The following prepositions occur with the Greek articular infinitive: *meta* and accusative (*after* the action); *en* and dative (*during* the action); *pro* and genitive (*before* the action); *dia* and accusative (showing *cause* or *on account of*); *eis* or *pros* and accusative (showing *purpose* or *for the purpose of*).

One final example: *meta de to ton Joannen akousai en to desmoterio ta erga tou Christou.* First, the infinitive (*akousai*) literally is "to hear." Second, the article (*to*, third word) combined with the infinitive means "hearing." Third, adding the preposition *meta* ("after") we have "after hearing." Fourth, with the Greek subject of the articular infinitive in the accusative case (here between *to* and *akousai*) we translate so far "after John's hearing." Add the last two phrases—"in the prison" and "the deeds of Christ"—we render the Greek as "after John's hearing in the prison the deeds of Christ." By practicing these four steps, the articular infinitive, which equates the gerund or verbal noun in English, should gradually cause less and less trouble in reading the New Testament in the original language.

14. The *article with the Greek correlatives men/de emphasize contrast.* Basically *men* means "on the one hand" and *de* means "on the other hand." These two correlatives occur so frequently on many pages of Greek text that a literal translation becomes cumbersome. So when they appear with the Greek article, an abbreviated rendering is preferable. For example, *ho men...ho de* (literally "he on the one hand...he on the other hand") become "the one...the other." In the plural *hoi men...hoi de* (literally "they on the one hand...they on the other hand") are better rendered "some...others."

Also if *men* and *de* occur without the Greek article, the literal rendering is awkward and an abbreviation is preferable. For instance, "I on the one hand am a Roman, you on the other hand are a slave" is more suitably translated: "I am a Roman, but you are a slave"—that is, omit a translation of *men* and render *de* as "but" or "and."

At times there is no *men* in the first clause, but *de* appears in the second clause with the article. This construction marks a change of subject, and *ho de* would be "but he," while *hoi de* would become "but they." An example might be: "I called my brother, but he (*ho de*) did not hear."

15. The principle which apparently is least understood and least applied by translators, commentators, and theologians in general concerns the implications of *pas, pasa, pan with and without the Greek article* present with the noun. According to Maximilian Zerwick, S. J.

(*Biblical Greek*, p. 61, par. 188) the principle is illustrated in the Greek word for "law" (*nomos*). With *pas* in the attributive position and the noun having the article, *pas* denotes the thing or class taken as a whole. Thus *ho pas nomos* indicates "the law in its entirety." In the predicate position and the noun having the article *pas* means "all (the)...." So *pas ho nomos* refers to "the entire law" without exception of any precept. Without the article, however, *pas* denotes "every" or "all" in a distributive sense. *pas nomos* would imply "every kind of law" and the plural would be "all kinds of laws."

Since the article in Greek originally served as a demonstrative, its purpose is "to point out...to set apart from others, to identify as *this* or *these* and not simply "such" (op. cit., p. 53, par. 165). "The omission of the article shows that the speaker regards the person or thing not so much as this or that person or thing, but rather as *such* a person or thing, i.e. regards not the individual but rather its nature or quality" (op. cit., p. 55, par 171).

Likewise Bauer-Arndt-Gingrich-Danker distinguishes between *pas, pasa, pan* with the article (1c) and without the article (1b). With the article it means "the whole" or "all." For instance, "the whole herd" (Matthew 8:32); "the whole creation" (Mark 16:15). Without the article the translation is "every kind of" or "all sorts of." Examples are: "all kinds of sickness and all kinds of disease" (Matthew 4:23); "they are full of all kinds of uncleanness" (Matthew 23:27); "from every kind of nation" (Acts 2:5); "(evil) desire of every kind" (Romans 7:8); "every kind of sin" (1 Corinthians 6:18).

Professor Basil Gildersleeve in his *Syntax of Classical Greek* has the fullest discussion of *pas, pasa, pan* available, which he treats in thirteen pages of small print (vol. 2, pp. 304-316). Under the paragraph entitled "*pas* with Anarthrous Substantives" he writes: "With anarthrous [i.e. without an article] singulars *pas* means *every, every kind of*; with abstracts, it is often translated by *perfect, complete*; with anarthrous plurals, it means *all, all kinds of...*" (p. 312, par. 651). Then he lists numerous examples, one of which is: *stephanos hapas*, "a wreath of any kind" (Demosthenes, 22.75). The findings of Gildersleeve, the "dean" of classicists and grammarians, reveal that the implication of *pas* without the article is rooted in the Greek language already in the age of Classical Greece.

We began this section by affirming that the implication of the principle concerning *pas, pasa, pan* and a noun *without the article* is least understood and applied by translators, commentators, and theologians. To evaluate this statement we checked various translations in references to several passages which have *pas* and a noun *without the article*. The following table gives the results the concerning the correctness of the renditions:

	NKJV	NIV	NET	NASB
Matt. 4:23	yes	no	yes	yes
Matt. 5:11	yes	yes	yes	yes
Matt. 9:35	no	no	yes	yes
Matt. 10:1	yes	no	yes	yes
Luke 12:15	no	yes	yes	yes

Note the confusion that is apparent among the translators—except in the NASB and NET, which in our examples show an understanding and application of the principle under discussion. The NIV reveals the most confusion.

Also *A Grammatical Analysis of the Greek New Testament* by Max Zerwick and Mary Grosvenor has the correct notes concerning *pas* on the four passages cited above from Matthew.

What does all of this discussion mean? It is most important doctrinally, especially for commentators and theologians. Take, for instance, three of the above passages: Matthew 4:23; 9:35; 10:1, which speak of the healings performed by our Savior. That Jesus healed "every kind of sickness and disease" (NET and NASB) implies something vastly different from "every (all) sickness(es) and disease(s)" in the NIV. The renditions in the NIV would seem to bolster the position of charismatics, who could deduce that after Jesus left a town or locality no one was ill, for sickness shows a lack of faith—also today—as our Lord desires everyone to be well. I always told my Greek students that I would teach them no rule of syntax which does not have a doctrinal application. Here is another example—the distinction between *pas* with a noun with and without an article.

But wait! The application of the principle concerning *pas without the article* on two additional and important passages may not earn me "brownie points" among our theologians. Nevertheless, theology must be based on exegesis and not *vice versa*. So, here goes!

In 2 Timothy 3:16 we read: *pasa graphe....* There is no definite article. According to the principle being discussed the absence of the article reveals that inspiration belongs to Scripture *as such*. Or, without the article the phrase could be rendered: "Every kind of Scripture"—that is, historic, poetic, prophetic. The addition of an article would be needed to imply that all the existing Scripture was inspired. The NASB gives an alternate rendition in a note: "Every Scripture inspired by God is also profitable." Perhaps our theologians should reconsider this passage.

Another passage which merits some study is Romans 11:26, where Paul refers to *pasa Israel* as being saved. I was informed that Professor George Stoeckhardt deduced that this term could not refer to the Jewish people because not every Jew will be saved. But such a view would demand a definite article in the Greek text. Since the article is absent, the translation could be: "And so Israel as a whole (or, people from all Israel) will be saved."

Compare *pasa Ierosoluma* in Matthew 2:3. This phrase may be viewed as a hyperbole (exaggeration), since we can be sure that not every Israelite—not even all in Jerusalem—was troubled by the news of the birth of a baby. Just as when we read that "all went out to hear Jesus," certainly some were sick in bed, or had other things to do, on that day. The New Testament contains frequent figures of speech, including hyperbole. But we must first note the absence of the Greek article. So the passage may be rendered: "People from all over Jerusalem were troubled."

Likewise, the absence of the article in Romans 11:26 must be evaluated by our theologians in interpreting whether the reference is to Jewish persons or to the new Israelites, the believers in Jesus—without resorting to the argumentation of previous theologians.

16. A comment should be made concerning the presence and absence of the article with *hagion pneuma*. There is much to be said in favor of the theory that *when the article appears* with this term, the reference is to the *person* of Holy Spirit, and the *absence of the article implies His activity*. Paul writes (1 Thessalonians 1:5): "For our gospel did not come to you in word

only, but also *en dunamei kai en pneumatic hagio kai en plerophoria polle....*" The omission of the article with *en pneumatic hagio* seems to imply that Paul is speaking not so much of the third person of the Trinity as of His activity—of a certain divine inspiration experienced by the apostle—and therefore he correctly places it on the same level with *dunamis* (power) and *plerophoria* (conviction), which are likewise divine gifts. See also the use of *pneuma hagion* without the article in Luke 1:15,35,41,67. The *decision* between a reference to the third person of the Trinity and His activity *must rest on the context* of the passage as in 1 Thessalonians 1:5 (above). Difficulties in decision at times arise because one or two other principles concerning the article may also be involved: 1) the presence of the article with proper names (see no. 2 above); 2) the absence of the article in prepositional phrases (see no. 1 above).

17. Finally, we may add what is almost a grammatical rule concerning the Greek article. If a noun used with a following genitive is itself without the article, the article generally is omitted also with the genitive. See *pneuma theou* (Romans 8:9) and *to pneuma tou theou* (1 Corinthians 3:16); *logon theou* (1 Thessalonians 2:13) and *ho logos tou theou* (1 Thessalonians 1:8).

We trust that our discussion of the definite article in Greek will be of value to all who attempt to derive theology from proper exegesis.

References to Work of R. G. Hoerber on Plato

Essentials of Greek and Roman Classics, by Meyer Reinhold (Great Neck, N.Y.: Barron's Educational Series, Inc., 1956) p. 369.

Plato's Republic: Interpretation and Criticism, edited by Alexander Sesonske (Belmont, California: Wadsworth Publishing Company, Inc., 1966) p. 141.

Plato's Meno: Texts and Criticism, edited by Alexander Sesonske and Noel Fleming (Belmont, California: Wadsworth Publishing Company, Inc., 1965) p. 116.

Plato: The Dialogues - First Period, by Paul Friedlander ("Bollingen Series," LIX-2.) (New York, N.Y., Pantheon Books, 1964) pp. 311, 313, 316.

Plato: The Dialogues - Second and Third Periods, by Paul Friedlander ("Bollingen Series," LIX-3.) (Princeton, N.J., Princeton University Press, 1969) p. vi, 477, 491-2, 509.

Studies in the Styles of Plato, by Holger Thesleff ("Acta Philosophica Fennica," Fasc. XX.) (Helinski: Akateeminen Kirjakauppa, 1967) p. 180.

The Socratic Paradoxes and the Greek Mind, by Michael J. O'Brien (Chapel Hill, N.C.: University of North Carolina Press, 1967) pp. 100, 103, 107.

Plato: Euthydemus, by Rosamond Kent Sprague ("The Library of Liberal Arts," 222.) Indianapolis, Indiana: The Bobbs-Merrill Company, Inc., 1965) p. xiv.

Plato's Meno, by R. S. Bluck (Cambridge: Cambridge University Press, 1961) p. 465.

"Plato (1950-1957)" by Harold Cherniss in *Lustrum: Internationale Forschungsberichte aus dem Bereich des Klassischen Altertums* (Gottingen: Vandenhoeck & Ruprecht, Band 4, 1959; Band 5, 1960—pages numbered consecutively) pp. 60, 97, 100, 136, 156, 194, 197, 239, 318, 456, 593, 595-596, 631.

Platonic Studies, by Gregory Vlastos (Princeton, N.J.: Princeton University Press, 1973) pp. 136-137 n. 73, p. 408.

Essays in Ancient Greek Philosophy, edited by John P. Anton with George L. Kustas. (Albany, N.Y.: State University of New York Press, 1971) pp. 253 n. 45, 315, 341 n. 2, 646.

A History of Greek Philosophy, Volume IV: Plato The Man and His Dialogues: Earlier Period, by W. K. C. Guthrie (Cambridge: Cambridge University Press, 1975) pp. 2 n. 2, 102, 102 n. 1, 110, 112, 125 n. 1, 125 n. 2, 134, 135 n. 2, 142 n. 1, 143 n. 2, 146, 147, 175 n. 1, 186 n. 4, 434 n. 1, 434 n. 2, 455, 456, 464, 465, 480 n. 1, 483 n. 3, 485 n. 2, 528, 528 n. 3, 531 n. 2, 570, 597.

Plato and Socrates: A Comprehensive Bibliography, 1958-1973, by Richard D. McKirahan, Jr. (New York: Garland Publishing Inc., 1978) pp. 138, 159, 167, 168, 172, 187, 189, 191, 222, 242, 247, 296, 553, 554, 556, 572.

Honors and Offices

Fellow in Greek—Washington University - 1942-44

Phi Beta Kappa—Washington University - 1944

Vice-President for Missouri of the Classical Association of the Middle West and South - 1954-65

Vice-Chairman of Classics Section for Missouri State Teachers' Association - 1956-57; 1959-60

Chairman of Committee on Resolutions at meeting of the Classical Association of the Middle West and South - Columbus, Ohio - April, 1957

Assistant Chairman of Program Committee for the Tenth Annual Latin Institute of the American Classical League - Oxford, Ohio - June, 1957

Chairman of Committee on Scholarships for Summer Study at Athens and Rome - American Classical League - 1957-64

Program Committee for the Eleventh Annual Latin Institute of the American Classical League - Oxford, Ohio - June, 1958

Member of Council, American Classical League - 1958-64

Representative of Classical Association of the Middle West and South to the American Classical League - 1961-70

Member of Executive Committee, American Classical League - 1962-64

Chairman of Classics Section for Missouri State Teachers' Association - 1962-63

Memberships

American Philological Association

Classical Association of the Middle West and South

American Classical League

Phi Beta Kappa

Society for Ancient Greek Philosophy

Society of Biblical Literature and Exegesis

Lutheran Academy for Scholarship with rank of FELLOW

Catholic Biblical Association

Studiorum Novi Testamenti Societas

Notes

Notes

Notes

Notes

Notes

Notes

Notes

Notes

Notes

Notes